NOTES

on Bible Readings

1990

INTERNATIONAL BIBLE READING ASSOCIATION
Robert Denholm House, Nutfield
Redhill, Surrey, RH1 4HW, England

© 1989 International Bible Reading Association

ISSN 0140-8275
ISBN 0-7197-0671-8

Cover picture: Nile fisherman
Photograph by Maurice Thompson, Bible Scene Slide Tours

Typeset, printed and bound in Great Britain by
BPCC Hazell Books Ltd,
Member of BPCC Ltd,
Aylesbury, Bucks, England

CONTENTS

IBRA International Bible
Reading Association

Dear Friends,

There is nothing like a good story. At any family gathering or meeting of friends it will not be long before people start sharing stories — familiar incidents from the past. These shared experiences are part of what binds people together as a family or a group of friends.

Stories can tell us who we are, help us to understand life and give us values to live by. Story-tellers have always been valuable members of the community in every part of the world. In some places today the role of story-teller has been taken over by films, radio or television. But, whether it is through a small group of people or through modern technology, stories play an important part in our life.

For Christians, stories are particularly important. Our faith is centred around the story of God's love. The Bible is full of stories reminding us that we are God's people. These stories give us a sense of personal identity and belonging, and help us to understand ourselves and the world in which we live.

We make a mistake if we only see the biblical stories as being about other people of long ago. All good stories invite us to enter them in our imagination. However, the Bible story — which begins and ends with God — does more than that, for **our** lives are also part of this story. Like Abraham, Moses, David, Isaiah, Peter, Paul and all the other very human people we meet in the pages of the Bible, **we** have a part in the story of God's loving purpose for the world.

As *Notes on Bible Readings* helps us to explore various parts of the Bible story this year, let us pray that:

● *our reading may help us see how God has worked in and through people in the past and give thanks;*

● *we may be alive to God working in and through us to write the next episode of the story.*

Simon Oxley

IBRA Staff: Simon J Oxley (General Secretary)
Joy R Standen (Editor)

INTRODUCTORY NOTES

These notes may be used with any version of the Bible. However, for convenience, the versions on which the authors have based their notes are named in the introduction to each section. Quotations are from this version unless otherwise stated. Abbreviations used in this book are given below. Sometimes it is suggested that you read the Bible passage after reading some of the notes and this is indicated by the symbol ▶. Each day there is a short prayer or an idea for meditation and these are marked by the symbol ✳. After each Saturday's notes a question is given for personal thought or for discussion in a group. These are not necessarily the work of the authors of the notes. Helpful information on the questions is given in *Bible Study Handbook*, and more details about this are to be found on page 15.

ABBREVIATIONS AND ACKNOWLEDGEMENTS

We are grateful for permission to quote from the following Bible versions:

AV   *Authorised Version*

GNB   *Good News Bible* (The Bible Societies/Collins Publishers) – Old Testament © American Bible Society 1976; New Testament © American Bible Society 1966, 1971, 1976

JB   *Jerusalem Bible* (Darton, Longman & Todd Ltd) © 1966

LB   *The Living Bible* (Tyndale House Publishers Ltd) © 1971

NEB   *The New English Bible* (Oxford and Cambridge University Presses) © 1970

NIV   *The Holy Bible, New International Version* (Hodder and Stoughton) © 1978, New York International Bible Society

RSV   *The Holy Bible, Revised Standard Version* © 1973, Division of Christian Education, National Council of Churches of Christ in USA

We are also grateful for permission to quote from:

The hymn 'Lord Jesus Christ (Living Lord)' by Patrick Appleford © 1960 Josef Weinberger Limited (reproduced by kind permission of the copyright owners) on February 13

The hymn 'Tell out, my soul' © Timothy Dudley-Smith on March 13

The hymn 'In Christ there is no east or west' by John Oxenham on May 18

Prayers of Life by Michael Quoist (Gill & Macmillan Limited) on May 20

Further, we are grateful for permission to include the map of Palestine on page 29, from the *Good News Bible*, © British and Foreign Bible Society 1976.

Other IBRA BOOKS 1990 UK prices

LIGHT FOR OUR PATH   £2.25
shorter notes for adults

BIBLE STUDY HANDBOOK   £2.00
for group leaders (see page 15)

PREACHERS' HANDBOOK   £2.00
sermon outlines (see page 49)

DISCOVERING THE BIBLE   £2.00
for teenagers (see page 25)   each part

BIBLE BREAKTHROUGH   £2.25
for young people (see page 59)   each pack

BIBLE TRAIL   £2.00
for children (see page 134)

BIBLE STORYTIME   £1.60
for young children (see page 77)   each book

LOOKING AT THE CROSS   £2.25
(see page 44)

LOOKING AT ADVENT   £2.25
(see page 177)

EVERYDAY PRAYERS
MORE EVERYDAY PRAYERS   £2.50
FURTHER EVERYDAY PRAYERS   each book
(see page 153)

BASICS   70p
for new Christians (see page 83)

All prices include postage for the UK

JAMES

Notes by the Revd Brian Haymes, MA, PhD

Brian Haymes ministered in Baptist churches for sixteen years before he became a tutor, and then Principal, of the Northern Baptist College in Manchester, England. He is the author of 'Looking at the Cross' and 'Looking at Advent' (see pages 44 and 177).

The notes in this section are based on the Good News Bible.

New Year resolutions are better when they are precise and practical. It is usually easy to cope with generalisations, but hard to ignore definite, practical challenges. **James** is a book of practical religion in which the author puts out a call to thoughtful, real discipleship. He wrote at a time when early enthusiasm for the gospel was waning, persecutions were beginning, and temptations to conform to what everyone else was doing seemed more compelling than the radical ways of Jesus.

The teaching in **James** is expressed in vivid language, with illustrations that live on in the imagination. Among the issues raised are the control of our tongues, wealth and poverty, times of testing, snobbery and prejudice, as well as some direct pastoral matters of prayer and healing. The Christian faith is full of practical implications. So why not let **James** help you shape your resolutions for 1990?

Suggestion for further reading

The General Epistle of James: An Introduction and Commentary by R V G Tasker, New Testament Commentaries (Inter-Varsity Press)

Monday January 1   **James 1.1–8**

It is a great day when an ocean-going liner is launched. However, before it is finished, it has to undergo sea trials. Only in this way will its true quality and performance be developed.

In a similar way, the writer of **James** sees trials as essential for our growth as Christians. Some say that the 'trials' of verse

7

2 are persecutions, but this is not necessarily so. They may simply be everyday troubles and temptations. **James** depicts the Christian life in dynamic terms, like a journey. Therefore, faith involves enduring, growing and moving on. The difficulties in being a Christian are causes for thankfulness. After all, if we never experience 'trials' we are probably not trying; and if we are not trying, we are not growing.

Often, our problem is in not knowing the way forward. We are told to pray for **wisdom** – wisdom, in its Old Testament sense of practical knowledge. We are not to ask God to make us clever but to help us live his way.

The promise is that what is necessary will be given to us by God, generously and ungrudgingly. But, if we are not single-minded and really in earnest about discipleship, how can we ever receive God's gifts?

✷ *Lord, help me to mean it when I say I really want to follow you this year.*

Tuesday January 2

Wealth and possessions always present a 'test' for Christians. Our consumer society, heavy with its advertising and January sales, challenges us. How can we live without being possessed by our possessions? If all we have is what we own, then we have our reward already. But God has abundant blessings for those whose lives are concentrated on him and his will – blessings that nothing can destroy.

▶ Read **James 1.9–18**.

It is easy to blame others for our attitude towards possessions. After all, we need to go on producing and buying in order to keep the economy strong. We find reasons for what we do and, if we are not watchful, our riches become the most important thing in our life.

James shows quite clearly that **we** are responsible for our lives. We cannot blame God. Our problems are within us. God does not test us with evil – we test ourselves. It all centres on the question of where our heart is (see Matthew 6.21). We can resist temptation better if we keep in our minds one of the favourite themes in **James**, which is affirmed in today's reading – the generosity of God.

✷ *Save me, Lord, from self-deception. Keep my heart fixed upon your goodness and your will.*

Wednesday January 3 **James 1.19–27**

Yesterday we noted the danger of self-deception, especially in matters of religion. Christians can become very careful about words and deeds in church, almost obsessively so, but what of the **whole** life that we lead? How do we avoid the trap of religiosity and live a truly Christian life?

There are two essential steps to take. The first is a matter of time and application. We live at such a pace that we seldom stop and listen. Christian living begins with listening to the word of God. All too often, in the rush of everyday life, we hear the words, our eyes skim the page, but the result is all on the surface. We glance, but do not look, We hear, but do not listen. Really looking and listening is the crucial way for God's word to take root deep in our existence and so begin to produce fruit.

If we have taken the first step, then the second is a natural consequence. We **do** the word we have heard. We are obedient and practise our faith, naturally. We are concerned not simply to say the right things in church but in all our conversation. We are glad of God's law within our hearts because we know it sets us free to live God's way.

✱ *Slow me down, Lord; help me listen to you; and may I serve you in perfect freedom.*

Thursday January 4 **James 2.1–13**

If possessions present one 'test' for Christians (see January 2), another is social discrimination. We can be very partial in our likes and dislikes about people. Our society is riddled with distinctions which challenge the gospel. Just think of some of the social, economic and racial issues that face us.

Have you heard the story of the poor man who hammered on the closed door of a church, and how the Lord came and told him that he had been trying to get in there too? None of us is entirely free from prejudice and at the heart of prejudice is fear. People who are different can easily disturb us.

The Church is called to be an alternative society. This is because God has no favourites. He 'treats everyone on the same basis' (Acts 10.34). His heart is full of love for all, the kind of love that casts out fear.

Our Christian calling is to have our lives shaped by God's own will and law, and not by the standards of our society. If God does not discriminate in his love, then that is to be our

way too. God's law is clear – love your neighbour as yourself.
Right living is inseparable from right belief.

✴ *Lord, forgive my little love. Fill me with the love that casts out fear, your own love for us all.*

Friday January 5   James 2.14–26

Verse 26 has a startling image – of faith dead as a corpse!
Dead faith makes no difference; it produces no fruit; it does
nothing. We long for **real living** faith – faith which shows
itself in actions. This point is illustrated in today's reading in
two ways:

● First, **in logic**. Faith implies works. The reference to the
poor is very challenging. How does our faith show itself?
To send the desperate away, telling them to do what is
impossible for them, is not faith. No more is faith just a
matter of right doctrine (see verse 19). Right belief shows
itself in loving actions. That is the logic of faith.

● Secondly, **in Scripture**. Abraham was obviously a man of
faith. He was obedient and trusting. And, to drive the point
home, the Gentile prostitute, Rahab, is recalled. With these
people, faith in God showed!

Read verse 24 again, and then Romans 3.28. These may
seem to contradict one another. But this is not really so,
because both Paul and the writer of **James** knew that faith
means obedient trust in God. It is a whole way of life.

✴ *Lord, I believe in you. May my life show it, in love.*

Saturday January 6

A sign of maturity is self-control. Without it we can create
havoc in the lives of others. Think of the pain caused by those
who say things they immediately regret because they have
not learned when to control their tongues.

▶ Read **James 3.1–5a**.

The position of teacher was an honoured one in the early
Church and many sought it; but not all were called and gifted.
The choice of teachers was an important business because of
the very considerable influence they had. That remains true
today. Great power and, therefore, far-reaching responsibility
is theirs. All teachers have a special claim upon our prayers.

It is a deep insight of **James** to stress control of the tongue.

The two illustrations – the horse's bit and the ship's rudder – make this point but also raise the questions: Who holds the reins? Who steers the helm? One of the most popular songs of this generation is, 'I did it **my** way'. But what if my way is less than perfect? What practical difference would I expect to see if I gave my life over into God's control?

✴ *Lord, be in my mind and in my speaking. Hear me, as I pray for all teachers.*

For group discussion and personal thought

Read and discuss **James 1.22–27**. How would you define 'pure and genuine religion' (verse 27)? Think of up-to-date examples of what you have in mind. How can you better practise 'genuine religion' in your church?

Sunday January 7

'Sticks and stones may break my bones but words can never hurt me.' That saying simply is not true. Words sting. They break hearts. They start wars. Words are frighteningly powerful.

▶ Read **James 3.5b–12**.

Are these verses fair? The writer's thought seems so negative. Is our speech all that bad? We do say some kind, creative, loving words. The right word at the appropriate moment can bring comfort, hope and faith.

But, for all that, the observation of **James** is true. We have a problem with our tongues – or, rather, with what is within us. When we think of what we sometimes say, are we masters in our own house? For the writer of **James** much of the 'fallenness' of our lives, and that of the world, shows itself through our tongues. We know it ought not to be so. The very fact that we can use our tongues to praise God only heightens the seriousness of our predicament. One test of being Christlike, and of our living in God's salvation, is the ability to control our speech – to have tamed what otherwise seems to be untameable.

✴ *Lord, help me to control my tongue. May your salvation be heard through the words of all your people.*

Monday January 8

What would you say are the characteristics of a wise person? Being wise is something more than knowing a lot. Some of the most knowledgeable people have also been the most wicked. Some may be very clever and yet lack wisdom – such people are dangerous.

▶ Read **James 3.13–18**.

The writer may well be referring back to those teachers mentioned in verse 1. He is arguing that for anyone to claim to have wisdom but to be without self-control is to live in delusion. A teacher like that can have devastating effects on others. Claiming to be inspired is not enough, because inspiration may be demonic.

James gives us some criteria for discerning true teachers. The words of a wise man will build up the community in peace and well-being. Compassion and good deeds will be present in the teacher's life and in the lives of the taught. We recognise again how much **James** is drawing on Jesus' words about the importance of our inner life and the fruits by which we are known (see Matthew 15.18–19; 7.15–20).

✷ *Lord, give us good and wise teachers. May we grow in the wisdom that is from above.*

Tuesday January 9

It is strange but true to record that saints are more concerned about sin than the rest of us. As a hymn has it:

. . . they who fain would serve thee best
Are conscious most of wrong within.   *Henry Twells*

Most of us become captive to the values of our own society. We adopt the envy-making desires suggested by powerful advertising. Our lives are shaped by these pressures and so we become conformed to this world. It happens almost without our noticing.

▶ Read **James 4.1–10**.

Christians are not called to be morbid, breast-beating kill-joys. Nor are we called to be careless and casual, as if the little sins of life do not really matter and we can laugh them off. There is a profound 'having-gone-wrongness' about the world which is always with us. This is not to be morbid – it is to be realistic. The cross reveals the sin of which we are capable. It also reveals the saving love of God. There is a deep seriousness in the perspective of the writer of **James** that drives him desperately to the grace of God.

✳ *Lord, may I seek your kingdom above everything else and live in quiet trust of your goodness and mercy.*

Wednesday January 10   **James 4.11–17**

There are two kinds of atheism – one intellectual, the other practical. Intellectual atheism denies that God exists, while practical atheism means **living** as if God did not exist. People may say they believe in God but if, in fact, that belief makes no difference to the way they live then, practically speaking, they are atheists. Today's reading contains two examples of practical atheism:

● **Verses 11–12.** There are people who speak about others in unfair and derogatory ways. They pass judgements even against fellow Christians. Do they think they are above God's command to love their neighbours?

● **Verses 13–17.** There are people who organise their lives as if they alone were in control. Have they no thought of living before God? What about the desire to do God's will? All personal boasting means that God is not in the centre, but at the margins, of their life.

Simply saying the right things about God does not make us believers. Jesus said, 'How happy are those who hear the word of God and obey it!' (Luke 11.28)

✳ *Lord, may what I say and what I do express your rule alone.*

Thursday January 11   **James 5.1–6**

Ten children were asked to come to the front of the church. They stood in a row and the minister gave some sweets to the first four. There he stopped. One of the remaining six called out, 'It's not fair. What about us?' And the point was made. Over half the world's people are hungry and it's not fair.

In world terms, if today we have enough and to spare we are among the rich. Some countries have a slimming industry while others are desperate for food. We have learned that much of the wealth of the rich countries comes at the expense of the 'undeveloped' nations.

All of which makes today's prophetic reading hard-hitting and disturbing. We are told that God hears the cry of the needy. Do we hear it too? There is a stern note of judgement, not to be taken lightly. Riches bring great temptations, not least that of avoiding the challenge to seek a more just economic and social order. The writer of **James** saw that challenge implicit in the gospel.

✳ *Pray for international aid agencies, for those who serve with them, and those who need their ministry.*

Friday January 12   James 5.7–11

You could make out a good case for calling our generation the 'instant generation'. 'Take the waiting out of wanting,' says the advertiser persuading us to buy now. We have 'fast food' industries and we drink instant coffee. A conference even advertised a way to 'instant spirituality'.

Some things cannot be rushed and forced. The growth of Christian character is one. This takes time, God's time. The farmer knows he cannot hurry the grain. There is no point in him getting flustered. He must do his part – and wait.

Patience is a Christian virtue. Impatience shows itself when we become agitated and begin to blame others. Christian patience is not the passive indolence of doing nothing. Rather, it shows itself in a steady determination to get on with our calling, to endure if necessary, but always trusting in the divine mercy and compassion, and waiting upon God's time. The words of **James** about the Lord's return are both a warning and a consolation.

✳ *Lord, forgive my impatience and readiness to blame others. May I live in quiet trust of your unfailing goodness.*

Saturday January 13   James 5.12–20

The book of **James** has been no soft option. At times it has been disturbing. The writer's purpose has not been to moralise and make us feel bad but to underline the seriousness of sin, the demands of discipleship and the utterly faithful nature of God.

In the concluding verses, which emphasise above all the gift of prayer, the writer thinks of our life before God. Whether good or ill comes our way we can turn to God in praise or prayer. In times of particular need, when the fellowship and ministry of the Church matter more than usual, it is not human action that **James** emphasises but the promise of God's responsive healing presence.

It is true that religion can be reduced to morality and life become all duty with little joy. But this is not the life **James** commends, nor the gospel we must proclaim. Christian living is not without cost, but it is undertaken in answer to the call of God – the God known in Jesus, whose presence always goes with us and whose mercy never fails.

✻ *Lord, thank you for the gift of prayer, the fellowship of the Church, and for your forgiveness, healing and salvation in Christ.*

For group discussion and personal thought

Look again at **James 5.13–16**. These verses give us a glimpse into the pastoral life of the early Church. Discuss the importance of prayer in the healing ministry of the Church. How does 'healing faith', as described in **James**, differ from 'faith healing' as practised in some places today?

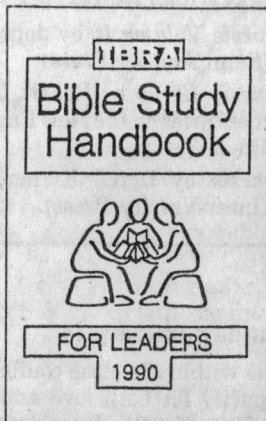

GENESIS 37 – 50

Notes by the Revd Michael J Townsend, BA, MPhil, BD

Michael Townsend is a Methodist minister in the Huddersfield Pennine Circuit, Yorkshire, England. He is the author of 'Our Tradition of Faith' (Epworth Press), and has contributed articles on biblical, theological and homiletical subjects to various periodicals.

The notes in this section are based on the New International Version.

The story in **Genesis 37–50** is vividly written. The characters, especially Joseph and his family, come to life from the pages. They exhibit human emotions with which we are familiar, and they wrestle with problems which still come to us today. Above all, the story is an exciting one. Those who come to it for the first time find themselves eager to know what happens next. This is the secret of the enduring appeal of these chapters.

Yet, they have a deeper purpose. Through the story of Joseph we learn something about the way in which God's purposes for human history are worked out in the sometimes difficult circumstances of daily living.

Suggestions for further reading

Genesis Volume II by John C L Gibson, Daily Study Bible (Saint Andrew Press)

Genesis 12–50 by Robert Davidson, Cambridge Bible Commentaries on the New English Bible (Cambridge University Press)

Genesis by Derek Kidner, Old Testament Commentaries (Inter-Varsity Press).

Sunday January 14   **Genesis 37.1–11**

It is within the close confines of family life that the greatest capacity for both love and hatred is present. Here, at the beginning of the Joseph story, two reasons are given for the hatred Joseph's brothers felt towards him:

- The first was that Israel (Jacob) 'loved Joseph more than any of his other sons' (verse 3), and as a sign of this presented him with a special robe. We cannot be quite certain what this was like, but such favouritism is psychologically bad, although understandable, considering that Joseph was the son of Jacob's old age.
- The second was Joseph's claim, implicit in his two dreams, that he would become more important than any of the rest of his family. We can well understand that such a claim was not likely to make him popular.

What would we have made of Joseph if we had been a member of his family? Might we have thought of him as a spoilt brat? Perhaps he was! Yet God, who does not always choose the most likeable of people, had indeed destined Joseph for a special purpose. Against that purpose human wickedness could not be allowed to prevail.

✳ *Think about your own family life. Thank God for the good things and pray about the weaknesses.*

Monday January 15   Genesis 37.12–35

The story of how Joseph's brothers sold him into slavery is told compactly and realistically. Why did Judah and Reuben restrain the others from killing him? Probably because, although what they did was bad enough, murder would have been even worse and their guilt so much the greater. If they had killed Joseph they would have had to conceal the fact, to 'cover up his blood' as Judah pointed out (verse 26).

So Joseph was sold to merchants at a fair price for a young slave. Yet Jacob still had to be provided with 'proof' that his son was dead, and the robe dipped in goat's blood provided this. No doubt the brothers found considerable satisfaction in using the hated symbol of Joseph's special status in this way.

The real poignancy, and irony, of this story, comes with Jacob's grieving for Joseph (verses 34–35). As a young man he had deceived **his** father (see Genesis 27.1–29). However, Jacob does not know that he is being deceived – his grief is real and intense. It seemed like the end of the Joseph story. With the events told in today's reading Joseph could have disappeared from history. That he did not was because God had a plan for him.

✳ *Thank you, Father, that what so often seem to us to be endings are, in your providence, new beginnings.*

The colourful story of Joseph in Potiphar's household has both
an overall theological purpose and, along the way, lessons
about proper behaviour. 'The Lord was with Joseph' (verse 2)
and, as a result of this, although still a slave, he won the
favour of Potiphar who gave him responsibilities and privileges. Potiphar trusted him.

The attempt by Potiphar's wife to seduce the handsome
young slave, and the way her thwarted desire turned to vin-
dictive hate, is quite psychologically credible. Moreover, she
had the upper hand, for Potiphar would certainly have taken
his wife's word against his slave's. Yet Joseph resisted the
woman's invitation. As he expressed it, his reasons were a
combination of ordinary human decency and awareness of
God's will in such matters (see verses 8–9). That Joseph was
unwilling to abuse the trust placed in him was to his credit.
That he recognised such abuse as a sin was remarkable. It
reminds us that sin is always against God. (see Psalm 51.4).

Yet, despite the worst that circumstances could do, the Lord
was still with Joseph (verses 21–23). All the evil stories and
false accusations of human beings could not prevent Joseph
from fulfilling his God-given destiny.

✴ *Thank you, Lord, for those who stand firm in time of temptation. Help us to follow their good example.*

Wednesday January 17   **Genesis 40.1–23**

Dreams are powerful; they are also mysterious. Some doctors
use people's recollections of their dreams to help towards a
greater understanding of the human personality. Yet we do
not understand very much about dreams, and relatively
primitive societies understood even less. It should not surprise us if God does use dreams to communicate some aspects
of his will.

Pharaoh's chief cupbearer and chief baker each had vivid
dreams. They could not turn to those in Egyptian society who
were recognised as interpreters of dreams, but they told
Joseph about them. His comment, 'Do not interpretations
belong to God?' (verse 8) was confident. With great skill, he
separated those aspects which were important from those
which were not and, as the story unfolds, we see how accurate
he was. Once again this was seen to be proof that the Lord
was with him.

The natural outcome of this **ought** to have been that Joseph earned his release from prison through the gratitude of the cupbearer. But matters were not quite so simple. When some good thing does not come to God's servants it is sometimes – but not always – because he has something better in store. However, at the time it may be difficult to see that.

✳ *Lord, when things do not go the way we want or expect, help us to have patience and to trust you.*

Thursday January 18

To feel forgotten by everyone is an unpleasant experience. As Joseph languished in prison for a full two years after the departure of the cupbearer and the baker, he must have wondered if even God had forgotten him. Although Joseph could not have known it, something very special was in store for him, which would be worth waiting for.

▶ Read **Genesis 41.1–16**.

The character of Pharaoh's dreams were very strange indeed and he was extremely disturbed. Only after fruitless recourse to those who would normally have interpreted such things did the cupbearer suddenly recall Joseph's skill in his own case. Perhaps he felt guilty that he had previously forgotten Joseph.

However, the main thrust of today's reading is in verses 15–16. Pharaoh assumed that the power to interpret dreams belonged personally to Joseph, and said so. What a temptation it was for Joseph to go along with that assumption and thus ensure his good standing and future advancement! But instead Joseph gave the glory where it was due – to God (see verse 16). In that reply is a model for all God's servants.

✳ *Lord, when you work through us, may we always give to you the glory and never claim the credit for ourselves.*

Prayer for use during the Week of Prayer for Christian Unity, January 18–25

Father of all, as you have called all Christians to your service, so bind us closer together in love and understanding.

What immediately strikes us about Joseph's interpretation of
Pharaoh's dreams is its simplicity and clarity. The dreams
themselves seemed very strange, but the meaning of them
was quite simple. It was this simplicity which enabled Joseph
to move from interpretation to practical suggestion!

If matters were as clear as Joseph said, then the course of
action which must be followed was equally straightforward.
It seems to have been this evident common sense which commended Joseph's interpretation to Pharaoh. How else could
he have taken the word of an unknown and imprisoned slave
unless the explanation carried its own conviction!

Sometimes we say of some event or idea, 'Yes, of course,
how could it be otherwise?' It is as if our eyes have suddenly
been opened to something which is simple, even obvious, but
which we had never seen before. Once we have seen it the
situation becomes plain. And, often, the proper response for
us, as for Pharaoh, is to take practical steps to deal with
matters. All this is the work of God's Spirit in our lives. He
makes the mysteries of God plain to those who believe (see 1
Corinthians 2.12).

✴ *Pray that your eyes may be opened to where and how God
calls you to action and service.*

Joseph's brothers could not possibly have expected to see him
in Egypt. They did not know he was there; and, even if they
had known, they would not have anticipated him being second
in rank only to Pharaoh (see 41.40–41)! But it was different
for Joseph. When he heard that people were travelling from
Canaan to buy food he would have realised that sooner or later
members of his family would be among their number.

The story of their meeting is touching. The brothers sus-
pected nothing, and their attitude of reverence and subservi-
ence reminded Joseph of his dreams which had caused so
much of the trouble in the first place (see 37.5–11). It seemed
like a fulfilment of those dreams.

Joseph's long-term plan was, of course, to bring the whole
family to Egypt for safety, and in the process to test whether
his brothers had changed in character over the years. It was
to this end that he kept Simeon in Egypt and commanded the

bringing of the youngest brother, Benjamin. Joseph's brothers could not have known this. They saw only the testing, and thought it harsh.

✳ *Father, when times of testing come into our lives, help us to trust that through them all your purposes will become plain.*

For group discussion and personal thought

Read **Genesis 37.1–11**. What were the problems in the relationship between Joseph and his family, and how might they have been resolved? What does this story teach us about our relationships within our families and within our churches?

Sunday January 21

▶ First, read **Genesis 42.25–29, 35–38**.

When Joseph replaced his brothers' money in their sacks perhaps he intended it as a sign of his love and care, but the brothers were only puzzled and afraid.

There are some lessons in life that we only learn from hard and bitter experience. This was true for Joseph's brothers – and for Jacob. Joseph's demand that Benjamin be brought to Egypt was resisted by him (verse 38), but the famine went on longer than expected and there seemed to be no choice.

▶ Now read **Genesis 43.1–15**.

The circumstances that Jacob so resented turned out to be a cause of blessing to him and the whole family. However, not knowing this, he had to accept the inevitable first. We can see, too, how the brothers had begun to change. Judah's solemn personal pledge to his father regarding Benjamin's safety (verse 9) is in great contrast with the brothers' original cynical deception of Jacob concerning Joseph. The hard test to which they had been put was teaching them new values and morals. It is a sign of spiritual growth when we can learn from events and circumstances how to grow in grace and faith.

✳ *Ask God to help you to discern his presence even in unpleasant circumstances, and to grow in grace through them.*

Joseph's strategy for separating Benjamin from the rest of his
brothers seems a strange, even a cruel one to us. But it was
certainly effective. The brothers knew that they were innocent
of the crime of which they were accused (verse 7). When the
cup was discovered they could find no rational explanation for
its presence. The ancient world largely held an objective view
of guilt and innocence. If the cup had been found, then they
must accept that as a judgement of guilt from God, even
though they did not understand how it had come about.

Joseph's aim, to keep Benjamin with him and send the
others back, was designed to put his brothers in a situation
similar to that in which they had been many years before.
Once again they faced the prospect of returning to their father
without their youngest brother. This time they would even
have an excuse of sorts for doing so.

Joseph wanted to see how much his brothers had really
changed. Judah's offer to remain behind instead was a fulfilment of the pledge he had given to his father (see 43.9). In the
contrast between their former and present attitudes towards
their father we can see the change of heart for which Joseph
had been hoping.

✻ *Father, forgive us that sometimes we forget that your grace
can change people, ourselves included.*

Tuesday January 23

If we have ever experienced a reunion with family or close
friends from whom we have long been separated, we will know
what an overwhelming experience that can be. Even if we
have not ourselves shared in such an occasion, it is not difficult
to imagine its impact. So it was for Joseph and his brothers.
Considering the circumstances in which they had last been
together, strong emotion could be expected on both sides.

▶ Read **Genesis 45.1–11, 25–28; 46.1–4**.

However, it is not just the experience which matters; it is
also the understanding which is attached to that experience.
When Joseph said to his brothers, '. . . it was not you who
sent me here, but God' (verse 8), he was referring to the way
in which all the experiences of his life, even the most unprom-
ising, had finally served the purposes of God. In the most
practical way Joseph's position in Egypt enabled him to save
his family from the effects of the famine. Joseph's insight

needing to be considered, Joseph would show that he still held a grudge against them for what they had done so long before.

Their message to Joseph received a reception which encouraged them (verse 17) and this led to a personal meeting – always the best way to resolve problems! In his reply, Joseph made it plain that he could see God's hand in what had taken place. If God had forgiven them, so could he. Evil had been done, but God had brought good out of it. What more was there to be said?

It should go without saying that Christians, who know through Jesus how much God loves and forgives them, should never hold grudges. If a wrong has been done to us we have to trust God to bring good out of it. If we do, he will.

✳ *Reflect on whether you still hold a grudge against someone. If so, offer that to God and ask him to heal the pain and use what was done for good.*

For group discussion and personal thought
Consider **Genesis 45.1–11** and **50.15–21**. How did God bring good out of evil in the story of Joseph? Recall times when he has done this in your life. How should we respond to these experiences? Should we always expect God to bring good out of trouble? Why, or why not?

MARK 1 – 10

Notes by the Revd Leta Hawe

Leta Hawe is a Presbyterian minister in the Burwood United–St Kentigern's parish in Christchurch, New Zealand. She has recently completed a term as Moderator of Christchurch Presbytery.

The notes in this section are based on the Good News Bible.

It is widely accepted that **Mark** was the first of the four Gospels to be written, the author drawing on oral tradition and Peter's reminiscences. It is also believed that the authors of **Matthew** and **Luke** used **Mark** when writing their Gospels. Although some uncertainty surrounds the identity of the author of **Mark's Gospel**, tradition has ascribed it to John Mark and, in these notes, we shall refer to the author as 'Mark'.

Compared with the other Gospels, **Mark** has less of the teaching of Jesus. On the whole, the events are left to speak for themselves. There is a sense of urgency in Mark's narrative as he moves quickly from one incident to the next.

In this first section of **Mark**, we shall read of Jesus' ministry in Galilee ending with his journey to Jerusalem via Jericho, before his triumphal entry. The rest of **Mark** will be read in the four weeks leading up to Easter.

Suggestions for further reading

The Gospel of Mark by William Barclay, Daily Study Bible (Saint Andrew Press)

Saint Mark by D E Nineham, SCM Pelican New Testament Commentaries (SCM/Penguin Books)

The Gospel of Mark by Hugh Anderson, New Century Bible Commentaries (Eerdmans/Marshall, Morgan & Scott)

Sunday January 28   **Mark 1.1–13**

How differently each Gospel writer sets the stage for the beginning of the ministry of Jesus Christ, Son of God! Mark's style is straightforward and vigorous. The curtain on the divine drama of salvation is raised quickly. He sees no need for a detailed genealogy as is found in the opening chapter of **Matthew**. He gives us no angelic chorus, no homage of shepherds or wise men. There is no royal fanfare to mark the commencement of Jesus' ministry.

A desert region seems a most unlikely and unproductive setting, but our God is a God of surprises, constantly breaking through our narrow, restrictive expectations. Mark has little to say about John the Baptist. This preparer of the way receives more attention in Matthew 3.1–12 and Luke 3.1–20. However, Mark does tell us two things about him:

- He preached a baptism of repentance for the forgiveness of sins.
- He clearly regarded himself as preparing the way for one greater than himself.

✱ *Lord, may my words and actions point others to you.*

Monday January 29   Mark 1.14–20

The authority and compelling personality of Jesus is obvious right from the beginning of his ministry. There is no sign of a 'gentle Jesus, meek and mild', but every evidence of the strong Son of God. This authority is seen in:

- the announcement that the hour had now struck – the time fixed by God had fully come.
- the call to repent and believe – unlike John the Baptist, Jesus proclaimed not merely judgement, but a gospel.
- his calling of the first disciples – there was something compelling about this man and his invitation.

Notice that Jesus came to the fishermen at their place of work. Do we sometimes fail to notice the presence of Christ in the ordinariness of our working-day, because we assume his coming is restricted to special times and places?

Every place, however ordinary, can become holy ground for us, as it was for Moses (Exodus 3), for the travellers of the Emmaus road (Luke 24.13–32) and for these fishermen.

✱ *Lord Christ, I may not know very much about you, but I am eager to learn and to let you make of me what you will.*

Tuesday January 30   Mark 1.21–34

Capernaum was one of the most important towns in Galilee, and an appropriate place for Jesus to begin his public ministry. His teaching in the synagogue impressed and astonished the worshippers. Other teachers of the law always quoted from great rabbis. Jesus, however, spoke the truth without reference to the wise men of the past.

The effect on the people was electric. One man was clearly affected and gave voice to his feelings. Whatever the exact nature of the man's illness, he recognised the authority and uniqueness of the preacher and his message. While many would label the man as mad, he gave voice to a cry that was to be echoed again and again during Jesus' ministry (verse 24).

Many regarded Jesus as too threatening – a disturber of their way of thinking and living. Do we, too, see the Christ as coming to destroy? Does his presence and his teaching shatter our complacency? Have we pleaded, 'Leave us alone . . . let us stay as we are'? We are fortunate that Jesus does not always do for us as we ask!

✳ *Lord Christ, disturber and renewer, your presence demands a response. Let me rise to your challenge and follow you.*

Wednesday January 31   Mark 1.35–45

The last incident of an eventful twenty-four hours is found in verse 35. Despite a busy, exhausting Sabbath, Jesus was up before dawn, away in search of solitude. Such withdrawals were characteristic of Jesus. In the solitude he sought renewal of strength in communion with his Father.

However, could there also be another motive here? Did Jesus see in his popularity a temptation to turn from the true purpose of his ministry? Jesus had come to win people to God. As he had resisted the temptation to turn stones into bread (see Luke 4.3–4), so now he resisted the temptation to gain people's allegiance by way of miracle cures. He had already committed himself to the patient, costly way of love. There was to be no turning from that chosen path.

This did not mean that healings would stop – needs would continue to be met. There was, however, a danger that the wants of people would overshadow their real needs. The demand to satisfy wants must be refused in order that greater blessings might be received.

✳ *Lord Jesus, give me the desire to reach out for the fullness of all you have promised me. Let me never be satisfied with less.*

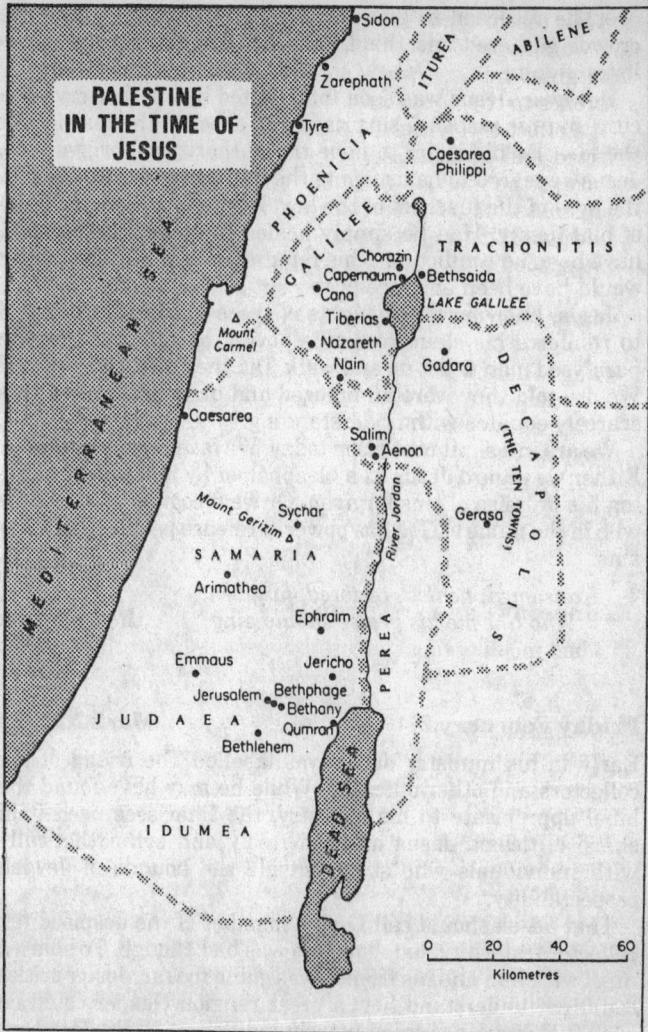

PALESTINE IN THE TIME OF JESUS

Sidon

ITUREA

ABILENE

Zarephath

Tyre

PHOENICIA

Caesarea Philippi

GALILEE

Chorazin

Capernaum

Bethsaida

TRACHONITIS

Cana

LAKE GALILEE

Mount Carmel

Tiberias

Nazareth

Nain

Gadara

D E C A P O L I S (THE TEN TOWNS)

Caesarea

Salim

Aenon

Mount Gerizim

Sychar

Gerasa

River Jordan

SAMARIA

Arimathea

Ephraim

PEREA

Emmaus

Jericho

Jerusalem

Bethphage

Bethany

JUDAEA

Qumran

Bethlehem

DEAD SEA

IDUMEA

MEDITERRANEAN SEA

0   20   40   60

Kilometres

Thursday February 1   **Mark 2.1—12**

Jesus was back at Capernaum again. He had left because
things had begun to go wrong. People were attracted by the
miracle cures, but did not want to accept his teaching. How-

ever, he returned to give them another chance. Again, the crowds gathered and this time seemed to be more ready to listen to him.

However, Jesus was soon interrupted by another cry for a cure, but his response surprised and shocked the teachers of the law. By his claim to have the authority to forgive sins, Jesus appeared to be usurping the authority of God. This, in the eyes of the teachers of the law, laid him open to a charge of blasphemy. Had he simply healed the man, there would have been no conflict, and his reputation as a miracle-healer would have been enhanced.

Jesus, knowing the thoughts of these teachers, proceeded to reinforce his claim to divine power, by commanding the paralysed man to get up and walk. Did they now understand? We are told they were all amazed and praised God, but this scarcely equates with understanding.

We are in a similar position today. We face two alternatives. Either we regard Jesus as a blasphemer by ignoring or denying his promise of sins forgiven. Or we recognise him as One who in the name of God has power to release people from their sins.

✳ *Ransomed, healed, restored, forgiven,*
Who like me his praise should sing?   *Henry F Lyte*

Friday February 2   Mark 2.13–22

Early in his ministry Jesus was labelled 'the friend of tax collectors and other outcasts'. While he may have found the label appropriate to his ministry, the Pharisees used it in sharp criticism. Jesus mingled freely and sympathetically with individuals who stood outside the bounds of Jewish respectability.

That Jesus should call Levi, a member of the despised tax collector fraternity, to follow him was bad enough. To share a meal with him and his friends was going too far. Jesus' critics could not understand how a great religious leader could do such a thing. He seemed utterly indifferent to the fact that laws concerning foods and ritual cleanness were violated during the meal.

Jesus answered his critics with words they could not fail to understand. He was not dismissing his ministry to good people, but was pointing out that such people often felt no need of the gospel. God does not wait for sinners to become righteous, but loves them as sinners. This is the Christian gospel – good news for all people, regardless of status or race.

✳ *Lord Jesus, your love includes all people – including me. Secure in that love, I can risk reaching out to others.*

Saturday February 3   Mark 2.23 to 3.6

The question of Sabbath observance continues to surface from time to time. Few of us would welcome a return to the strict pleasure-less Sabbaths of earlier years, yet we need to guard against the other extreme of allowing Sunday to become a day which is no way different from the other six.

'The Sabbath was made for the good of man' (verse 27) is still a relevant statement for us. Whether we think of it in terms of a Sabbath or a Sunday, the sabbath-idea directs us toward keeping one day in seven as a day of rest, relaxation and renewal. In today's society the maintenance of essential services requires many people to work on Sunday. For their own good it is important that they have time and space for re-creation on another day of the week.

Jesus' positive attitude toward the Sabbath and his claim to have authority over the Sabbath, gave the Pharisees more fuel to inflame their anger. They had looked for a Messiah who would stand with them in their observance of the law. However, Jesus, by word and action, showed that people matter more than systems. Human need comes before slavish obedience to the letter of the law.

✳ *Lord, help me to use my Sundays in such a way that their renewing power may stay with me all through each week, even in my busiest hours.*

For group discussion and personal thought
This week's readings have shown that Jesus very quickly became both widely popular and bitterly criticised. What can we learn from both reactions which will help us to see how we should respond to Jesus?

Sunday February 4   Mark 3.7–19
From the beginning of Jesus' ministry there was a clear sense

of purpose; and, as Mark tells it, a sense of urgency as he went about his work. Demands and opportunities were increasing to the extent that Jesus had to enlist others to carry his message and to ensure that the work he had begun would continue after his death. The word Mark used for 'called' (verse 13) indicates not an invitation, but an authoritative summons. Those whom Jesus chose were:

- **to be with him** – as they accompanied Jesus, they would learn; they were also to provide support in a shared ministry.
- **to be sent out** – the Christ who had said, 'Come,' would also say, 'Go and tell' (see Matthew 28.19–20).

Judged by human standards, the men Jesus chose possessed no notable qualifications. They were as ordinary and as varied a company as we could find anywhere – people very much like us. But Jesus looked beyond what was, to what they might become. He saw their potential and chose them with confidence.

* *Lord Jesus, in the work of your kingdom, let me not be unemployed.*

Monday February 5   Mark 3.20–35

When Albert Schweitzer, a gifted musician and scholar, turned his back on a promising and lucrative career to give medical aid to African people in Lambarene, many people were dismayed and confused.

When Jesus left the carpenter's shop at Nazareth to become an itinerant preacher, those closest to him found his actions and his controversial teaching embarrassing and disturbing. They also had good reason to fear for his safety. He was taking risks no prudent family member should be allowed to take.

At the other end of the spectrum, the experts in the law accused Jesus of being in league with the prince of the demons – that it must be from this evil source that his power came.

However, Jesus' mission involved him in confronting and challenging the powers of evil. He would continue to do this, whatever the cost. If this meant some degree of alienation from his immediate family and brought him into direct conflict with authority, so be it. His first priority was at all times obedience to his Father's will.

* *Lord Jesus, let your will be my will, that I may be included among those whom you call **your family**.*

Tuesday February 6 Mark 4.1–9

In today's complex world, where so many conflicting voices clamour for our attention, courses are being offered to enable people to sharpen up their listening skills. All too often what we hear reaches us through the sieve of prejudice, tradition or our own expectations.

Jesus was anxious that those who heard his teaching really received the truth of the gospel. He was an excellent communicator, quickly assessing where people were at, and starting from that point. As he preached and taught outside the synagogues, he used people, scenes and things familiar to his hearers. He began at the point of people's knowledge and led them into areas of new truth.

Educationalists and communicators today endorse such a method. Abstract ideas are difficult to grasp. Introduce a teaching session with 'Once there was . . .', and we are more likely to gain people's attention and stimulate their interest.

One of the great qualities of the parables Jesus used is that a child may glimpse the truth, and a theological scholar never fully exhaust its meaning.

✳ *Lord Jesus, let not familiarity with the gospel dull my sense of hearing. May its truth take root and shape my living.*

Wednesday February 7 Mark 4.10–20

The word 'parable' is Greek in origin and means 'a comparison'. We can thus define a parable as a comparison made from ordinary life or from nature to teach some spiritual truth.

As we consider the parables Jesus used, we find that the truth contained in every parable is not easily discerned. A parable is intended to make us think, and then to lead us to decision-making and to action.

The parable of the sower, the seed and the soil challenges us to ask, 'What kind of soil am I? How do I respond to the word of God?'

● Has familiarity with the truth made me hard and unresponsive to new insights?
● Is the soil too shallow for seed to thrive?
● Have I allowed other interests and concerns to choke out my initial response to the gospel?
● Has the seed been well-received and constantly nourished?
● Is there something of the four soils in me?

✳ *Speak, Lord, for I am listening, ready to act upon your word.*

Verses 21-25 give us four different sayings which are recorded here in two pairs. This is unlike **Matthew** where each of these sayings is recorded separately (5.15; 10.26; 7.2; 25.29). Let us consider each pair as **Mark** gives them:

● **Verses 21-22.** There is no such thing as secret discipleship. Either the secrecy will destroy the discipleship, or the discipleship will destroy the secrecy. Our Christian faith must be obvious. Like Paul we should be able to declare 'I am not ashamed of the gospel' (Romans 1.16, RSV).

● **Verses 24-25.** Jesus was not advocating generosity for the sake of personal gain. Nor was he saying that we should give now to accumulate merit marks in the hereafter. Rather, Jesus was affirming the 'echo principle' of life. If we are prepared to invest ourselves, our time and energy in worthwhile pursuits, we will benefit accordingly. This is true of sportspeople, willing to put time and effort into training programmes. It is true of scholars who in due time find their studies rewarded. It is true for the Christian who is prepared to go against the 'give me' cry so frequently and loudly heard today.

✳ *Generous God, may I be as willing to give to others as you are to give to me.*

The sea of Galilee was notorious for its sudden storms. Nevertheless, on this occasion, according to the reasoning of the disciples, the journey across should have been smooth and trouble-free. For, not only were they obeying their Master's instructions, but they also had Jesus with them. They discovered, as we discover, that the Christian way is not a 'no danger' insurance cover. Christian commitment and obedience, and even the presence of Christ, do not prevent trouble from coming to us.

In today's reading there are three questions to consider:

● **'Teacher, don't you care?'** (verse 38). The disciples, looking for proof of Jesus' caring, did not find it in a sleeping companion. It was not the first, nor the last time, this question was asked.

● **'Why are you frightened?'** (verse 40). Did their faith not assure them that nothing in the whole created universe

could separate them from God's love and care? (See Romans
8.38–39.)

- **'Who is this man?'** (verse 41). The disciples knew that only
  God could rule wind and sea. Now Jesus had done it. That
  could only mean that God was present with them in Christ.

✳ *Companion Christ, help me to know your presence and to
trust your power even when life's storms swirl about me.*

Saturday February 10   Mark 5.1–20

As Jesus brought peace to frightened disciples amid the
storm, so here he brought calm and wholeness to a troubled
spirit. This particular incident is regarded by many as one of
the most bizarre stories in **Mark**, because it speaks a
language no longer ours, and some of its details are strange
and confusing. Yet, it would be a pity if for that reason we
chose to ignore it. We can learn much from this account if we
are prepared to take time to look beneath the surface.

Here was a man who needed deliverance. Whether he was
actually demon-possessed or suffering from manic delusion is
not the most important factor. In Jesus' eyes, this man who
was despised by many, was important and of value. In his
confused state he needed not only a cure, but proof of a cure.
The sight of the herd of pigs taking fright and rushing down
a cliff into the lake, gave the man the assurance he needed.

Ironically, the response of the local people was to beg Jesus
to leave the area. They saw Jesus – the giver of peace to the
demented man – as a disturber of their peace.

✳ *Pray for those whose minds are disturbed or have not
matured. May we see them as persons, not problems.*

For group discussion and personal thought
Look again at the reading and notes for **February 10**. How
does Jesus disturb us today (a) in our personal lives, (b) in our
church and (c) in our community? In what circumstances do
we expect Jesus to bring us comfort and peace?

Sunday February 11   Mark 5.21–34
Jairus' appeal to Jesus for help pointed to a new development

in Jesus' ministry. It appears that before this time only outcasts had come to Jesus acknowledging his power to make them whole. However, here it was an official of the local congregation who came. At once, **Mark** says, Jesus went with him.

Along the way their journey was interrupted. Jesus, Jairus, and all who followed could have chosen to ignore the woman's need. After all, was she not less important than Jairus? But interruptions can be God's opportunities. There is no indication of impatience or frustration on Jesus' part. Here was an opportunity not only to demonstrate his power to heal, but also to show that, in the sight of God, all people are of equal value.

Like Jairus, the woman was sure Jesus could heal, but she wanted no fuss. Perhaps she saw herself as of little importance and not worthy to interrupt Jesus. Or she might have been too shy to come forward openly.

Jesus did not criticise her. He recognised in her faith a starting-point and used that to build on. In the presence of the compassionate Christ the woman gained not only physical healing but affirmation of her value as a person. She had been made new and whole.

✷ *Jesus, generous and compassionate, may I find in your presence confidence to overcome my hesitancy and so receive your gift of wholeness.*

Monday February 12   Mark 5.35–43

'It's too late now!' could have been the reaction of Jairus when the messenger arrived with the chilling news that his daughter had died. While there is life, there is hope, is the human stance. However, where there is hope, there is life, is the Christian affirmation.

Jesus acted quickly. He did not give Jairus the chance to apologise for wasting his time, or to give up. He continued on his way as though nothing had happened.

In the face of death Jesus was still confident (see verse 36). With similar words of comfort he later prepared his disciples to face his own death. He urged them, 'Do not be worried and upset. Believe in God and believe also in me' (John 14.1).

Jewish mourning customs recognised the reality and finality of death, and gave expression to sorrow and despair. However, Jesus' attitude to death was in complete contrast. In today's reading we see the resurrection hope of the Christian foreshadowed, and know that we can trust the one who on another occasion said, 'I am the resurrection and the life. Whoever believes in me will live, even though he dies' (John 11.25).

✳ *In life, in death, beyond death, we are not alone, for God is with us.*

Tuesday February 13   Mark 6.1–13

When Jesus returned to Nazareth, there was a clear indication that 'familiarity breeds contempt'. Although impressed and astonished by his ability to teach and preach, the locals were not prepared to honour him as 'local boy made good'. They were critical of him for two reasons:

● **Isn't he the carpenter?** What right had he then to set himself up as an authority on religious matters?
● **Isn't he . . . the son of Mary?** They knew his family background too well to take his claim seriously.

As a result of their scepticism Jesus was unable to exercise his ministry to the full in Nazareth – his home town. The writer of **John's Gospel** had every reason to write at a later date: 'He came to his own country, but his own people did not receive him' (John 1.11).

Jesus will not impose his presence on those who do not want him. When he left the area, the people of Nazareth were the losers. They had missed their chance.

✳ *Lord Jesus Christ,*
   you have come to us,
   you are one with us,
      Mary's Son.   *Patrick Appleford*

Wednesday February 14   Mark 6.14–29

The mission of the twelve disciples had been fruitful. News of Jesus had spread throughout the country. Many had found healing and relief, but to the high and mighty Herod in his palace the news of Jesus and his followers brought judgement and humiliation. His smouldering guilty conscience was fuelled by the verdict of those who saw in Jesus, John the Baptist come back to life.

What Herod heard reminded him of the murder of John.

He remembered how John denounced his marriage to his brother's wife – something forbidden by the Jewish law. The troubled ruler recalled all that led to John's death – his foolishness in collaborating with Herodias and his weakness in failing to go back on his impulsive promise. As he remembered, Herod was tortured further by the realisation that he must take responsibility for John's death.

In **Mark** we have an unfinished story. We are left wondering what Herod did about it all. However, that is not the important issue for us. What matters is our response to the One whose word not only judges us, but also offers us mercy.

✳ *Lord, there is much of Herod in me – so many things I would rather forget. Let me seek your mercy and know your peace.*

Thursday February 15

▶ First read **Mark 6.30–32**.

There is a rhythm to the life of a Christian. This is clearly seen in the ministry of Jesus and his disciples. First, there is the 'Come to me'; then, 'Go and teach' (see February 4). Now the twelve have returned and Jesus says, 'Let us go and rest a while.' He recognised the need for rest and renewal.

As always, the rest and renewal were preparation for further service. The disciples had important lessons to learn.

▶ Now read **Mark 6.33–44**.

Aware of the physical hunger of the crowd that had gathered and listened long to Jesus, the disciples were anxious to send them off to find food. Jesus, however, surprised them by suggesting that they – the disciples – should deal with it. They had to learn to accept responsibility and to use what they had to meet the needs of the people.

The disciples were practical men and saw only the difficulties, but Jesus enabled them to see the possibilities. Taking the Master at his word, and working with him, the disciples became part of the miracle.

Very often our response to human need is to look at what we have and to consider it too little to be of any practical use. When we offer all we have to God, he can use it to achieve results far beyond our imagining.

✳ *Let us give thanks and praise 'to him who by means of his power working in us is able to do much more than we can ever ask for, or even think of' (Ephesians 3.20).*

Mark does not explain why Jesus sent the disciples and the
crowd away before going to the hills by himself. We have to
rely on **John** for a clue. There we read that the crowd, seeing
the mighty work that Jesus had done, desired to take him and
make him king by force (see John 6.14–15).

If the crowds had had their way, Jesus' plan of action would
have been overturned with disastrous results. The disciples
could not have been left with the excited, milling crowd, lest
they too became caught up in the crowd's desire. So Jesus sent
them away before going off alone to talk it over with God.

The disciples found that, even when obeying the Master's
orders, it was not all plain sailing. We find them facing
adverse conditions and getting nowhere. Could it have been
that they were so confused by recent events that they were
unable to give their full attention to the task in hand?

Jesus saw their situation and came to them, calming their
fears, but adding to their sense of surprise and confusion. The
disciples still had much to learn about their Master. They
would continue to be both surprised and confused – all the
way to the cross and beyond.

✼ *Lord Jesus, even now, may I hear you saying, 'Courage! It
is I. Don't be afraid!'.*

Jesus had come so that people might have life in all its fullness
(see John 10.10b). However, Jesus' interpretation of this new
life frequently brought him into conflict with the religious
leaders.

Through the years the Pharisees and the teachers of the
law had amplified the original law as set out in the ten commandments and the first five books of the Old Testament, so
that all of life was hemmed in and restricted by rules and
regulations.

Jesus condemned them for their hypocrisy, reminding them
of Isaiah's description of the religion of his day – full of religiosity but empty of reality (see Isaiah 29.13). It was all built
on their own ideas of how God should be served. Instead of
listening to God, they listened to, and were persuaded by, the
clever arguments of men. This led to two major errors:

● **separation** from all unholy people and things (the name
  'Pharisee' means separated ones).

- a **division** between duty to God and duty to other people.

In his rejection of their attitude, Jesus declared there could be no division or competition between service to God and service to others.

✷ *Lord, may my love for you find expression in my love for others.*

For group discussion and personal thought

Jesus knew what his disciples needed when they were tired (see **Mark 6.30–32, 45–48**, and the notes for **February 15 and 16**). How should we, as Christians, cope with the times when we are busy or tired?

Sunday February 18   Mark 7.14–23

The Pharisees made another great error (see yesterday). They imagined that by following fastidious washing rituals they were ensuring holiness and gaining God's favour.

Jesus shocked them by declaring that the source of pollution is not outside at all. Pressed by the disciples for an explanation, Jesus declared that it was a question of the heart. Food cannot defile because it does not affect the heart. All that is useless or harmful is purged away through the ordinary process of digestion.

It is a person's attitudes and actions, emanating from the heart, that will be judged clean or unclean. The evil we do is the outward sign of heart-sickness. This disease cannot be eradicated by rituals, rules or regulations.

Heart transplants have become a feature of modern medical practice and have frequently given the recipient a new beginning, offering better health and a changed life-style. The Christian gospel offers to us all a new heart, cleansed from its present diseased condition of evil. A renewed heart will produce a changed life-style and a new desire to serve God and our neighbours.

✷ *Create a pure heart in me, O God,*
and put a new and loyal spirit in me.   (Psalm 51.10)

Monday February 19   Mark 7.24–30

In **John's Gospel** we often find that an account of some great

act of Jesus is followed by teaching which brings out its meaning. Here in Mark 7 this procedure is reversed. Earlier in the
chapter we read about Jesus in dispute with the Pharisees,
as he taught new truths. Now, in today's reading, we see him
practising what he had already preached.

Jesus had rejected the narrow, restrictive practices of the
Pharisees. Then, by going into Gentile country, he was declaring that Gentiles were not unclean. They, too, belonged within
the scope of God's kingdom.

To our ears the conversation between Jesus and this woman
(verses 27–28) is strange. However, we are not present to hear
the tone of his voice, or to see his expression.

While the Jews might claim exclusive rights to Jesus' attention, here was a woman whose humility and faith opened the
door to Jesus' compassionate healing, and revealed to all the
scope of the kingdom.

✳ *Lord, when my faith is tested, let me continue to trust in*
  your mercy.

Tuesday February 20   Mark 7.31–37

'How well he does everything!' (verse 37). As news spread of
yet another miracle performed by Jesus, so the admiration
and wonder of the crowds grew. We, too, can marvel, not only
at the outcome of the deaf man's encounter with Jesus, but at
the way Jesus responded to the request for help.

● There was Jesus' sensitivity. The deaf man had for long
  enough been the recipient of pity and put-down. Jesus took
  him away from the crowd, showing him respect and consideration.

● Jesus treated him as a person – not simply as an interesting
  case or as an object of derision.

● The methods Jesus used were appropriate in this particular
  situation. Jesus dealt with him in a way that the man could
  understand, using signs and movements he could see, feel
  and interpret.

This incident reminds us that people who have one specific
impediment should not be treated as if they were totally without other abilities. Disabled people are often angered by the
lack of understanding shown to them. Frequently they find
themselves ignored or treated as being less than fully human.

✳ *Compassionate Christ, let me see others as you see them and*
  be as sensitive to their needs as you were.

Mark takes us quickly from the needs of one person to the needs of a large crowd. The size of the challenge made no difference to Jesus. His compassion was wide enough to embrace all.

His concern for the crowd found expression in practical action. Some Christians may earn the criticism of being 'so heavenly minded as to be of no earthly use' – but not Jesus! He was very much aware of the physical condition of the people. He did not dismiss their hunger as being of no concern of his. Rather, he set about satisfying their needs.

On the other hand, the disciples could be labelled 'too earthbound' in their approach. Jesus challenged their caution and their excuses.

Why wait until circumstances are perfect and supplies are considered adequate before doing anything? Begin now with what you have. Be willing to share that and see what happens.

✳ *Take what I have, Lord, that through my giving other lives may be enriched.*

Modern medical skill has done much to counteract eyesight defects. Corneal transplants have brought new sight to many. Great is the joy, wonder and gratitude of those now able to see more clearly.

Mark is the only Gospel which records this particular incident – possibly because the cure was not instantaneous. There are nevertheless, some interesting features to notice.

● We see Jesus as a very humane healer. Instead of effecting the cure in the midst of a curious crowd, he took the man aside and led him outside the village.

● Jesus used a method understood by the man. Saliva was believed to have healing power. How often have we sucked an injured finger to gain relief?

● Jesus was not prepared to leave the man only partially cured. The patient may have been satisfied with some improvement in his sight, but for Jesus this was not good enough.

There is symbolism here. How many of us are satisfied to wander in some twilight zone of faith, while all the time Jesus is ready to lead us on to discover and experience a much more satisfying Christian life?

✳ *Lord, may I not be content with a half-faith. Lead me on to the fullness of life you came to make possible.*

Friday February 23

Opinion polls are frequently held to ascertain what people are thinking about particular issues, or how they rate certain well-known people. Such market research is important and necessary for planning future direction and priorities.

▶ Read **Mark 8.27 to 9.1**.

Jesus had been with his disciples long enough for them to have formed their own opinions about him, but sometimes they seemed so slow to understand. Time, however, was not on their side. If Jesus could be sure of their understanding and their commitment, then he could open up new dimensions for them. But he could not proceed until he was certain that they were ready.

The first question Jesus asked his disciples (verse 27b) was reasonably safe. He had a good idea what the answers would be. The disciples voiced the popular opinions and reports. Then came the more important question (verse 29). How would they reply? Who would speak for the group?

Peter, so often the spokesman, gave the answer that must have gladdened Jesus' heart. If they were really convinced he was the Messiah, the anointed One, he could risk revealing something more of the way ahead – the way of the cross.

✳ *Jesus, may I not be ashamed or afraid to own you as Lord, whatever the consequences may be.*

Saturday February 24   Mark 9.2–13

Peter's confession of faith at Caesarea Philippi was followed by Jesus' warning of the suffering and death that lay ahead. Peter's reaction indicated something of the confusion in the minds of the disciples (see Mark 8.31–33). They very much needed to have their faith restored and strengthened.

Obviously Peter, James and John had already become an inner circle. When Jesus went to raise the daughter of Jairus these same three had been chosen to be with him (see Mark 5.37). Later when he needed the support of friends as he prayed in Gethsemane, the same three were invited to go with him (Mark 14.33).

The exact nature of the experience known as the **transfiguration** is difficult to describe. Was it really a vision? And if it was, what did it signify? The 'reality' of any vision depends not on its form, but on its spiritual content.

In some inexplicable way the three disciples 'saw' Jesus' place within salvation history. The law, represented by Moses, and the promise of the prophets, represented by Elijah, were fulfilled in Jesus.

In this experience, God confirmed Peter's confession (Mark 8.29b). The disciples were given something to steady their faith and to take with them as they entered the valley.

✴ *Thank God for the 'mountain-top' experiences that have dispelled your doubts and enabled you to accept what you could not understand.*

For group discussion and personal thought
Study **Mark 7.31–37; 8.1–9, 22–25** and look again at the notes for **February 20–22**. What do these three miracles suggest about the things that Jesus can and must do for us?

LOOKING AT THE CROSS

This book by Brian Haymes focuses on the last few hours of Jesus' life on earth. Primarily a Bible study, examining the differences in the four Gospel narratives, it is about Good Friday – a day to pray, to wait, to wonder . . . to look at the cross. A helpful book to read during Lent.

● *UK price:* **£2.25**

44

'Mountain-top' experiences are valuable for they give us new
insights, and widen our horizons, but they are not the sub-
stance of our living. They equip us for the present moment
and for the journey ahead. However, we have to come down
from the mountain to the earthy demands of people.

In today's reading Jesus and the three disciples found themselves right in the centre of human need and confusion. The
teachers of the law were making the most of the disciples'
failure to cure the boy. Embroiled in arguments, they were all
ignoring the real need. How often in the history of the Church,
has a war of words prevented urgent human needs from being
met! Scoring points and claiming power has become more
important than the willingness to minister to need.

The expectations of the father were not unreasonable, for
Jesus had given the twelve authority over evil spirits (Mark
6.7). However, having the authority was not enough. The disciples found themselves unable to act. The ability to act was
not to be found in their own cleverness but in a deeply prayer-
ful relationship with God.

✷ *Lord, I believe. Help me where my faith and prayerfulness*
falls short, so that I am not a hindrance to needs being met.

Ask anyone to name six of the world's great people, and it is
likely you will receive the names of world leaders – the powerful people. Jesus, however, used a very different measure of
greatness. He said that the truly great are those who have
chosen the way of humble service.

The patience of Jesus must have been tested again and
again as he watched and listened to the disciples. Only a short
time before he had been speaking again of his suffering and
death. Had the disciples still not understood Jesus' way? Or
was it that they chose not to accept his warning?

Clearly, they were still confused about the meaning of life
and the nature and values of the kingdom of God. The concept
of a suffering Messiah was alien even to his closest friends.
Are we any more willing than they to accept this complete
reversal of human values which Jesus expressed not only in
his words but in all his living?

Albert Schweitzer said: 'The only ones among you who will

be truly happy are those who have sought and found the way to serve.'

✳ *Teach me, good Lord, to serve you as you deserve;*
   to give and not to count the cost.   Ignatius Loyola

Tuesday February 27   **Mark 9.42–50**

Jesus moved from the thought of service to others to the opposite one of hindering or obstructing others. This was expressed in strong pictorial language which was characteristic of Jesus. The saying in **verse 42** is couched in general terms, but it could have been directed particularly at the teachers of the law. These men not only refused to enter the kingdom of God themselves, but also prevented those who wished to enter (Matthew 23.13).

In **verses 43–48** Jesus moved next to a warning, equally intense, about hindrances to oneself. The kingdom of God is worth any sacrifice. Anything, therefore, which might prevent us from participating in the kingdom, regardless of how good it is in itself, should be ruthlessly sacrificed.

In contrast with his warnings about hindrances to receiving God's grace, Jesus then spoke about the helpfulness of salt – see **verses 49–50**. Salt adds flavour, purifies and preserves. It is the task of the Christian to bring a new zest to life, and to bring a cleansing, purifying influence to bear on the corruption of the world. Salt was also a symbol of concord. So, with a reference back to their quarrelling, Jesus was urging the disciples to keep their fellowship intact.

✳ *Lord, may I be a 'salty' Christian, a diffuser of those things*
   which make life good and worthwhile.

Ash Wednesday, February 28   **Mark 10.1–16**

A recently published report reveals that in New Zealand fewer marriages are taking place, while divorces have increased considerably each year. Divorce was also common in Jesus' day. However, according to Jewish law, a wife could not divorce her husband, while a husband could divorce his wife on the flimsiest of grounds – for example, if her cooking failed to please him! Jesus was aware of the unfairness of the law and used this opportunity to affirm the rights of women.

The question posed by the Pharisees was an attempt to bring Jesus into conflict with the Jewish law. However, Jesus avoided becoming involved in the legal wrangles. Instead, he lifted the whole concept of marriage out of the area of legal arguments, and placed it on the highest plane – within the creative purposes of God.

Rather than use Jesus' reply in a legalistic way to condemn divorce, we should remember that Jesus' teaching in nearly every instance was in general terms, and so in particular cases we must interpret it with compassion. To do otherwise would make us guilty of the same 'hardness of heart' of which Jesus accused his own people.

✳ *Prayer for Ash Wednesday* *Lord Jesus, draw us, your people, along the way of the cross. Speak to us again of the love which took you to Calvary. As we journey with you, deepen our love for you and for others.*

Thursday March 1   Mark 10.17–31

Taken at its face value, the question in verse 17 would appear appropriate and acceptable. But Jesus was not content to take things at surface value. He probed deeper.

'What must I do?' said the man. The belief that salvation can be gained by **doing** any one thing, or a number of things, is utterly false. Such a belief persists today and hinders many a person from turning to God – on the grounds that they consider themselves not good enough.

The demand of Jesus for the rich man to give all his goods to the poor was not a requirement he made on all who would be his followers. But, in this instance, Jesus had perceived that his wealth stood between him and full commitment to the purposes of God. The disciples were staggered that Jesus should make entrance to the kingdom so difficult for someone who seemed so keen and promising.

It has been suggested that 'the eye of the needle' refers to a very narrow gate in Jerusalem. However, it is much more likely that it is a picturesque metaphor used to describe what is well-nigh impossible.

✳ *Lord Jesus, set me free from the tyranny of the trivial, that I may follow you with singleness of purpose.*

Friday March 2   Mark 10.32–45

We now sense that the climax to the Gospel story is approaching. The goal of the journey – Jerusalem – is disclosed and Jesus led his disciples on with steady stride.

This third prediction of Jesus' passion (verses 32–34) is the most detailed (see also Mark 8.31 and 9.31). The awe and amazement of the disciples as they followed Jesus probably reflected a heightened sense of something imminent, but not yet understood. Their failure to understand is seen in James' and John's request for earthly power. The disciples were still blinded by visions of thrones, crowns and seats of honour. Jesus was telling them that without the cross there could be no crown.

Jesus was not denying the ultimate victory of resurrection, but was emphasising that this victory must 'pass through' the pain and suffering of Gethsemane, Jerusalem and Calvary. 'The cup' (verse 39) referred to the life to which God had called Jesus (see Mark 14.36). The disciples assured Jesus they were able to share the bitter experience through which he must pass. However, it is one thing to feel confident when the testing time is still some distance away. How their profession must have mocked them when they were actually put to the test – and failed!

✳ **Prayer for (Women's) World Day of Prayer**
O Saviour Christ, in whose way of love lies the secret of life and a better tomorrow, we pray for quiet courage to match this hour. Let the problems of this age challenge us, its discoveries excite us, its injustices anger us, its possibilities inspire us, for the sake of your kingdom.

Saturday March 3   **Mark 10.46–52**

This story is notable for the persistence of the blind beggar, and for the attention Jesus gave to one lowly individual in a great crowd. For Bartimaeus, this was an opportunity to be grasped – his chance to be healed! For the crowd, it was their opportunity to hear Jesus, and they were not going to let anyone deprive them of this chance.

Again we see Jesus reversing the commonly-held scale of values. To him, one person with a need was given priority and his full attention. The crowd could wait.

'Jesus stopped' (verse 49) – in these two words we see the graciousness of Jesus; his readiness to put another's need before his own. Remember, at this time the shadow of the cross had darkened over his way. At Jericho he was only about fifteen miles (24km) from his goal.

Bartimaeus knew exactly what he wanted. There was nothing vague or hesitant about his request. Only one thing really mattered – he wanted to be able to see again. His faith was rewarded. Then, having received his sight, he followed Jesus along the way.

We all sit in blindness and poverty until Jesus comes and makes us whole. The experience of Bartimaeus is a picture of what it means for us to follow Christ.

✳ *Lord, how do I answer your question, 'What do you want me to do for you?' May I walk humbly and gladly in your way.*

For group discussion and personal thought

Read **Mark 10.17–31** and look again at the notes for **March 1**. What sacrifices does Jesus call us to make when we follow him? What is there in our lives which is a hindrance to our relationship with Jesus? Is it ever possible to sacrifice too much? Can you think of specific examples?

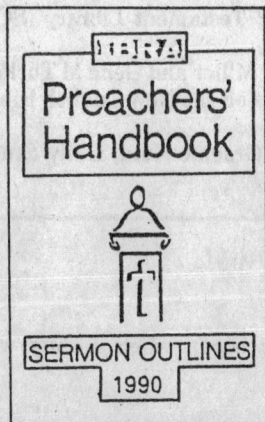

JOSHUA

Notes by the Revd Alison R Goodwin, BA, BD

Alison Goodwin is the minister of Lee Mount Baptist Church in Halifax, England. She worked as a prison psychologist and then with the Leeds Truancy Project research team, before training for the ministry.

The notes in this section are based on the New English Bible.

The main part of the book of **Joshua** tells of the Israelites' conquest of Canaan – the promised land – and the subsequent dividing up of the land among the tribes. Many people have difficulty in seeing how books like this are relevant to our everyday Christian living. If we only read **Joshua** as history, then this might well be true. However, **Joshua** is much more than history, for it tells of a community ready to listen to God and of God in action fulfilling his promises especially to his chosen people.

We shall see that **Joshua** is a book concerned with faithfulness and trust among a community which has been through hard times and is faced with an uncertain future. Thus it has a message for all who seek to be pilgrims today.

Suggestions for further reading

Joshua by J Alberto Soggin, Old Testament Library (SCM Press)

The Book of Joshua by J Maxwell Miller and Gene M Tucker, Cambridge Bible Commentaries on the New English Bible, (Cambridge University Press)

Joshua, Judges and Ruth by A Graeme Auld, Daily Study Bible (Saint Andrew Press)

1st Sunday in Lent, March 4

A new stage in Israel's history began when Joshua was appointed as Moses' successor.

▶ Read **Joshua 1.1–11**.

The Lord's words provided hope and encouragement to Joshua as he faced a monumental challenge. God had been with his people in the past and, because of this, they could trust him absolutely to go with them into the future. With this promise went a command – that the people should be careful to obey God's law (verses 7–8).

We often worry when we find ourselves in difficult situations but, in those times, we must trust God just as Joshua did. We must trust his promises to us, because he has called us and he will be with us whatever we have to face.

God wants us to be obedient and to make room for spiritual things in our lives, not because we fear punishment, but so that the way we live our everyday lives matches what we claim to believe. This is so that we may gain the strength to set out in confidence to tackle the tasks we are called to do each day.

✳ *Jesus calls us! By thy mercies*
 Saviour, may we hear thy call,
Give our hearts to thine obedience,
 Serve and love thee best of all.   C Francis Alexander

Monday March 5   Joshua 2.1–16

Jericho commanded a key defensive position in the Jordan valley. From there, spies would have a good overall view of the central area of Canaan. In sending these spies Joshua continued to prepare for entry into the promised land.

Rahab, a poor prostitute at the bottom of the social scale, hardly seems a good prospect for helping to achieve God's purposes. Or was she? The Bible contains many stories of how God uses unlikely people to help in his work. Rahab offers hope to us all and shows us that we can leave behind our past sins and work for God.

Rahab reminds us of some 'dubious' women whom Jesus met, notably one who disturbed a meal so that she could kiss his feet and anoint his head (Mark 14.3–9). Both Rahab and this woman demonstrated faith in their actions and are still remembered.

What we make of Rahab may reveal our own prejudices. Often we may be tempted to write people off – perhaps even ourselves – as not good enough to serve God. Rahab reminds us that we can all serve and no one is beyond his reach. God has always used unexpected and unlikely people to further his purposes.

✳ *Pray that you may be open to learn from all the sources and people that God may use.*

Tuesday March 6   **Joshua 3.1–17**

The story of the Israelites advancing under God, led by the
Ark of the Covenant, is presented as an act of worship led by
priests, rather than as an army marching to war. The people
had been spiritually prepared for this occasion (verse 5). When
they crossed the Jordan there was a real sense in which the
living God gave the new land to the people and crossed the
Jordan before them (verse 10).

Today's reading is centred on the Ark of the Covenant. This
was a portable altar, signifying the living presence of God
with his people. The Ark no longer exists, but for Christians
this does not matter since we can turn to Jesus for assurance
of God's presence. Jesus is the perfect symbol of God's presence with us. We can be sure that he is always ahead of us
whatever unknown circumstances we may have to face.

✳   *Christ of the upward way,*
        My guide divine,
    Where thou hast set thy feet
        May I place mine:
    And move and march wherever thou hast trod,
    Keeping face forward up the hill of God.

                                        Walter J Mathams

Wednesday March 7   **Joshua 5.1–12**

This celebration of the Passover Festival marked the end of an
era for the Israelites and their new beginning in the promised
land. Only men who had been circumcised could celebrate the
Passover; so before the celebrations began, the rite of circumcision had to be carried out. This rite seemed to have lapsed
while the Israelites had been on the move in the wilderness.

Today, in our Christian communities, celebrations are held
to mark the end of one era and the start of another – perhaps
at the beginning of a new ministry or a special anniversary
such as a centenary. These celebrations always include
elements of thankfulness for the past and hope for the future.

A strong sense of past thanks and future hope was the
essence of the covenant promise to the Israelites, and this is
true for us. God **has been** with us; God **is** with us; God **will
be** with us. For Christians this is a cause for thanksgiving
and hope every day, and especially each time we share the
bread and wine at Holy Communion. We celebrate with

thanksgiving and hope, remembering Jesus Christ 'the same yesterday, today, and for ever' (Hebrews 13.8).

✳ *O God, our help in ages past,*
  Our hope for years to come.   *Isaac Watts*

Thursday March 8   **Joshua 5.13 to 6.11**

The battle of Jericho was the first of a series of campaigns led by Joshua, each of which was concerned with an important local centre in the promised land. This was no ordinary battle, but firmly set within a religious context. Joshua was even instructed to respect the sanctity of the place where he was given his orders for the day (verse 15)! The leader himself was led by God. Recognising God's holy presence, Joshua was willing to listen, and in listening received strength and encouragement for the task ahead.

Holy wars are still fought today but are unwelcome by most Christians. The plans for taking Jericho remind us that not all battles in which Christians engage for their Lord will be violent. Notice the strange weapons in the story – religious symbols – trumpets of rams' horns and the Ark of the Covenant. Victory was promised without a blow being struck.

Whatever we make of the Jericho story, it reminds us that God fights battles in a different way from us – often with unlikely resources. God's methods and ways are not the same as ours; and he requires us to obey and trust him before he can use us for anything.

✳ *Ponder God's words to Paul: 'My grace is all you need; power comes to its full strength in weakness.'*
                                        (2 Corinthians 12.9)

Friday March 9   **Joshua 6.12–27**

The orders Joshua received for taking Jericho were strange by anyone's standards. They involved an unusual ritual of quietly marching around the walls of Jericho each day. Then, it is recorded that, on the seventh day with a loud shout and the blast of horns the walls fell down flat.

Archaeologists have provided evidence of substantial destruction to towns in Canaan which coincide with the time of the military invasion of this land by Israel. However, many of these places do not seem to be mentioned in **Joshua**; and the excavations at Jericho do not appear to support the biblical account of its destruction. So why has it become one of the best-known stories in **Joshua**?

Perhaps this is because it was the **first** of the battles fought by the Israelites, and through it they learned many valuable lessons. For example, the Lord kept his promise of victory to Israel because Joshua had fully obeyed the instructions he was given. Obedience to God has been essential for all generations of God's people. The word of God is only powerful when we obey it. All kinds of barriers and walls will fall before God's word, whether shouted from the roof-tops or whispered from the quietness of our hearts!

✳ *Lord, help us to be obedient to your word. Grant us the strength to work where we are to overcome evil with good.*

Saturday March 10   Joshua 7.1–20a

Throughout the book of **Joshua** God's people are being called to have faith in God and to trust the God who had chosen them from the beginning and called them to be obedient. In yesterday's reading we saw how obedience to God's commands led to success, but today we see that disobedience – even by a single individual – led to failure for **all** the people.

The idea that behaviour is either rewarded or punished is ancient and was commonly believed in Israel at this time. The penalty paid by Achan, following his confession, was severe. This was to reinforce the terrible thing he had done – keeping some silver and gold for himself. The spoils from Jericho should have been placed in the Lord's treasury. To keep them was a desecration and had to be punished.

This story is a lesson to all of us when we are faced with the issue of obedience and disobedience. We are free to choose whether or not we obey God's word; but if we really believe in Jesus, we will desire to follow his commands. Deceit and disobedience have no place in the kingdom of God. However, when we do make a mistake, unlike Achan who was punished by death, we have the opportunity to receive God's forgiveness and start afresh if we are truly sorry.

✳ *Thank God for the forgiveness we are offered in Jesus.*

For group discussion and personal thought

Read and study **Joshua 1.5–9**. What characteristics of leadership did God require of Joshua? How do this week's readings show that Joshua lived up to these requirements? What can we learn from Joshua about leadership?

2nd Sunday in Lent, March 11   Joshua 8.1–8, 28–35

Joshua 8 records the second attempt to capture and destroy the city of Ai following the previous failure because of Achan's disobedience. Today we may find it difficult to come to terms with the bloodiness of this destruction. This may be particularly so when it is recorded that God himself takes the initiative, giving instructions to Joshua along with the promise of success (verses 1–2). The capture and destruction of the city is a straightforward ambush story. Victory was total as the enemy was thrown into a panic by shrewd tactics rather than a miracle. However, the victory was still interpreted as the work of the Lord.

After the battle Joshua reminded the people of the blessings which they would receive if they obeyed God's word, and the curses which would come if they disobeyed. Verses 30–35 record a pause in which the Israelites renewed their devotion to God before pressing on with the next task. Here we have an important lesson for all those who are engaged in the Lord's work.

We need to take time to 'recharge our batteries' – just as Jesus did – in prayer and worship. Let us renew and refresh ourselves, regularly rededicating ourselves to God's service.

✳ *Jesus said: 'Come to me, all whose work is hard, whose load is heavy and I will give you relief.' (Matthew 11.28)*

Monday March 12   Joshua 9.3–27

The story in today's reading has the hallmarks of a folk-tale to explain why the Gibeonites served as menials in Israel. It may also have been an attempt to reconcile the theological idea that all the original inhabitants of the promised land were to be killed, with the well-known fact that many of them survived.

The story is also a wonderful example of ancient cunning in which Joshua and the Israelites were outmanoeuvred by the Gibeonites. Verse 14 is the key verse – they 'did not at first seek guidance from the Lord'. This meant they made decisions and promises which they later regretted, but which could not be broken.

In our daily lives, when we are faced with important decisions we often forget to consult God – and we, too, suffer the consequences. Before rushing into making such decisions we need to seek God's guidance. If we learn to do this each day, we shall not become trapped as Joshua did.

✸ *Take time to be holy, let him be thy guide;*
And run not before him, whatever betide;
In joy or in sorrow, still follow thy Lord,
And, looking to Jesus, still trust in his word.

                                                 W D Longstaff

Tuesday March 13

Joshua 10–17 contains the account of Israel taking possession of the promised land. The different territories of captured land were allocated to various tribes. Today's reading is set in Shiloh in the central hill country and concerns seven tribes who had still not taken up their inheritance in the promised land.

▶ Read **Joshua 18.1–10**.

Joshua urged the seven tribes to get on with taking up their inheritance (verse 3)! They were to allocate the territory by casting lots. This was not leaving matters to chance like our tossing of a coin, or drawing straws, but was an activity done 'in the presence of the Lord' (verse 6) in a sacred and reverent way.

God had promised the land to the children of Israel, but it was their responsibility to take it up and pass it on to the next generation. In much the same way, today, the Lord invites each of us to claim his promises to us for ourselves. We need to take up our own heritage of faith – a living relationship with God – and then pass it on to the next generation.

✸ *Tell out, my soul, the greatness of the Lord*
  To children's children and for evermore!

                                           Timothy Dudley-Smith

The background to today's reading is Exodus 21.12–14 where
God told the people that he would provide cities of refuge for
them. These were to be six places (verses 7–8) where people
who had unwittingly committed a crime could find safety and
receive a fair trial. At this time in Israel the system of justice
presumed that in a case of a murder, the victim's next-of-kin
would avenge the death by killing the murderer.

Most judicial systems try to differentiate between deliberate and accidental crimes. However, sudden death and other
serious crimes often lead to anger and the seeking of revenge
before the facts can be established. So there is still the need
for places of refuge today.

Throughout history many people have sought refuge in a
church or other holy place. Today, there are many people – for
example, refugees, immigrants, the homeless and the men-
tally handicapped – who find themselves in difficult circumstances, perhaps through their lack of awareness or
intolerable living situations. Are our churches still places
where people can be protected, find safety and be assured of
fair treatment?

✳ *Pray for those who seek sanctuary in the Lord's house, and
those who endeavour to care for and protect them.*

The story begun in Joshua 1 is almost concluded. The conquest of the land was completed, all Israel was settled, and
the Lord had kept all his promises (verse 43). However, before
the Israelites settled down to ordinary living in the promised
land, Joshua called a gathering of the tribes whose land was
on the eastern side of Jordan. They had been required to help
their fellow Israelites take possession of Canaan.

Joshua acknowledged their obedience to his orders. But,
because their territory was separated from the rest, he urged
them to take care to remain faithful to the Lord. Finally, he
sent them back home with his blessing.

The success of the conquest of Canaan came about because
all the people of Israel operated in unison under Joshua's
command. God's purposes were achieved through co-oper-
ation and not quarrelling.

Today, much is being achieved for the kingdom of God
because Christian groups are working together rather than

competing with one another. In many ways we are co-operating under our one leader – Jesus Christ; and in continuing to do so we shall more effectively win the world for Christ.

✳ *Lord, help us to co-operate with one another.*

Friday March 16   Joshua 23.1–16

Joshua, now an elderly man, made a farewell speech to all the people. This address was very important because in ancient Israel, as in some parts of the world today, the parting words of tribal leaders and heads of families were highly regarded. Joshua encouraged his people to remember their recent history and reminded them of all that God had done for them. However, his primary concern was to appeal to them to keep God's law and remain faithful to him. If the people of Israel were not faithful to God, then they could not count on God's protection or blessing in their lives.

Finally, Joshua pointed out the consequences of obedience and disobedience to God – blessing or curse! His entire speech was a call to devotion – to be resolute . . . observe and perform everything in the book of the law of Moses, without swerving to right or to left' (verse 6).

Today's reading contains words of encouragement and advice for all those who belong to God, and who seek to follow Christ in their daily living. It reminds us that we need to make a conscious effort to **remember** all that God has done for us. As we think about his great faithfulness to us, let us willingly respond to him with love and obedience.

✳ *Lord, how great is your faithfulness to me – each day!*

Saturday March 17   Joshua 24.1–2a, 14–31

Joshua's last public act was to lead his people in renewing their covenant with God. He knew that the success of the nation of Israel depended upon them serving the Lord wholeheartedly. Joshua made it very clear that the people could not follow God **and** cling to their old ways. He challenged the people to forsake all other gods and idols and serve only the Lord. But it was up to them to **choose for themselves** if they would do this (verses 14–24).

Every generation must **exercise the choice** of following God for themselves. We cannot live on the faith and stories of a previous age. Neither is it possible for **us** to be faithful to God and also to follow 'other gods' – particularly the god of 'selfism' which is so deeply entrenched in our society today. We must heed the words of Jesus when he reminded his followers that they could not serve two masters at the same time. He said that they would either 'hate the first and love the second or . . . be devoted to the first and think nothing of the second' (Matthew 6.24).

As we conclude our readings from **Joshua**, let us come afresh to God and respond to his challenge to renew our covenant relationship with him.

✳ *Come, Holy Spirit, renew us. Lead us always into a deeper relationship with the God who has done so much for us.*

For group discussion and personal thought

Read **Joshua 20**. Think of examples today where churches or other holy buildings are used as places of refuge. Who are in need of refuge today? As Christians, should we ever refuse to give refuge to a person seeking sanctuary? How should we respond to those who seek the Church's help?

MARK 11 – 15

Notes by the Revd Allan J Bowers

Allan Bowers is a Methodist minister. He has served as a chaplain to the army in Hong Kong and Korea, and in several circuits in England. He is now retired after forty years' ministry, and is living in Sidmouth.

The notes in this section are based on the Revised Standard Version.

In **Mark 11–15** we trace the ministry of Jesus in Jerusalem during the last few days of his life on earth. These chapters tell of his triumphal entry into the city, and of specific acts and teaching, culminating in his arrest, trial, crucifixion and burial. At the centre of these highly important narratives is Jesus himself and his redemptive work for all humankind.

Suggestions for further reading – see page 26.

3rd Sunday in Lent, March 18   Mark 11.1–11

The story of Christ's entry into Jerusalem is one of supreme courage, sustained by faith. He was courageous, because he knew that the Jewish leaders were plotting to kill him (see John 11.57); and because the colt he was to ride on was unbroken. Perfect control would be needed by Jesus to master this young donkey.

Some years ago I attended a rodeo in Oregon, USA, at which none of the cowboys succeeded in breaking in the untamed horses – their hands simply could not hold them. But what powerful, yet gentle, hands Jesus must have had as he mastered, guided and soothed the unbroken donkey, despite the fact that the people around were shrieking 'Hosanna' in its ears, waving palm branches before its eyes (John 12.13), and throwing clothes in front of its feet!

If we submit our wills to Jesus, those same hands can guide and control our mulish, undisciplined lives. However, perhaps more than anything else, we need **self-control**. Jesus, as no other, can make this possible, for self-control is one of the fruits of his Spirit (see Galatians 5.23).

✳ *Direct, control, suggest, this day,*
   All I design, or do, or say.
      That all my powers, with all their might,
      In thy sole glory may unite.   *Thomas Ken*

Monday March 19   Mark 11.12–19

The account of the cleansing of the temple demonstrates once
more the superlative courage of Jesus and his unusual self-
control. Notice how vividly the narrative reads – this is a
special characteristic of **Mark**. There is no doubt that Jesus
was roused to anger at the defilement of God's temple, just as
Moses had been roused to anger at the idolatry of his people
(see Exodus 32.19–20).

It was a brave thing for Jesus to declare within the precincts
of the temple that God's house should be called a house of
prayer for **all the nations**, because it was well-known for its
Jewish exclusiveness. This was a strong reminder that God's
love reaches across the whole world to all peoples.

It is always wrong to lose one's temper, but it can also be
wrong not to be angry – for example, at the ill-treatment of
children or the taking of innocent hostages. Ephesians 4.26a
says, 'Be angry but do not sin.' A Christian should be expected
to keep his anger under perfect control at all times. Jesus
alone makes this possible.

✳ *Lord, grant us by your grace, the ability to control our*
   emotions at all times.

Tuesday March 20

It is clear that Jesus insisted that we must play our part before
faith becomes an active power in our lives. We all know what
it is to face 'mountains' of difficulty. However, we often find
that, if we face the mountain resolutely and pray for the faith
that puts forth effort, what appeared as a mountain becomes
a molehill.

▶ Read **Mark 11. 20–25.**

These verses have a special word for us today. Part of our
malaise is that we are waiting for God to remove the mountain
for us, while we look on. We require will-power, and it is God
who empowers our will. Ephesians 3.20 says, 'By the power
at work within us (he) is able to do far more abundantly than
all that we ask or think.'

One day, while watching a huge crane lifting tons of material in the construction of a block of flats, I noticed on the window of the crane driver's cab the words, 'I believe in God'! Here was a witness to the crane driver's faith, but it also reminded me that, if we have faith in God, then we will know that he is the best 'weight-lifter' in the world. However, like the crane, he still needs the driver!

✻ Pray that the Lord will help you to 'be alert; stand firm in the faith; be valiant and strong' (1 Corinthians 16.13, NEB).

Wednesday March 21   Mark 11.27–33

In the charming town of Chipping Campden in England, there is a house called 'Controversy' – a strange name for a house. Yet, there can surely be few houses where there has never been controversy on some issue of importance.

In today's reading the controversy was over the authority of Jesus, which had been challenged by members of the Jewish Council because of his moral courage in cleansing the temple court and his daily teaching. Jesus was aware that their question (verse 28) was a trap, an attempt to get from him an admission that would warrant the death penalty. In his own inimitable way Jesus reduced his opponents to silence, and suggested that there was a close connection between his ministry and the ministry of John. Both acted with authority from heaven – from God.

The refusal of his disputants to answer Jesus' question (verse 30) freed him from replying to their initial challenge. Encapsulated in this incident is the conviction of Jesus that his authority was from God.

Likewise, authority in the Church is to be found in the enduring life of Christ in which we all share, and which is the body of Christ in the world today.

✻ Pray that, with renewed trust, you may accept the authority of God.

Thursday March 22   Mark 12.1–12

'Is it relevant for me?' asked a woman in the bookshop when she was recommended to read a certain book. The parable in today's reading seems so remote from everyday life and experience that we may well ask, 'Is it relevant for me?' Yes, it is relevant, because in telling this parable Jesus makes us think about three things concerning God.

- **The cost to God.** In sending Jesus into the world it cost God the life of his Son. It has been said that 'No man able to command force would risk a beloved son among ruffians.' Yet is this not precisely what God did, at the cost of the life of his Son? That which has cost God so much, cannot be cheap for us.

- **God's patience.** Martin Luther once said that if he had made the world he would have kicked it to pieces long ago. God treated the tenants with infinite patience. Does he not treat us in the same way?

- **God's grace.** God did not reckon his Son too dear a price to pay for our life.

In thinking about these things we can only say:

'This was the Lord's doing,
and it is marvellous in our eyes.'   (verse 11)

✳ *Lord, may I live, think, feel and act as one who is called to be your disciple.*

Friday March 23   Mark 12.13–17

God or Caesar? This is still the central question for Christians concerned with twentieth-century politics. Jesus handled the question with consummate skill. Had he replied that his fellow Jews should pay tribute to their masters, he would have been charged as a reactionary and an enemy. On the other hand, had he said that Jews should not pay tribute to Caesar, then he would have been inviting trouble with the Roman authorities.

The coin bore the image of Caesar. Jesus said to the Pharisees and the Herodians, that they must give to Caesar what belongs to Caesar and to God what belongs to God. This advice still stands today. The implication for all Christians, wherever they live, is that their supreme loyalty is to God. Therefore, if duty to God and duty to the State are in conflict it is duty to God that must have the paramount claim. Peter and the apostles learned the lesson well – they said, 'We must obey God rather than men' (Acts 5.29).

If, as in some countries today, Christians are confronted with laws which are immoral and an outrage against love, then they must defy them and bear the consequences.

✻ *Give us, Lord, the spirit to think and to do always those
things that are right, and live according to your holy will.*

Saturday March 24   Mark 12.18–27

W E Sangster told a story of a man who was telephoning his
wife from a call-box. While waiting to be connected, he sang
this hymn verse:

> My knowledge of that life is small,
>> The eye of faith is dim;
> But 'tis enough that Christ knows all,
>> And I shall be with him.   *Richard Baxter*

The operator said, 'Please, do sing it again.' The man did,
and she replied, 'Thank you, you'll never know how much you
have helped me.'

The idea of resurrection may seem a fantastic notion – the
Sadducees simply could not accept it. The question they put
to Jesus demonstrates that human logic is by no means divine
logic. Our knowledge of that life may be small but Jesus, in
his reply to the Sadducees, made it clear that there is a resurrection – that God 'is not God of the dead but of the living'
(verse 27). Death is a boundary which no one ever crosses
alive, and those who have died cannot tell us what the experience is like. Faith does not explain death, but those who live
by faith in the living God can entrust themselves to God and
know that because Jesus died and rose again, all is well.

✻ *Thank you, Father, that in the resurrection of Jesus we have
your confirmation that all is well.*

For group discussion and personal thought
Think of pictures you have seen of Jesus, both traditional and
modern. What do they tell you about Jesus? Now study **Mark
11.15–18**. How does this picture of Jesus differ from those
you have thought about?

4th Sunday in Lent, March 25   Mark 12.28–34

'God is love' is probably the greatest single statement about
God in the whole of the Bible. Our love for him and our neighbour can only be by way of response to his love for us. It is

important to understand this otherwise the two commandments in today's reading become impossible to practise, and then the danger is that they go unheeded.

The state of 'living in love' is not something we can achieve by our own effort or in our own strength; it is something which happens by God's grace. Love sees the life of my neighbour as 'my life'. In faith I recognise and value my neighbours and always seek their highest good.

In a small town two doctors – one a doctor of medicine and the other a doctor of divinity – lived in the same house. One day a man came to the door and asked the housekeeper if he could see the doctor. She replied, 'Do you want to see the one who preaches or the one who practises?' We may know the theory of what God expects from us, as did the scribe in today's reading, but what he expects from us carries a moral impulse to turn our hearing into doing, our preaching into practice.

✷ *Lord, make me a doer of your word so that my neighbour's welfare will be my concern.*

Monday March 26

▶ First read **Mark 12.35–37**.

Although these verses may seem difficult for us to understand, they would have been clear to Jesus' audience. The question he asked in verse 35 was to cast doubt on the credibility of the scribes' teaching. They taught that the Christ – God's promised anointed One – would be 'the son of David'. In other words, they were looking for an earthly king who would follow in the footsteps of his ancestor, David, and would bring freedom and prosperity to the kingdom of Israel.

The scribes believed that all the psalms were written by David, so Jesus quoted from Psalm 110.1 to show that even David referred to the promised One as 'my Lord' (verse 36b). This was to show that the Christ would be much greater than David and not merely an earthly king.

▶ Now read **Mark 12.38–40**.

Jesus continued his courageous attack on the scribes. He not only criticised their teaching but drew attention to their pride, vanity, hypocrisy and their love of people's praise. The claim that the scribes would 'receive the greater condemnation' (verse 40) reminds us of Jesus' words in Luke 12.48: 'Every one to whom much is given, of him much will be required.'

✷ Lord, you have given me so much, help me always to live according to your ways.

Tuesday March 27   **Mark 12.41–44**

'The widow who cast two mites into the treasury by doing so became rich; but had she kept them, she would have remained simply "a poor widow" ', so wrote Christina Rossetti. The poor widow was commended by Jesus for her generosity. Clearly it is not the amount of the gift that gives it value in the sight of God but the sacrificial generosity with which it is given. 'One coin out of a little,' said Saint Ambrose, 'is better than a treasure out of much; for it is not considered how much is given, but how much remains behind.'

In the church graveyard of a small village, in memory of a woman, who gave herself untiringly and without stint, is the epitaph; 'She hath done what she couldn't!' There are many demands made upon us to give to this and that cause. Should not all our giving be done in adventurous faith and in a selfless way? It is only in giving that our lives are enriched. That which draws everything into itself and gives nothing out becomes lifeless – like a stagnant pool.

✷ Lord, you know what I give and how I give it, help me always to give generously.

Wednesday March 28   **Mark 13.1–13**

These words of Jesus have an uncanny realism about them for frequently on our television screens we see the terrible effects of wars, earthquakes and famines – and we often feel helpless. Yet these dark symbols of despair for us can become bright signs of hope. Let us look at some of Jesus' words which are enormously challenging and encouraging:

● **'This is but the beginning of the birth-pangs'** (verse 8). Birth-pangs are painful, but after they are over there is wonder, love and joy at the birth of a baby. In our helplessness we lay life's happenings in God's hands, believing that through him there is indeed hope.

● **'Take heed to yourselves'** (verse 9). Our reaction to this should be to keep a firm watch on our own lives. Trials have to be borne and offer us the opportunity to strengthen our faith.

66

- 'The gospel must first be preached to all nations' (verse 10). This is the mind of Jesus on the proclamation of the good news to all peoples and should be our top priority.
- 'He who endures to the end will be saved' (verse 13b). It is in our endurance that we shall overcome, and find that the goal has been reached and the blessing of God received.

✽ *Lord, help me to link my earthly feebleness to your almighty power.*

Thursday March 29   Mark 13.14–23

Winter added a last horror to the catastrophe forecast by Jesus in this reading. However, what we see here, and what Jesus saw with penetrating insight, is God in human history. Although Jerusalem would be encompassed by armies and although there would be appalling suffering, none of these events was outside God's sphere of influence. God fulfils his purposes not only when we embrace his will, but even in our disobedience.

The miracles of the incarnation and the resurrection are God's guarantee that he holds the whole world in his hands, and that his will, which is obeyed in heaven, will be obeyed on earth. The reading ends with Jesus telling his hearers to 'take heed'. This is a strong reminder to us in today's world, as we see the result of people's inhumanity to one another, that disobeying God's laws leads to disaster and death.

✽ *Lord, help us to discover what will be best for the welfare of your creation and ourselves.*

Friday March 30   Mark 13.24–37

In Mark 13 there are four keywords: take heed, watch, endure, and pray. **Watchfulness** is the general theme, in view of the future return of Christ in glory. This method of speaking was used by Jesus to impress upon his hearers the lessons of watchfulness, and to warn them against the peril of not being ready. If the human situation in Jesus' day warranted such severe warnings, how much more are those warnings justified today? The possibility of global nuclear warfare is one telling proof of the perpetual relevance of these biblical warnings.

We must heed the warning signs of our own civilisation but we also need to know that things can never go so wrong that the living God is defeated. The good news is that nothing can separate us from God's love, and that no trials and tribulations can ultimately thwart God's purpose.

❋ *Who can faint, while such a river*
  Ever flows their thirst to assuage
Grace, which, like the Lord, the giver
  Never fails from age to age?   John Newton

Saturday March 31   Mark 14.1–2, 10–11

Some time ago I went on a house-to-house visiting campaign offering people free copies of **Mark's Gospel**. At one house a young man came to the door and I gave him the Gospel. 'Is it one of those whodunit stories?' he asked. I've never heard the Gospel thought of in that way before, but there is a sense in which the Gospel is the best whodunit story of all time.

As the story unfolds one thing is clear – Jesus is the central character, and we know why he died. But what about Judas? Do we know why this man, who was chosen by Jesus to be an apostle, betrayed him? No one can say with absolute certainty what happened to Judas, other than that he turned away from his apostleship (see Acts 1.25). As far as events take us he is presented as a man of despair and remorse, but not of sorrow. However, we cannot say what, in God's endless mercy, happened to the soul of Judas.

In Washington Cathedral, there are posts in the communion rail carved to represent each of the apostles. There is, however, one uncarved post that represents Judas. It is called 'The Unfinished Man'. We are filled with repugnance as we think of what Judas did, but how many of us are free from those sins which brought about the betrayal of Jesus? All of us are unfinished persons who need the 'master carver' to shape us into the likeness of Jesus.

❋ *Lord, refine my nature until the beauty of Jesus be seen in me.*

For group discussion and personal thought
Despite his teaching and his actions, some people failed to recognise who Jesus was. Read **Mark 13.33–36**. How do we recognise Jesus at work in our lives and in the world? What can we do to make ourselves ready and alert to see him?

Passion Sunday, April 1

Today is a day when we think of the **passion** – the suffering – of Jesus. Our reading is from **Isaiah**; and, from New Testament times, it has been linked with Jesus' death and passion. It depicts someone who has suffered severely for the sins of others. If we read these verses slowly they will help us to meditate upon Jesus' passion.

▶ Read **Isaiah 52.13 to 53.12**.

It is little wonder that the early Christians saw in these verses a vivid description of Jesus.

- They knew for themselves that his appearance had been marred (verse 14) by beatings and crucifixion.
- They, themselves had rejected him, hid their faces from him and caused him sorrow and grief (verse 3).
- They had heard that at his trial Jesus 'had opened not his mouth' and had been 'like a lamb that is led to the slaughter' (verse 7).
- And they were also beginning to realise the implication of the words: 'he shall . . . make many to be accounted righteous; and he shall bear their iniquities' (verse 11).

✳ *Man of Sorrows! What a name*
For the Son of God, who came
Ruined sinners to reclaim!
Alleluia! What a Saviour!   *Philipp Bliss*

Monday April 2   Mark 14.3–9

Before Mary Martin, a great star, went on the New York stage to play the leading lady in the muscial *South Pacific*, she received a note from the writer of the lyrics. The short but vibrant note read:

A bell is not a bell till you ring it,
A song is not a song till you sing it.
Love in your heart is not put there to stay,
Love is not love till you give it away.

Our reading today is a story of a woman who gave her love away. Not only had she broken the expensive alabaster flask of ointment to anoint Jesus, but she used it all. To some of the onlookers this seemed to be a waste of precious and costly ointment; but Jesus, who always saw further than anyone else, recognised it as an act of love's extravagance. The woman was willing to give away all she had to the Lord she loved. She had no inhibitions.

Jesus commended her for the beautiful thing she had done. The person who lives for others lives free of inhibitions. True love can never be held back.

✳ *Lord, help me to be like a free-flowing stream – as you pour your love into my heart, so may I give it out.*

Tuesday April 3   Mark 14.12–21

Jesus had made careful plans to share the Passover meal with his disciples (verses 13–15). Again we are reminded of Jesus' courage as he approached the time of his suffering and death. Then, in the upper room, while they were eating their supper, Jesus announced to his twelve closest followers that one of them was about to betray him. Was he reminded of the words of Psalm 41.9:

'Even my bosom friend in whom I trusted,
   who ate of my bread, has lifted his heel against me'?

The reaction of the disciples suggests that they were not proud and arrogant men whose self-confidence assured them of their ability to remain loyal to Jesus no matter what the cost. Being in the presence of Jesus reminded them of their human weaknesses, so each was able to ask sorrowfully if it was he who would betray Jesus.

Jesus makes us sensitive to our sins. When Peter first came into close contact with Jesus, he had said, 'Depart from me, for I am a sinful man, O Lord' (Luke 5.8). Yet, as we claim fellowship with Jesus, we can look to him with confidence, knowing that in our weakness he will give us his strength.

✳ *Fan the flame of faith and hope and love in me, Lord, so that I may always remain loyal to you.*

Wednesday April 4   Mark 14.22–31

Leonardo da Vinci, in his famous picture, *The Last Supper*, shows originality not only because in muted colours he depicts the last supper but also shows the moment of the announcement of the betrayal. The quiet superiority of the noble figure of Jesus dominates the scene which is filled with human emotions and agitation. As we think of Peter we see a soul which seems to have been a battleground of cowardice and courage, conflict and emotion. He was so human; and we can identify with him. We can also know that, just as the strong hand of Jesus turned the shifting sand of Peter's nature into a rock, so Jesus can do the same for us.

A Syrian custom tells us that when someone was about to go on a journey, he gathered his friends around him to assure them of his abiding love. The food and wine they consumed was a bond of love and a reminder that, whenever they partook of food and wine again, they would be bound together as one.

Therefore, it is a privilege for us as Christians to share in the Holy Communion, to be bound together as one with our Lord; and to know that, like Peter who denied Jesus and found forgiveness, we, too, can find forgiveness when we repent and believe in him.

✳ *We thank you Father, that you are 'able to do far more abundantly than all that we ask or think' (Ephesians 3.20b).*

Thursday April 5   Mark 14.32–42

In the garden of Gethsemane, Jesus said to Peter, 'Watch and pray that you may not enter into temptation' (verse 38a). But he, and James and John, continued to sleep; they neither watched nor prayed. We note two things:

● While the apostles slept, Jesus' enemies were active. It is likely that this incident was recalled when 1 Peter 5.8 was written: 'Be sober, be watchful. Your adversary the devil prowls around like a roaring lion, seeking someone to devour.'

● Jesus survived the onslaught of Satan by the power of prayer. We are always open to temptation and our spiritual decline takes place when we do not pray. In Gethsemane, Jesus set before us the need to pray and not to faint. It was during his prayer that Jesus' battle against the onslaught of evil was won and he could say, 'Not what I will, but what thou wilt' (verse 36). Let us learn the lesson that we will not survive without prayer, for it is as important to us as food or sleep.

✳ *Lord, teach me to pray as Jesus prayed, at all times.*

Friday April 6   Mark 14.43–52

Leslie Weatherhead wrote a book which he called, *Over His Own Signature*. This title could well be given to the last two verses of today's reading. The identity of the 'young man' can only be conjectured, but it could have been the author of this Gospel. Perhaps, in these two verses, he has painted a picture of himself.

The description of the betrayal and the arrest of Jesus appears to be the work of an eyewitness who, although in danger of his own life, continued to follow Jesus when all the others had fled. We see here, in the moment of crisis, one who was prepared to follow Jesus even though armed men had attempted to seize him. Here we see faith on trial as well as faith in retreat – a reminder to us that every day we live our faith is on trial.

The Church is judged very largely by the conduct of its members. More than anything else Christ wants us to have faith in him; and to have faith in him is to make the witness of the Church strong.

✳ *Lord, help me by the reading of your word to have my faith rekindled, so that in times of testing I may never forsake you.*

Saturday April 7   Mark 14.53–65

No disciple was present at the trial of Jesus, but Peter had followed at a distance, right into the courtyard of the high priest. However, the room where the trial took place before the hostile Jewish Council was out of Peter's view.

There is no doubt that Peter loved Jesus and this can be seen in three ways;

● This love began with **concern**. Love is concern, but that is not enough. There is no better way of understanding a situation than by being in it, but Peter kept his distance!

● Love is **involvement**. Peter was still heavily involved, but afraid that involvement would be too costly.

● Love is also **commitment**. Peter's physical feelings of the cold indicated his inner spiritual state. Our love grows cold when we distance ourselves from Jesus, the Sun of righteousness.

As we continue to follow Peter's actions we shall see that, out of his weakness there came strength, and ultimately a love that knew the meaning of response and responsibility.

✳ *Lord, when I am weak, help me to know that your grace is sufficient for me, for your power is made perfect in weakness. (Based on 2 Corinthians 12.9)*

For group discussion and personal thought

How do we know what God wants us to do? Sometimes the way forward seems clear, while at other times we have to wrestle with the problem. How does the story of Jesus in Gethsemane (**Mark 14.32–36**) help us?

Palm Sunday, April 8

Today we turn to two readings from the Old Testament which Christians, from earliest times, have linked with Jesus' entry into Jerusalem on 'Palm Sunday'.

▶ First read **Zechariah 9.9–12**.

The king pictured in these verses is a king who identifies with ordinary people. He is humble and rides on an ass (verse 9). It was the custom for a king to ride on a mule to distinguish him from the ordinary people who rode asses (see David's instructions for the anointing of Solomon in 1 Kings 1.33). In Jesus' time the people of Israel sought a king with whom they could identify. However, they were still looking for an earthly king and did not understand the nature of God's kingdom. This is seen more clearly in the psalms they sang when he arrived in Jerusalem.

▶ Read **Psalm 118.21–27**.

This psalm is thought to have been written as a conqueror's welcome after Judas Maccabaeus, the Jewish hero, drove out a Syrian king, called Antiochius, from Jerusalem. Again the crowds showed how little they understood of God's kingdom when they displayed their hope that Jesus would liberate them from their Roman overlords.

✳ *King of creation, King of my life, enable me to understand your ways which are not the ways of this world and are so often unexpected.*

Monday April 9   **Mark 14.66–72**

Peter seems very close to us as we picture him warming himself in the courtyard. We can identify with his conflicts and emotions, his strength and his weakness, his deep desire to be heroic and his disastrous failure. At Caesarea Philippi

Peter had affirmed that Jesus was the Christ, the Son of the living God (see Matthew 16.16). But here, frightened by an ordinary servant girl, he denied that he knew Jesus, saying, 'I do not know this man of whom you speak' (verse 71b). This statement made by Peter seems extraordinary, but in the light of his fear we can understand it.

How well did Peter really know Jesus? And how well do **we** really **know** Jesus? Such a question should present us with a spiritual challenge. Do we hear the voice of Jesus putting the same question to us as he put to Philip, 'Have I been with you so long, and yet you do not **know** me, Philip?' (John 14.9)

How can we know Jesus? Like Peter, we must affirm him as 'the Christ, the Son of the living God'; we must repent and begin a fresh venture with Jesus – a fresh exploration. There can be no other way of knowing him.

✳ *Lord, as I think of Peter today, may I know that as you forgave him so you can forgive me for my sins.*

Tuesday April 10   Mark 15.1–15

It was the custom at the Passover to release a prisoner and the crowd was aware of this. Barabbas was a robber and also guilty of rebellion against Rome. In all probability the crowd included people who were not there to see what happened to Jesus, but were supporters of Barabbas.

The crowd begged for Barabbas to be released on the authority of Pilate. Ironically it appears that the full name of Barabbas was Jesus Barabbas. The drama increased when the choice of the mob was not for Jesus Christ, the righteous one, but for Jesus Barabbas, the rebel.

This incident so impressed itself upon the followers of Jesus that it is recorded in all four Gospels. Inevitably it raises the question of choice. Which Jesus is to be chosen? And, in our own day, are we to choose Jesus Christ who represents all that is beautiful, true, loving and good; or someone who regards the use of violence as the only means of changing the economic and political climate of the world?

✳ *Pray that your choice will always and in all circumstances be for Jesus Christ.*

Wednesday April 11   Mark 15.16–22

Exhausted from his night-long trial and his scourging, Jesus was then subjected to the mental anguish of mockery. We do not know whether the soldiers mocked him in jest or with malicious contempt. Nevertheless, for Jesus it was a painful time of waiting while they prepared for his crucifixion.

A condemned person had to carry his own cross to the place of crucifixion. The longest route possible was taken so that all could see the reason for execution and be warned! Jesus could not manage his cross by himself, so the soldiers ordered an African visitor to Jerusalem – Simon of Cyrene – to help Jesus with his burden.

We have reason to believe that Simon's encounter with Jesus on the way to the cross profoundly changed his life. It is thought that Rufus in verse 21 is the same Rufus as is mentioned in Romans 16.13; and that Simon (Simeon) is again mentioned in Acts 13.1. At first Simon may have resented being called upon to help in this way, but perhaps that resentment was later turned to gratitude and joy. We, too, can be called to unpleasant tasks, but let us remember that these very tasks may bring us closer to Christ.

✳ *Lord, help me to take up my cross daily.*

Thursday April 12　　　　　　　　　　Mark 15.23–32

In this reading we see that there were three crosses at Calvary – the cross of Jesus and those of the robbers on either side of him. The central cross will always be the symbol of victory for Christians. It is this victory that Jesus offers to every man, woman and child. It is victory over suffering.

Jesus was offered wine mingled with myrrh to deaden his pain, but he would not take it. He wanted to die with an unclouded mind, knowing the intensity of human pain. Ever since, people in their suffering have found immense strength through the cross, not only for their bodies and souls but also for their hearts.

On the cross the victim became the victor. Because Jesus would not come down from the cross (verse 32), he gained victory over cruelty, hatred, pride and prejudice. For all time, and for all people, he brought sufficient hope, love, joy and faith to take us through the dark journey of suffering and death.

The arms of Jesus outstretched on the cross are God's demonstration of victory won and of welcoming love. The outer crosses tell of redemption available for everyone.

✳ *Victorious Lord, as I think about your suffering and death,*
help me to trust you in my times of testing and pain.

Good Friday, April 13

When I was an army chaplain I met a man who had fought in
the battle of the Somme in the First World War. He told me
of one particular day when shells were bursting dangerously
near him, and he felt utterly forsaken by God. In desperation,
he prayed for help and, in the terror of the moment, dug his
hands in the mud. When the shelling ended he scraped the
mud from his hand and found a silver crucifix. He seized the
crucifix and his thoughts turned to Calvary. He felt the presence of Christ and a peace came over him and his fears van-
ished. For forty years since then he had carried the crucifix,
and loved and served Christ who came to him in a special way
on the battlefields of France.

▶ Now read **Mark 15.33–41**.

The darkness described in verse 33 was an outward symbol
of the spiritual darkness which surrounded Jesus. The cry of
dereliction (verse 34) was a quotation from Psalm 22. However, that psalm taken as a whole is anything but a cry of
despair; rather it is an amazing utterance of faith in God.
Today's reading ends with a centurion's words of recognition
– words of a soldier who saw and affirmed Jesus to be God's
Son.

The help that Jesus brought to a soldier on the battlefields
of France and the response of the centurion at the foot of the
cross indicate the help that he can bring to us as we turn and
look at him on the cross.

✳ *Meditate on the cross of Jesus.*

Saturday April 14   Mark 15.42–47

In the absence of any of Jesus' relations being able to provide
a respectable burial for him, Joseph of Arimathea asked Pilate
for his body and had it placed in a tomb hewn out of rock.
Little is known about Joseph of Arimathea, other than that
he was a wealthy Israelite, a member of the Jewish Council
and a good and righteous man. John says he was a disciple of
Jesus, but secretly for fear of the Jews (see John 19.38). In the
light of the fact that the disciples had fled (see Mark 14.50), it

was a courageous act for Joseph to go to Pilate and ask for
Jesus' body.

Simone Weil wrote in her book *Waiting on God*: 'One of the
principal truths of Christianity, a truth which goes almost
unrecognised today, is that the **looking** is what saves us.'
Joseph of Arimathea looked for the kingdom of God (see verse
43). He was obviously sympathetic towards the mission of
Jesus. Jesus said, 'Seek first his kingdom' (Matthew 6.33a).
Could it be that Joseph's daring venture to obtain the body of
Jesus for a proper burial was a demonstration of his seeking
for God's kingdom?

✳ *Father, hold before us the vision of your kingdom, that in
seeking it we may discover it and truly become your disciples.*

For group discussion and personal thought
Where do we see crosses most frequently today, and what do
they signify? Now read **Mark 15.33–41**. How do the crosses
we have thought about compare with the cross of Christ? Does
the rough agony of crucifixion challenge our comfortable faith?

77

JESUS IS ALIVE

Easter readings

Notes by the Revd Donald H Hilton, BA

Donald Hilton is Moderator of the Yorkshire Province of the United Reformed Church in the United Kingdom. He has previously held pastorates in three English churches and was Christian Education Secretary for the Congregational Church. He has also written and compiled several books published by the NCEC.

The notes in this section are based on the New English Bible.

The pattern of the Christian year is a series of rising peaks, each one leading to the next. Advent rises to Christmas, which itself points to Lent. Lent leads us to the high point of Good Friday, where the suffering Servant's obedience reveals the majesty of the love of God. Now the towering peak of Easter is before us – God's mighty act in raising Jesus from death.

To celebrate the message of Easter we begin with the story recorded in the Gospels. However, the mighty power of resurrection bursts out to touch our personal lives and the life of the Church. The apostle Paul goes further and triumphantly asserts that the whole universe is waiting for its resurrection.

We shall never exhaust the message of Easter. Resurrection holds truths that challenge all human knowledge and imagination. In this short section we explore afresh what resurrection meant for Jesus, and what it means for us.

Suggestions for further reading

The First Easter: What Really Happened? by Hubert J Richards (Mowbray)
True Resurrection by Harry A Williams (Fount Paperbacks)
A Matter of Life and Death by John V Taylor (SCM Press)

Easter Sunday, April 15

By coming to live among us, Christ accepted all the limitations of a human life. The Creator of all things was contained in a human body! The King of the universe walked the roads of

78

one small country! At the end, the Lord of life accepted human death! A stone blocking the doorway of a tomb is a striking symbol of this 'imprisonment' of Christ.

▶ Read **Mark 16.1–8.**

The Easter message is of Christ's release from all chains:
- He broke out of the tomb where he had been placed.
- He broke the bonds of death to live a risen life.
- He was no longer constrained by time or place. He appeared in Jerusalem and Galilee, in a garden and on a beach.

And we now **know** what the first disciples could hardly have guessed – he strides down the generations offering his healing and challenge to every successive age. He leaps the oceans to be with his faithful people in every continent.

When the first American astronauts landed on the moon they broke a piece of bread, poured wine into the chalice normally used in their local church, and celebrated the Communion Service. They were not claiming the moon for Christ. They were affirming that he was already there. He had gone before them.

✳ *Christ the Lord is risen again!*
Christ has broken every chain!   *Michael Weisse*

Monday April 16

The original version of **Mark's Gospel** probably stopped at verse 8. Today's reading is a collection of other stories discovered later. One of their common themes is the doubt of the first disciples.

▶ Read **Mark 16.9–20** noticing the following pattern:

- **Disbelief** (verses 11 and 13). The disciples did not welcome the first Easter by saying, 'This is exactly what we thought would happen!' It took them by surprise and **Mark** was honest enough to say so.
- **Commission** (verse 15). Uncertainty and faith mingled together as, led by the risen Christ, they realised the enormity of their task – to preach the good news to all creation.
- **Confidence** (verse 20). Knowing that the Lord was with them 'they went out to make their proclamation everywhere'.

That pattern of discipleship reoccurs in us. We should not be afraid of our doubts. So often, as we share them frankly with Christian friends we find the Lord speaking to us within

our uncertainty and pointing to fresh challenges which lead
to growing confidence.

It is still relevant to ask what would have happened if those
first disciples had failed their Lord in the early years of the
Church. It is no less relevant to ask what will happen if we
fail him now.

✷ *Lord Jesus Christ, use my doubts and hopes, my mingled
faith and confidence, to proclaim your truth to all peoples.*

Tuesday April 17   1 Corinthians 15.12–26

Clearly, the Corinthians had doubts about their personal resurrection after death. In writing to them about this Paul used
an argument which is based on 'solidarity'. Our own experience of sin shows our solidarity with Adam. He sinned and
brought death into the world. In the same way, we also sin
and die. But if we are thus united with Adam, a mere man,
how much more readily will we be united with the living
Christ! Living in solidarity with him, we will share his resurrection. What is this solidarity? It is the solidarity of:

● **Faith**. We cannot **prove** what happened to Jesus, nor what
  will happen to us after death, but faith looks in hope beyond
  the grave.
● **Suffering**. None of us will suffer as Jesus suffered, but we
  bear the pain and grief of life and so glimpse what it meant
  for him.
● **Service.** As we serve others we are united with our servant
  Lord.

Our resurrection to eternal life is not a prize for suffering
and service. It is rather that these things so unite us to Christ
that, belonging to him and sharing his sorrow, we go on to
share his glory.

✷ *Made like him, like him we rise;*
  Ours the cross, the grave, the skies.   Charles Wesley

Wednesday April 18   Ephesians 2.1–10

We tend to confine our idea of resurrection either to what
happened to Jesus long ago, or what we hope will happen to
us when we die. Resurrection is far more than that. It is about
now. In today's reading Paul contrasts the death-producing
ways of 'this present age' with 'life with Christ' which is past
and future, but also **now**.

In his book, *A Matter of Life and Death,* John Taylor tells of an event in an old people's home. The elderly sat day after day 'half-dead' in their chairs until a young visitor played some music and danced around them. Very soon, the old folk, shedding their 'deadness', began to move in time to the music. That is resurrection **now**.

Another author tells of a marriage which was alive in name only. All freshness had gone from it and the couple lived together, made love, and entertained friends as a dull routine. When tragedy struck them they had to look afresh at their life and relationship. The task was painful but it led them to a new and vital marriage relationship. That is also resurrection.

We are not an audience watching the resurrection of Christ, nor are we only 'waiting in the wings' until death makes it our turn. Resurrection belongs to ordinary, everyday life in the here and now.

✶ *What experiences have you had of which you might say, 'That was a kind of resurrection for me'?*

Thursday April 19   **Ephesians 4.1–16**

One of the most powerful arguments for the resurrection of Jesus is the Church itself. In the early days after Jesus' resurrection, a group of disconsolate disciples were suddenly revitalised and the Church was founded. Time and again since then, the Church has sinned and failed, but later found the power within itself to rediscover its faith and purpose. Persecuted and scorned, the Church has found an inner strength to survive.

Human effort is not enough to explain these facts. Some external power is at work in the Church. Can it be less than the power of the risen Christ?

The Scripture to which Paul refers in verse 8 comes from Psalm 68.18. Traditional Jewish teaching related it to Moses who ascended Mount Sinai and brought back the gift of the law. Paul reinterprets the verse to refer to Christ who once 'descended' to earth, conquered it by the power of love, and then 'ascended' again, giving gifts to his Church as he departed. The gifts described in verse 11 are the gifts which have sustained the Church when it has failed through its own fault or has suffered persecution. They are signs of the protective love of Christ for his people.

* *Lord Jesus, you have given us gifts. As we use them in your service make your presence known to us.*

Friday April 20   **Philippians 2.1–16**

Resurrection is for me but it does not belong to me; it is personal but it is not private. It is God's gift to the whole community of his people. Note all the words and phrases in verses 1–4 which suggest a community understanding of the Church.

What kind of a community should the Church be? At best it is a Jesus-community modelled on his life. It is a **humble** community because he was born and lived in humility; an **obedient** community because Jesus was obedient enough even to accept death; and a **resurrection** community because Christ calls us to share his resurrection. (Note the carefully-structured poetry in verses 6–11. Many believe that these verses were an early Christian hymn. Only such a Church community is able to engage in its essential task of mission and be like 'stars in a dark world' (verse 15).

The Church has been called 'the Community of the Resurrection'. What do you think that means . . .
- when two members have a difference of opinion?
- when a newcomer attends worship and enquires about membership?
- when the Church plans for children in its life?
- when an older person grows too frail to attend church?
- when a church sees a problem in its local area?

* *Lord Jesus Christ, for the faith you have given me, for the faith I share with others, thanks be to God!*

Saturday April 21   Romans 8.18–25; Ephesians 1.9–10

We began the week by looking at Christ's personal resurrection and affirming that he burst out of the tomb to be in every age and place. We have affirmed his risen power in our lives, present and future. We have also seen him in the community of his Church. Paul held out one more triumphant mystery – that the whole universe is to be brought to new life by Christ's resurrection. He cannot be held even within his Church or the world we know. He is the cosmic Christ, Lord of the entire universe!

The early chapters of **Genesis** show an idyllic world in

which all is harmony. But the picture is spoilt by human sin which causes even the earth to be cursed (Genesis 3.17). Look again at Romans 8.18–25. Paul declared that the very universe would feel the splendour of resurrection power.

J S Stewart expressed his belief that the purpose of the resurrection of Jesus was 'to shatter history and remake it in a cosmic, creative event, ushering in a new age'.

When we say our personal prayers, confess our personal faith, and sit in our local church, we are more than simply individuals. We are caught up in a world-shattering, history-creating event which began long ago and will find fulfilment in a new earth and a new age.

✳ *Yea, amen, let all adore thee,*
  High on thine eternal throne!   *Charles Wesley*

For group discussion and personal thought

Many people fear suffering and death more than anything else. Why is this so? How does the resurrection of Jesus help us to overcome these fears? (Look especially at **Mark 16.1–7** and **1 Corinthians 15.12–26**.)

THE REIGN OF DAVID
Readings from 2 Samuel 5 to 1 Kings 2

Notes by the Revd Christopher Ellis,MA,MPhil

Christopher Ellis is a Baptist minister serving an ecumenical congregation in Swindon, Wiltshire, England. He previously ministered in Cardiff and Brighton.

The notes in this section are based on the New International Version.

The story of the **reign of David** is an exciting one – it tells of the struggles of an emerging nation and the greatness and failures of a famous leader. David was only the second king of this collection of tribes through whom God had chosen to reveal himself and his way. Jews still look back to this time as a golden age; and they refer to the Messiah as the 'Son of David'.

Yet **2 Samuel 5 to 1 Kings 2** provides us with a blunt picture of human reality. The value for us of these chapters lies in this very frankness, for they tell of emotions and influences which we still know and recognise in the world today.

Suggestions for further reading

Samuel by David F Payne, Daily Study Bible (Saint Andrew Press)

Second Book of Samuel by Peter R Ackroyd, Cambridge Bible Commentaries on the NEB (Cambridge University Press)

Sunday April 22 2 Samuel 5.1–12

As a collection of tribes, Israel was often threatened by division. There was a strong north/south divide between the tribes of Judah and Benjamin in the south and the other ten, fiercely independent tribes in the north. David first proved himself to be a capable king in the south; and then, seven and a half years after the death of Saul, the northern tribes decided to invite him to lead them as well.

David's anointing was part of a compact between the king and the tribes (verse 3). Here was no absolute monarch or dictator – David held a position of responsibility as well as power. The lad who had shepherded his father's flocks on the Bethlehem hillsides was now called to shepherd a nation.

David's concern for unity soon led to the conquest of Jerusalem, a city which belonged neither to the north, nor to the south. This became the seat of government and the focus of the nation.

Some 1,000 years later, Jesus came as the 'Son of David', and called himself 'the good shepherd' (John 10.11). He demonstrated his leadership by washing feet and has confronted each generation with questions about the use and abuse of power.

✳ *Pray for leaders in local and national government, that they may put the welfare of those they govern, or represent, before personal privilege and advantage.*

Monday April 23

David tried to centralise the worship of God in an attempt to reinforce national unity.

▶ Read **2 Samuel 6.1–11**.

The 'ark of God' was a chest made of acacia wood. It held the stone tablets on which were carved the ten commandments, given to Moses by God at Mount Sinai. The Israelites carried the ark through the wilderness on their way to the promised land, and into battle against their enemies. So it became for them a symbol of God's presence, a powerful reminder that he was with them wherever they went – that he was not restricted to a holy mountain or a temple.

Ancient commentators ascribed the death of Uzzah to the wrath of God. We might be unhappy with such an explanation but consider the following:

● As the symbol of God's presence, the ark was supposed to be venerated. Had the people become too familiar with it?
● The ark was supposed to be carried on poles threaded through rings on its side in an attempt to avoid such contact. The indignity of an ox-cart suggests undue haste and lack of preparation. Sometimes the best plans founder because of hasty and inadequate planning.

✳ *Lord, help me to plan well, yet still leave all to you.*

Tuesday April 24   2 Samuel 6.12–23

Yesterday's reading reminded us of the holiness of God. Yet

such an awareness need not lead to stiff formality and stern piety. If God is to be the Lord of our lives then enthusiasm must find its place in our worship. This will mean different things for different people. The cold reaction of Michal is as much a clash of cultures as it is a disagreement about what is dignified. David danced before God in an outpouring of emotion and joy. His dance and its critic challenge us to note two important aspects of worship:

- **We need to be natural before God.** Many of the psalms, perhaps written by this same David, express an openness before God which includes celebration and complaint. When there is no place for pretence in prayer, we will be led to a depth of private devotion and a richness of shared worship.
- **Our worship may involve all kinds of artistic expression,** including dance and drama. What we must not do is criticise what is helpful to **others** simply because it does not help us.

∗ *Thank God for composers, musicians, poets and artists who help us to worship God.*

Wednesday April 25   2 Samuel 7.1–16

Discovering God's will does not only mean finding out **what** is right, but also discovering **who** should act and **how** and **when**. David's concern to build God's house was a noble one which should challenge us. 'God deserves better' was the implication of David's words to the prophet Nathan. We often put our own comfort and priorities before God and his way. The Church usually has to make do with what we have left after we have done our personal budgeting. God's house is often less well-kept than our own homes.

David had a point, yet he was told that the temple was not to be built by him but by his son. It is not always easy to leave others to do what we want to do. Over-enthusiastic lack of delegation can hinder God's work in the Church as much as neglecting God's place in our life. Putting God first, and putting others before ourselves, go hand in hand. We often need to be set free from the kind of self-centredness which thinks that we can do things better than anyone else. That is only a short step to believing we can do it better than God!

∗ *Think about these words of Paul: 'Do nothing out of selfish ambition or vain conceit, but in humility consider others better than yourselves.' (Philippians 2.3)*

Thursday April 26

Nathan's words to David had included the promise that David was within God's plan and that his throne would be established for ever (2 Samuel 7.16). This covenant promise was not to be worked out in terms of political continuity. Rather, there would be a 'Son of David' who would be the salvation of humanity and the Lord of all. David's response to the covenant promise was to offer a prayer of praise and thanksgiving.

▶ Now read **2 Samuel 7.17–29**.

The main theme of David's prayer was a sense of God's grace, both in his saving of Israel from slavery in Egypt and in the chosing of David as king. Here was a man of action who acknowledged that what he had achieved rested not on his own efforts but on the goodness of God. His concern that God would accomplish that which he had promised was based on the promise that the whole world might know the glory of God.

✳ *What are the things for which* **you** *want to thank God? What are your concerns for the future which you wish to place in his hands?*

Friday April 27

From time to time we are fortunate to encounter politicians and monarchs who warrant the title of 'statesmen'. They demonstrate a largeness of heart, a breadth of vision, which enables them to see beyond the immediate advantages of a situation to the longer-term benefit of the whole community. On a number of occasions during his reign David demonstrated such vision and generosity. It found expression in his forgiving of opponents and in his reconciliation with the family of Saul.

▶ Read **2 Samuel 9.1–13**.

On a personal level, we can see that David's welcome of Mephibosheth may well be based on his deep friendship with Jonathan (see 1 Samuel 20). It is true that the disabled Mephibosheth could not have been much of a threat to King David. However, his special place at court must have won many friends for David from among those loyal to Saul and his offspring. Reconciliation and faithful commitment are major themes of the Bible and activities to which all Christians are called.

Saturday April 28

For the next few days we shall be reading the story of David
and Bathsheba. This story contains all the ingredients of a
best-selling novel – sex, violence, political intrigue and the
private failures of a great man. When reading about David's
attempt to cover up his affair with Bathsheba we must
remember that the penalty for adultery laid down in the Jewish law was **death** for both the man and woman (see Leviticus
20.10).

▶ Today read **2 Samuel 11.1–13**.

The tension of the story is heightened by the portrait of Uriah.
The soldier's code laid down that he would abstain from sexual
relations while on active service, and so his trip to Jerusalem
was spent chastely. This very virtue led to his death. Perhaps
the most surprising aspect of this story is that it is told at all!
However, the Bible is frank in its description of the people
whom God uses. Here the king, who led the people of God into
a golden age, is shown to be guilty of breaking the commandments, a prisoner of his own excesses and passion. Yet the
redemption story continues for it is God at work through the
ups and downs of human history.

❋ *Pray for marriage counsellors and all who provide support*
  for marriages and relationships under stress.

For group discussion and personal thought

Read, in **2 Samuel 6.14–15**, how David freely expressed his
joy before the Lord. How important are exuberance and
enthusiasm in our worship and how should they be expressed?
What hinders us from expressing our joy freely today?

Sunday April 29   2 Samuel 11.14–27

A mixture of desperation and arrogance led David to send
the fateful message to Joab via Uriah himself. One sin led to
another as David compounded his wrongdoing. What began
as an adulterous affair not only led to the murder of the hus-

band, but also to the deaths of innocent soldiers caught up in the deadly tactics of David and Joab.

Sins are not easily isolated into individual offences. The way of the world seems to draw in other actions and misdeeds so that we find ourselves trapped in a whole web of misfortune and guilt. The story of David might seem too lurid and violent to touch our own lives, but its lessons are clear:

- **Sin grows.** As adultery led to murder, so things that we do wrong are difficult to control and slide into a mess of frustration and hurt.
- **Sin does not choose its victims carefully**. The victims of David were an innocent husband and his comrades. Sin spreads in the hurt it inflicts.

✳ *Reflect on those you have hurt in recent days. Pray for forgiveness and the grace to heal what you have broken.*

Monday April 30   2 Samuel 12.1–14

There are parables in the Old Testament as well as in the New, and today's reading is a great example of how a parable can confront someone with the reality of their situation.

Nathan needed to show David how badly he had sinned. If he had simply condemned him in plain language the king might easily have ignored him or even punished him for his impudence. In order to demonstrate that even the king is not above the law, the prophet engaged him in a case of injustice and invited his judgement. When David responded with righteous indignation the trap was sprung and David realised that he had condemned himself.

Note the violence of David's condemnation of the rich man in the parable. Whenever we point a finger at the sin of others, we would do well to examine ourselves first. Jesus warned against pointing out a speck of sawdust in another's eye while ignoring a plank in our own (Matthew 7.4-5)!

✳ *Lord, show me my self as I really am, that I might seek your forgiveness and be transformed by your love.*

Tuesday May 1   2 Samuel 12.15–25

It is difficult for us to see the death of Bathsheba's child as a punishment from God, yet this was how Nathan and David would have come to terms with what had happened. Once the infant was pronounced dead, his father grieved and picked up the threads of his life again. Life could not be the same again – too many people had been hurt – but life must go on.

Not only is King David shown in all his frailty, but we shall see later that the adulterous pair were to be the parents of the next monarch, Solomon. God continues to work through people like you and me – that is good news!

The New Testament shows that God does not punish people in the way this story suggests. Instead, he shares our pain and bears our sin upon the cross. Redemption is about good coming out of evil – the perseverance of the grace of God through faithfulness to people like David – to you and to me!

✳ *And when human hearts are breaking*
   Under sorrow's iron rod,
All the sorrow, all the aching,
   Wrings with pain the heart of God.   Timothy Rees

Wednesday May 2

David's several wives and the many sons that resulted, led the nation of Israel and David into a time of instability as different princes vied for succession to the throne. Absalom had already been exiled for the revenge killing of his half-brother Amnon (see 2 Samuel 13–14). When he was allowed to return he soon caused dissension by stirring up trouble against David.

▶ Now read **2 Samuel 15.1–15**.

There must have been genuine grievances in Israel for Absalom to be able to stir up so much dissent. The ageing David had to face the prospect of civil war and fled from Jerusalem to a safe place east of the river Jordan.

If justice is neglected it can lead to division and war. It is no good striving and praying for peace unless we also strive and pray for justice. David's neglect of his role as judge led to the fermenting of civil war. We need to commit ourselves to the search for justice if we are to be peacemakers.

✳ *O Lord, lead us in your way of justice so that the earth may be filled with your peace and righteousness.*

Thursday May 3   2 Samuel 17.24; 18.1–17

This is the political and military low point of David's reign. In fleeing across the Jordan to the fortified city of Mahanaim,

David had to rely chiefly on his standing army and bodyguard made up of mercenaries. Most of the soldiers of Judah and the northern tribes were marching under the banner of Absalom, the rebel prince. Throughout this story the private tragedy of a father at odds with his son is interwoven with the public tragedy of a nation at war with itself.

The disciplined army of mercenaries loyal to the king proved too much for the rebel army of part-time soldiers. There was a rout and in the confusion Absalom was caught in the branches of a tree. This graphic scene raises the question of political morality. Absalom hung at the mercy of his enemies. He had been exiled and had returned to continue his scheming for the throne. Joab's brutal stabbing of the prince was the action of a political realist. In human terms this was the best way to avoid further trouble in the future. However, the Christian gospel never gives up on people. We must not write anyone off – however sinful they may be.

✳ *Pray for those who make life-and-death decisions which affect others.*

Friday May 4 2 Samuel 18.19–33

Ahimaaz may have volunteered to take the news of victory because he had not heard about Absalom's death and wanted to be the bearer of what he thought would be a popular message. On the other hand, perhaps he did know about the prince and wanted to break the news gently. Joab did not want to risk the life of a valued courtier and the son of a friend, so he ordered a Cushite mercenary to take the news. This soldier ran directly across rough terrain while Ahimaaz, who had decided to break the unpleasant news gently after all, ran on a quicker route and reached the city first. Yet Ahimaaz' courage failed him and it was left to the Cushite to tell David the plain truth.

David took the news about Absalom's death badly. His lament was piercing in its pain. His personal grief wiped out the good news of victory. The loss of a son outweighed the winning of a kingdom. The cry that he would have preferred to die so that his son might have lived, is a cry familiar to all who have lost children – yet that cannot be. Even God has shared such pain in the cross of Jesus.

✳ *Pray for those who have lost children in war and those whose children have turned away from them.*

David had been anointed king in order to protect the Israelites
and to strengthen their unity as the people of God. He had
been called to shepherd this group of tribes and now their
unity had been split by civil war. The generosity and wisdom
of David's statecraft was needed more than ever. But the king
was immobilised by grief. The loss of his son loomed larger
than anything else and threatened the kingdom as much as
the rebellion had. Joab the realist, was brutal in his attempt
to get through to David.

Government depends on loyalty as well as obedience and
David needed to reassure and encourage the men who had
served him so well. His private grief had to take second place
if he was to save the disintegrating kingdom. A battle had
been won, but now the hearts and minds of the people had to
be won as well, and David had to begin with those who were
already loyal to him. People in authority must never take
those under them for granted.

✷ *Pray for those who have to put public responsibilities before
private concerns; and for people in authority that they
might praise and encourage those who work for them.*

For group discussion and personal thought

Study **2 Samuel 12.1–14**. Discuss the approach Nathan used
when he confronted David with his wrongdoing. How can we
confront people we know who are doing wrong, without dam-
aging our relationship with them?

Sunday May 6

Once David had set his hand to the task of healing the divisions of a war-torn land and winning back the hearts and
minds of those his army had defeated, we see his old qualities
of generosity and mercy returning. The treason of Judah was
more deeply felt by David than the rebellion of the northern
tribes because Judah was David's own tribe and he had been
their king first. Therefore, David put feelers out to invite the
Judeans to take a lead in his return.

▶ Read **2 Samuel 19.8b–23**.

The replacing of Joab by Amasa was a combination of vindic-
tiveness for the death of Absalom and an opportunity to win

back rebel hearts by confirming their general (2 Samuel 17.25) as the new commander-in-chief of the reunited nation. How often do we act with mixed motives?

The forgiving of enemies is not an idealistic fantasy which cannot be put into practice. Here David showed the political good sense of a policy which looked to future harmony rather than past division. 'Should anyone be put to death in Israel today?' (verse 22) recognised that there had been enough death and now was the time for life.

✳ *Pray for those who work for peace and reconciliation, and offer yourself as someone through whom the Spirit of God's peace might work.*

Monday May 7   **2 Samuel 19.24–40**

As the tide of events turned back in David's favour, he was confronted by a variety of people who claimed loyalty to him. Concerning these David had to make decisions for the future. Mephibosheth, Jonathan's disabled son, appeared at the Jordan with the visible evidence of mourning throughout the time of the king's absence. He had stayed in Jerusalem because of his lack of mobility during the urgent flight of the royal court and his disregard of material reward underlines the sincerity of his welcome.

Barzillai had been a staunch ally and lavish host during David's time east of the Jordan. Now he was offered recompense at the court in Jerusalem. His declining of the offer is an eloquent statement of priorities for the elderly. However, he offered his son (verse 37, NEB) to go with David and the king accepted the new courtier with a gracious twisting of the offer. Barzillai's devotion to the king was great and challenges us about the measure of our loyalty. Our prayers should not simply offer a polite greeting to God but should be a dedication of our whole being.

✳ *Teach us, good Lord, to give and not to count the cost; to labour and not to ask for any reward, save that of knowing that we do your will. (Ignatius Loyala)*

Tuesday May 8

As the narrative of the reign of David begins to draw to a close, we have a song of praise sung by the poet king as he reflected on his experience of God's salvation.

▶ Read **2 Samuel 22.1–7, 26–36**.

In political terms the reign of David had been a success. It had had its fair share of danger, of tumultuous intrigue and warfare. But this national leader, who was only the second king for an uneasy group of loose-knit tribes, became the symbol of a golden age for all time.

It would have been easy for David, or the official court historian, to speak only of his triumphs and victories and to play down the bad times and failures. Yet the history we have been following is candid in its account. David's recollection of his life is full of gratitude to God and lacking in any pompous, self-important propaganda. The shepherd of God's people was great, yet flawed; visionary, yet aware of his own sin and God's grace.

It is an awareness of God's mercy and salvation which enables us to face the truth about ourselves. His grace and forgiveness make it possible for us to face our sin and therefore face ourselves and our God.

✳ *In the knowledge of God's gracious salvation and love, confess your sin to him.*

Wednesday May 9   2 Samuel 23.8–17

The story of the life and times of a great king would not be complete without a list of other people who played a special part in the events. The list of David's mighty men is both a record of incidental deeds of courage which have not found a place in the broad sweep of the preceding chapters, and a reminder that even the greatest of leaders needs partners in his greatness.

David's largeness of heart was able to inspire people to deeds of courage, but we must not ignore the deeds themselves nor the other people through whom God was seen to be at work. The people of God then and now are a community and the task of its leaders is to inspire the **whole** community.

The story in verses 13–17 is a lovely example of the devotion of followers and the reason why David's followers were so inspired. The passing whim for fresh water led to a glorious and needless act of bravery. David saluted the courage of the men but at the same time showed that lives should not have been risked for such a reason. Something obtained at such risk could only be offered to God.

* *Thank God for those things that sustain and enrich our lives and which are provided for us by other people.*

Thursday May 10   1 Kings 1.1–10, 15–21

In this confrontation of the story of David, we are shown the portrait of an old man, whose powers were failing. Palace intrigue, concerning who would be the next king, came to the fore as the ageing monarch began to lose touch with day-to-day affairs.

We can see from 1 Kings 2.15, and the prominence of his supporters, that Adonijah was widely expected to succeed to the throne. The supporters of Solomon were not invited to the feast; this suggests that Adonijah was not concerned with healing divisions, but confident of liquidating all opposition in due course.

Although he was not the eldest living son, Solomon had been chosen by his father to succeed him. Government was too important to be left to an arbitrary matter of birthdays. Changes of leadership often produce periods of uncertainty and this is especially true when it is not known who the future leader will be. Part of the role of a leader is to plan ahead.

* *Pray for those in positions of leadership who are approaching the age of retirement, that they might judge wisely when and how to hand over to others.*

Friday May 11   1 Kings 1.32–52

David wanted to ensure that Solomon became the new king. He sent for Benaiah who was now in command of the army; Zadok who was joint priest in Jerusalem; and Nathan who was the most prominent prophet in Israel. David ordered them to anoint Solomon – taking with them his personal retainers and bodyguards (verse 33), who would provide both physical force and the symbolic presence of the king at Solomon's anointing.

Solomon was to ride David's own mule (verse 33). Horses had not yet been introduced in Israel, so the king rode a mule and everyone else rode asses. Solomon was being presented to the people with the trappings of royalty.

It is probable that Solomon's anointing did not make him sole king, in place of David, but heir apparent and co-regent until his father's death. However, anyone anointed was regarded to be under the special protection of God, and so this action was both a proclamation of Solomon's status and an insurance for his personal safety.

This story stands in stark contrast to Jesus, the 'Son of David' who was to know no special protection. He rode an ass like his people, was crucified with the lowest and his throne is in the hearts of his followers.

✳ *Lord, help me to follow your humble way of trusting obedience.*

Saturday May 12   **1 Kings 2.1–12**

The deathbed speech of David is a good place to end our story. It contains that familiar mixture of devotion to God, practical politics and private vengeance, that marks and flaws David's greatness.

Solomon acted promptly in carrying out David's instructions. The death of Joab and Shimei followed soon after that of Adonijah (see verses 13–46) and Abiathar was removed from the priesthood and banished from Jerusalem. The elimination of the opposition was brutal and swift, but it would be far from easy for Solomon to live up to the challenge of verses 2–4! Solomon was not to forget that as king he was the Lord's anointed – he was not ruler by right but was entrusted with shepherding the people of God. His own religious faith and practical actions needed to be within the guide-lines that God had provided.

The Christian life has been likened to a pilgrimage or journey. It is more than a sudden decision or flurry of activity. It is a life-long walking in the ways of God – but we are promised a companion.

✳ *Jesus, Son of David and Son of God, you are the way, the truth and the life; help me to walk in your way my whole life long.*

For group discussion and personal thought

Consider the advice David gave in his final words to Solomon in **1 Kings 2.2–4**. From your own experience, what factors (a) hinder and (b) promote obedience to God's laws? What can we do to promote obedience to God's laws in the lives of individuals and in our communities?

GALATIANS

Notes by the Revd Daniel Nicodemus,BSc,BD

Daniel Nicodemus, a Baptist minister, is Secretary of the All India Sunday School Association. He has previously served on the staff of the India Sunday School Union for twelve years, and as Executive Secretary of the Andhra Pradesh Christian Council, Secunderabad.

The notes in this section are based on the New English Bible.

The letter of Paul to the **Galatians** was written at a time of great peril. Paul had preached in the Roman province of Galatia and established churches there. His converts were making steady progress in the Christian life when **Judaisers**, a group of Jewish Christians who insisted that the Gentile Christians should receive the law of Moses along with the gospel, appeared on the scene. They began to persuade Christians to accept circumcision and the law of Moses. Paul was totally opposed to this. The Judaisers questioned Paul's credentials saying that the true exponents of the gospel were the original apostles. To meet such a grave situation Paul wrote this letter in a fighting spirit.

Although one could say that circumcision and the law of Moses are no longer live issues, this letter has a message which is always relevant to the life of the Church.

Suggestions for further reading

The Letters to the Galatians and Ephesians by William Barclay, Daily Study Bible (Saint Andrew Press)
The Letter of Paul to the Galatians edited by William Neil, Cambridge Bible Commentaries on the New English Bible (Cambridge University Press).

Sunday May 13   Galatians 1.1–10

For some the gospel of Jesus Christ seems to be too good to believe and too simple to accept. It was so in the case of the Judaisers who contended that to be a Christian one should not only believe in Christ but should also accept circumcision and the law of Moses. Paul, a one-time zealous advocate of the Jewish law, opposed this view. He pointed out that the greatness of the gospel of Jesus Christ lies in its very simplicity. There is no need to make any additions to it. Even if an angel from heaven were to preach a different version of the gospel, it deserved to be rejected. There is only one gospel, and what the Judaisers were preaching was a perversion of it.

The essence of Christianity is to receive the grace of Christ through faith. Whenever any condition, rite or ritual is made a prerequisite for receiving Christ, the warning given by Paul becomes relevant. The Christian gospel is simple truth, and is meant to be accepted as such.

✳ *Paul wrote: 'Miserable creature that I am, who is there to rescue me out of this body doomed to death? God alone, through Jesus Christ our Lord! Thanks be to God!'*
(Romans 7.24–25a)

Monday May 14   Galatians 1.11–24

It is evident from this reading that the Judaisers accused Paul of distorting the gospel which he had received from the authority of the original apostles in Jerusalem. But Paul contended that the source of authority for the gospel he was preaching was his own spiritual experience. A former fanatical upholder of the law and arch-persecutor of the Church, Paul, reversed the course of his life when the risen Christ met him on the road to Damascus (Acts 9.1–6). It was Christ who revealed to Paul the mission to which he was called.

The details Paul gives of his life after this experience show that he consulted no man but received the gospel direct from God (see verses 17–22).

For Paul, gospel was truth, proved in experience – and in this lay the authority of the gospel he preached to the Gentiles. It is the same for us who are called to share that gospel with others.

✳ *'. . . mine eyes have seen thy salvation, which thou hast prepared before the face of all people; a light to lighten the Gentiles, and the glory of thy people Israel.'*
(Luke 2.30–32, AV)

Tuesday May 15   Galatians 2.1–10

Paul continued to defend his cause against the onslaught of

the Judaisers. His second visit to Jerusalem took place after fourteen years during which time the Gentile church had come into being. This visit was the result of a 'revelation' – he had not been summoned to Jerusalem by the apostles. Of his own accord Paul presented to them his work among the Gentiles and the gospel he had preached to them. His companion Titus was not forced to be circumcised. It was agreed that Paul should continue the mission to the Gentiles.

In today's reading, Paul makes three statements which have important lessons for us as Christians today:

● The 'liberty we enjoy in the fellowship of Christ Jesus' (verse 4). This is a matter, not of laws and rites, but of faith and love.

● 'The full truth of the gospel should be maintained for you' (verse 5). Paul never ceased to care for his people – he was a true pastor. What is important in the gospel is not a formal doctrinal statement but a universal missionary appeal inviting people to receive Jesus Christ into their lives.

● 'God shows no partiality' (verse 6, RSV). God cannot be claimed to be the exclusive possession of any group of people.

✳ *Forgive us, O Lord, if we have made faith harder for others by presenting a gospel of good works and the keeping of rules rather than a gospel of the heart.*

Wednesday May 16   **Galatians 2.11–21**

The incident referred to in verses 11–14 took place in the church at Antioch. Peter (Cephas) had begun to have meals with Gentiles but then later withdrew because he deferred to the wishes of a visiting group of Jewish Christians from Judaea. Although Peter was the most senior apostle at Jerusalem, Paul felt he had to rebuke him openly for this. Note two significant points:

● Any apostle, whether Jerusalem based or not, was to live by the gospel. Paul therefore appealed to the authority of the gospel in correcting Peter and Barnabas.

● By taking up this issue openly in the congregation in which Jewish and Gentile Christians were present, Paul testified to the universal nature of the gospel. If Paul had been lax on this point, Jewish and Gentile Christianity might have gone in different directions.

Paul declared to the Galatian Christians that no one is justified – put right – through the works of the law 'but only
through faith in Jesus Christ' (verse 16). Thus Jewish Christians, having been justified, could not go back and try to introduce the law into the scheme of salvation.

Let us remember that we are justified through faith not
merely at the moment of conversion but throughout our life.

✻ *Lord, help me to live by faith in the Son of God.*

Thursday May 17   Galatians 3.1–14

Paul, addressing himself directly to the Galatians, wrote, in
a tone of exasperation: 'You stupid Galatians! You must have
been bewitched' (verse 1). He appealed to them to examine
their own experience.

In the early Church many of those who responded to the
gospel received the Holy Spirit in a visible way as is evident
in the book of **Acts**. Paul asked the Galatians to state whether
they had received the Spirit through the law or by believing
in the gospel. For Paul it was a terrible thing for anyone to
begin with a spiritual experience and end up obeying rules
and trivial regulations.

To meet the challenge of the Judaisers who based their
arguments on the law of Moses, Paul appealed to Scripture
and took the wind out of their sails by taking his case back to
Abraham (see verse 6 and also Genesis 15.6). This points to
the fact that Abraham had a relationship with God which was
more real than anything the law could offer.

Because no one could ever completely keep the law of Moses,
it only brought condemnation. But Christ's death on the cross
('a gibbet' – verse 13) for our sakes has brought us freedom
and blessing.

✻ *Pray for those who are seeking security in a type of religious
life which is dependent on keeping rules and regulations.*

Friday May 18   Galatians 3.15–25

In this rather difficult reading Paul explains the purpose and
the role of the Jewish law, contrasting it with God's promise.
The following points help us to understand what Paul is saying:

● A legal document, when once it is duly ratified, cannot be
  altered. Similarly, in response to Abraham's venture of

faith, God made his promise, and entered into an unalterable covenant relationship with him.

- The law which came later – at the time of Moses – could not alter that covenant based on Abraham's faith.
- The role of the law was to expose sin.
- The law was given through angels and a human mediator, Moses, and was therefore inferior to God's covenant with Abraham.
- While law is not opposed to promise, it cannot give life.
- The law, however, had a place in the divine plan, that of a custodian – a 'kind of tutor' (verse 24) – to care for us until the coming of Christ.
- Now that faith in Christ has become a reality we no longer need the law as a custodian. Through faith we become the sons of God in union with Christ, and when this happens there are no longer any distinctions between one person and another.

✳ *In Christ there is no east or west . . .*
But one great fellowship of love.   John Oxenham

Saturday May 19

An heir when still a minor was no better than a slave. He only obtained his rights when he reached the age set by his father. Paul used this legal analogy to illustrate the point that at an appointed time, God sent his Son to release men and women from the guardianship of the Jewish law.

▶ Read **Galatians 3.26 to 4.11**.

The words 'the elemental spirits of the universe' (verse 3) refer to the heavenly bodies and the spirit-powers which were thought by the Gentiles to control people's lives. Christ's coming changed everything, for he bought us from bondage to such powers and to the Jewish laws, and adopted us as sons and daughters.

The Holy Spirit assures us that we are God's children. *Abba* is an Aramaic word used by Jewish children when they talk to their father. Paul used the Aramaic word with its Greek equivalent to help Jewish and Gentile Christians to realise that they can approach God as children approaching their father.

Paul wondered how the Galatians, while enjoying the status of sonship through God's grace, could ever dream of turning to the slavery of the Jewish law. How often we drift into such bondage by our pet obsessions with rituals of one kind or another!

✳ *Think and pray about verse 7.*

For group discussion and personal thought
Read and study **Galatians 1.6–9**. Paul claimed that there was only one gospel. What is that gospel? What 'other gospels' are being proclaimed today? How do these measure up to the gospel of Christ?

Sunday May 20   **Galatians 4.12–20**

Here is a moving personal appeal by Paul to the Christians in Galatia. He recalled his first visit to Galatia (Acts 13–14). His illness was probably malaria which he might have contracted in the swampy coastlands of Pamphylia. In this illness Paul received every attention from the Galatians. The words, 'you would have torn out your very eyes, and given them to me' (verse 15), show the lengths to which they had been prepared to go in serving Paul. But now Paul was pained to find a change in them, a change which was the result of the influence of the Judaisers. His efforts to bring the Galatians back to simple faith in Christ cost him pain like a mother's travail.

Paul was not only an evangelist but also a loving pastor (see 2 Corinthians 11.28). Both evangelical and pastoral concerns must be combined and given equal importance for a truly effective ministry.

✳ *Help me to love, Lord,*
    not to waste my powers of love,
    to love myself less and less in order to love others more
        and more,
    That around me, no one should suffer or die because I
        have stolen the love they needed to live.   Michel Quoist

---

Monday May 21   **Galatians 4.21–31**

Paul had already made several references to Abraham in his letter. Now, to meet the enthusiasts of the Jewish law on their own ground, he used another Old Testament story, that of Hagar and Sarah, and allegorised it. The two women with their sons symbolise the two covenants. Hagar represents the Sinai covenant – the Jews in bondage to the law. Sarah, on the other hand, stands for the new covenant in Jesus Christ by which God is bringing all people, both Jews and Gentiles, into a living relationship with himself, not by law but by grace.

Paul continued the story to show that, just as the child of the slave-woman persecuted the child of the free woman, the Jews – the children of the law – were persecuting the children of grace. He reminded them that the child of the slave was cast out; and, in the same way, the legalists would be cast out, for they could not inherit the riches of the new covenant.

Those who make law the principle of life are in the position of slaves; while those who make grace the principle of life become heirs to God's promises, and are truly free.

✱ *Pray for those who, like Paul, are trying to help others to gain a true understanding of the Christian gospel.*

Tuesday May 22 **Galatians 5.1–15**

It was an 'either-or' choice that Paul placed before the Galatian Christians. They could not choose both ways. If they decided to receive circumcision, then they bound themselves to keep the law in its entirety, and this inevitably meant turning away from the way of grace.

The Galatians had already made good progress in the way of grace – but now they were turning back to the law. Paul reminded them that 'a little leaven leavens all the dough' (verse 9). For a Jew 'leaven' normally stood for evil influence. So unless some immediate action was taken to stop the influence of the legalistic movement, it would soon turn everyone to the wrong way.

Our situation is probably very different from that of the Galatians. But this truth still remains – wrong ideas can spread through a church and, like leaven, have a bad influence on the fellowship.

✱ *O Lord, strengthen and guide us through your Spirit that we may not be led astray by forms of religion which are not from you.*

Wednesday May 23 **Galatians 5.16–26**

Paul went on to explain at some length the kind of life expected of Christians who are following the way of grace. Freedom from bondage of the law should on no account be turned into licence – doing what we like. Rather, it is freedom for fulfilling a divine purpose, to live a life of love and goodness motivated by the power of the Spirit. Note that Paul calls it the **'harvest'** or **'fruit'** (RSV) of the Spirit. These words show us that this kind of life is not the result of human efforts, but is the result of the Spirit dwelling in us. The Holy Spirit gives us life that resolutely opposes the self-seeking activities of our lower nature.

Those who are bound to Christ by faith have 'crucified the lower nature with its passions and desires' (verse 24), and live by the Spirit. If God's Spirit is the source of our new life, then we must allow that Spirit to have full sway in our lives producing 'love, joy, peace, patience, kindness, goodness, fidelity, gentleness and self-control' (verses 22–23a).

✳   *O come and dwell in me,*
      Spirit of power within!
   And bring the glorious liberty
      From sorrow, fear, and sin.   *Charles Wesley*

Ascension Day, May 24   Luke 24.50–53; Acts 1.6–11

Today we turn from **Galatians** to the account of Christ's ascension. It is fitting that his ascension should end the Gospel of **Luke** and begin **Acts**, because it is both an end and a beginning. It marks the triumphant completion of our Lord's earthly ministry and the beginning of the Church's worldwide mission.

The apostles were those who had witnessed the marvellous events of the Lord's ministry and his death and resurrection. They had been given the awe-inspiring command to preach the gospel, heal the sick, raise the dead and cast out demons (see Matthew 10.7–8). This was the kind of programme which none could ever fulfil in their own strength. But when Jesus commands, he also empowers. 'You will receive power when the Holy Spirit comes upon you' (Acts 1.8a) was his promise, to be fulfilled soon afterwards at Pentecost (Acts 2.1–4).

All through the ages men and women have been called by God to undertake great ventures. Today he calls **us**, often to daunting tasks or difficult undertakings in his name. But the power to see the task through is available to us, too – 'when the Holy Spirit comes'.

* O God our Father, open our ears to your call and our lives
to your Holy Spirit.

Friday May 25   **Galatians 6.1–10**

Throughout his letter to the Galatians Paul opposed the arguments of the Judaisers who were upholding the law of Moses.
He quoted Scripture, appealed to experience and used illustrations from life. Having done all this, he himself upheld
another law – **the law of Christ**. This law is quite different
from the old law of Moses, for it seeks to help persons to grow
in their relationship with God. This is the law that Paul commends to all Christians. He wrote: 'Bear one another's burdens, and so fulfil the law of Christ' (verse 2, RSV).

Treating with gentleness those who do wrong with a view
to setting them back on the right course; helping others to
carry their burdens; never getting tired of doing good and
unceasingly working for the good of all – these are some of the
hallmarks of a life lived in accordance with the law of Christ.

A great responsibility thus lies on Christians. All our
actions are like seed which, depending on the nature of sow-
ing, either bring forth corruption or eternal life.

* Help us to help each other, Lord,
    Each other's cross to bear,
Let each his friendly aid afford,
    And feel his brother's care.   *Charles Wesley*

Saturday May 26   **Galatians 6.11–18**

Here, at the end of his letter, Paul took the stylus and wrote
the closing paragraph in his own hand. Many theories have
been advanced to account for the 'big letters' (verse 11), but
it seems most likely that Paul used them to underline the
importance of these final words. Verse 15 is the focal point of
the paragraph and, perhaps, of the whole letter. The outward
show of religion can be impressive but what matters most is
that, by the grace of God, we can become new creatures.

John Wesley was a remarkable example of how this
happens. Before 1738 his journal reveals a man trying by
works of charity and personal piety to win favour with God
and, gradually, discovering the fruitlessness of such a course.
But in May 1738 during a meeting in London he heard someone speaking about the change which God works in people's

hearts through faith in Christ. Suddenly 'the penny dropped' and he realised that **what God had done for him** far out-weighed anything he might try to do for God. He wrote, 'I felt I did trust in Christ, Christ alone for salvation.' From that day his life took a new direction.

✳ *Heavenly Father, help me to accept humbly what you have done for me in Jesus Christ and to live triumphantly to your glory.*

For group discussion and personal thought
Read **Galatians 6.1–5**. In verse 2 we are told, 'Help to carry one another's burdens' (GNB) – think of examples when you have received or have given help. Does this contradict verse 5 which says, 'Everyone has to carry his own load' (GNB)? What are some of the 'loads' – burdens, responsibilities and duties – which we have to carry ourselves?

JOEL

Notes by the Revd Michael J Townsend, BA, MPhil, BD

The notes in this section are based on the New International Version.

A small part of the book of **Joel** is familiar to Christians because it was quoted by Peter in his speech to the crowds on the day of Pentecost (See Acts 2.16–21). However, the rest of **Joel** is largely neglected by many Christian readers. This neglect is to our loss because this book has a message which is important for all generations.

We cannot be sure when Joel lived and worked, but most scholars would place him fairly late among the Old Testament prophets. Some elements of **Joel** resemble the biblical writings which we call 'apocalyptic'. Certainly Joel's vision was on a global scale. From an ordinary, though tragic, devastation of the land by a plague of locusts, he drew reflections on God's dealings with his people, culminating in his final triumph over evil. As R F Horton wrote in his commentary on **Joel**: 'Our study of this book should lead us to Christ and the baptism of the Spirit.'

Suggestion for further reading

The Twelve Prophets Volume 1 (Hosea, Joel, Amos, Obadiah and Jonah) by Peter C Craigie, Daily Study Bible (Saint Andrew Press).

Sunday May 27   **Joel 1.1–12**

We have become sadly familiar with television and newspaper pictures showing the dreadful effects of famine. One single picture of a refugee camp or of a parched and dried landscape tells us as much as pages of description, and hopefully moves us to action.

It is a tribute to the power of Joel's writing that we are moved by this opening description of the havoc and destruction wrought by the plague of locusts. Indeed, it is as vivid as any picture could be. The land had been stripped of everything. There was nothing to offer in God's house (verse 9); the destruction was total (verse 12). In their dramatic effect, the locusts resembled not so much an army or a tribe, as a nation (verse 6) which had invaded and conquered Israel.

A letter-writer to a newspaper recently urged a Christian leader to lift his eyes up from his prayer-book and look at the real world! Today's reading reminds us that the biblical writers did live in the real world and they did not flinch from describing its difficulties and cruelties. The Bible was not written by people in comfortable circumstances and it can speak to those who know hardship and disaster in every age.

✳ *Pray for those whose personal circumstances are so difficult that they cannot see any signs of hope.*

Monday May 28   Joel 1.13–20

Sometimes, when a terrible calamity has taken place, we find it difficult to see how matters could become worse. Yet, as today's reading shows, in addition to the effects of the plague of locusts there was also a drought to contend with (verse 20). What was to be done?

Joel did not say that the famine was a punishment from God, but he did see the destruction as a kind of foretaste of further and worse destruction which would come on the 'day of the Lord' (verse 15). He therefore called upon the priests to declare a fast and summon a solemn assembly of the people (verse 14).

There is an important distinction drawn in verse 13 between '**my** God' and '**your** God'. It seems that Joel was warning the priests that they were in danger of thinking of God as being satisfied with the ritual observances of grain and drink offerings. On the other hand, Joel's understanding of God was that he called for repentance. That is the authentic voice of God's prophets in every age and the message is as important for us today as it was for the people of Joel's time.

✳ *Help us, Lord, to know our need for repentance and true faith. Grant that we may offer our worship and service in that spirit.*

Tuesday May 29   Joel 2.1–11

It is very galling to human pride to have to admit that despite all our intelligence, strength and power, we are often powerless against mere insects. Yet it is so. Some writers on **Joel** have included pages of description, culled from the reports of those who have travelled widely in lands where locusts are a problem. An army of locusts was – at least prior to chemical means becoming available – quite invincible.

The vividness of Joel's language and imagery here would be a frightening reminder for any who had witnessed such things. But Joel's concern was not to frighten so much as to warn. The locust plague reminded him so strongly that a God of righteousness would bring judgement to pass upon an unrepentant people, that he wrote of the Lord as thundering 'at the head of his army' (verse 11).

For true repentance to be possible our pride often has to be brought low. When human beings start getting 'above themselves' it is sometimes the little things – like the locusts – which have to be employed to make us see sense again.

✻ *Lord, sometimes we think we can do all things. Forgive us*
our pride and teach us we can do nothing without you.

Wednesday May 30   Joel 2.12–17

It is sometimes too easy to say that we are sorry for something we have done or neglected to do. The motives for such repentance may not be right. When we were children we may have sometimes said, 'Sorry', because we were told to, but then added under our breath, 'I am not really!' As adults we may repent because we are afraid of being found out, or because of what others will think of us, or because it is expected of us. Yet the only real motive for repentance is the recognition that what we have done or failed to do is a sin against God, dishonouring our Christian calling and taking us further away from God's grace.

In God's name, Joel called upon the people to repent. They had to turn to him with all their heart (verse 12) and rend their hearts rather than their garments (verse 13). This might suggest to us a particular emotional state; but in biblical thought the heart was the seat of the moral will, not the emotions. Joel's appeal, therefore, was for people to offer their wills and decisions to God in repentance. Along with the words 'I am sorry', we have to add 'I want to do better'. God never leaves that prayer unanswered.

✻ *Our God is gracious, nor will leave*
The desolate to mourn.   *John Morison*

God keeps his promises. Indeed, he keeps them more fully and wonderfully than we have any right to expect. In today's reading we see how Joel foresaw the **material** blessings which would come to God's people when they had truly repented and returned to him with all their hearts. Those blessings would be, in every sense, a restoration of the damage done by the locusts (verse 25).

Note how the promised blessings in today's reading match, and then surpass, the previously described calamities. The fig-tree and vine would again yield their riches (compare verse 22 and 1.12); there would be ample rain (verse 23 and 1.20); there would be enough grain (verse 24 and 1.17); there would be more than enough to eat (verse 26 and 1.16) and all this would cause God's name to be praised (verse 26 and 1.9).

It is a poor thing for us, as Christians, to praise God just because he gives us things. Nevertheless, God does provide for us and he does keep his promises, and those are among the reasons we have for being thankful and living thankfully.

✴ *Count your blessings, slowly. Give thanks to God for each of them in turn.*

Yesterday we read about the material blessings which Joel predicted for God's repentant people. Today's verses are concerned with the **spiritual** blessings which they would also receive.

The greatest need of human beings is for a new relationship with God. This can only happen if God himself takes the initiative. In the first part of today's reading the prophet promised that the Spirit would come into the hearts of God's people so that his purposes in human history might be achieved. What happened in Jerusalem at Pentecost (see Acts 2.1–13) was seen by Peter as the fulfilment of Joel's promise (see Acts 2.16–21).

This reminds us that, as Christians, we have received the fullness of God's blessings. We live now in the last days. They began at Pentecost and they will end with the Day of the Lord. The second part of today's reading (verses 1–8) reminds us that there are those who, even after the Spirit has come, will remain God's enemies. For them there will indeed be judgement. However, our task is to respond to God's initiative in sending the Spirit by letting him control and direct our lives.

✳ *We wait the pentecostal powers,*
   The Holy Ghost sent down from heaven.

Charles Wesley

Saturday June 2   Joel 3.9–21

It is often difficult for us to believe that the gospel of Christ will prevail. After nearly 2,000 years of preaching and teaching the Christian message – and many centuries of Jewish faith before that – it is not always obvious that the kingdom of God has made great progress in the hearts of men and women. There is still much evil, hatred, oppression, lust and greed in our world; and those who trust God often seem to be in a minority. For our spiritual health, therefore, we need verses such as those in today's reading.

These verses indicate that, after the outpouring of God's Spirit (which we believe took place at Pentecost) human history will continue until, one day, God's great victory is established. That victory will involve punishment for those who have scorned and slighted God's people (verse 19) but vindication for the faithful. Like travellers on a journey who need to know what their destination is, spiritual pilgrims need a vision of the end of all things. The closing phrase of Joel provides it: 'The Lord dwells in Zion!' It is in that faith that we journey on towards our goal.

✳ *Lord, when I am worried by the amount of evil in the world*
   help me to remember that you reign, and always will.

For group discussion and personal thought

Joel called the **nation** of Israel to repent. Read again **Joel 2.12–14**. What does it mean for us to truly repent from the heart (a) as individuals and (b) as a church? How can a church repent, and how is this repentance shown in its everyday life?

ACTS 2 – 12

Notes by the Revd A Gordon Jones, BD

Gordon Jones is a supernumerary Methodist minister in East London, England. Previously he has worked with the Richmond Fellowship for Moral Welfare and Rehabilitation.

The notes in this section are based on the New English Bible.

In the New Testament there are two books which appear to be a two-volume work. They are **Luke's Gospel** and the **Acts of the Apostles**, both of which are dedicated to someone called Theophilus. These two books are a careful attempt to explain about the founder of the new religion – Christianity – which was causing such a stir in the first century AD, and how this religion was growing. Although we cannot be certain about the author, many believe that he was Luke, a doctor, who accompanied Paul on some of his journeys.

Acts is a tremendously exciting and important book. It relates the memories of how Christianity began – the deeds, mistakes and experiences of the very first Christians. An **act** is something done; and an **apostle** is someone sent out. We today, who are **sent out** into the world, can learn much of what we should be **doing** through reading **Acts**. In the next five weeks we shall be looking at chapters 2 to 12.

Suggestions for further reading

Acts of the Apostles by William Barclay, Daily Study Bible (Saint Andrew Press)

Acts of the Apostles by William Neil, New Century Bible Commentaries (Marshall, Morgan & Scott)

Whit Sunday, June 3   Acts 2.1–13

This tremendous event took place on the Jewish day of Pentecost, which was a celebration of God's giving of the law to Moses on Mount Sinai. Today's reading shows how he, who had come to 'complete' or 'fulfil' the law (See Matthew 5.17), revealed this fulfilment to all people.

What words can we use to describe a vivid spiritual experience? In the Bible 'wind' and 'fire' are frequent symbols of God's activity (for example, see Exodus 19.16–19; Psalm 104.3; and Luke 3.16). An awareness of God working in a person seemed like the power of the wind, and the devouring and purifying of fire.

John Wesley described his experience of the power and love of God in terms of his heart being 'strangely warmed'. His brother Charles wrote a hymn which begins:

O thou who camest from above
 The pure celestial fire to impart,
Kindle a flame of sacred love
 On the mean altar of my heart.

So it was with the Holy Spirit coming at Pentecost. But not only were their hearts set aflame; it seemed that they were speaking in many languages (verses 5–12). The gospel was not just for the Jews but for **all the world**.

✷ *Holy Spirit, fall afresh on me. Revive my faith and send me forth to proclaim it in words and deeds.*

Monday June 4

Those who were in Jerusalem when the Holy Spirit came upon the disciples were amazed. They could not believe that this motley band of people – many of them simple Galileans, including fishermen, a tax-collector and even women – could be talking sense. They must be drunk! Surely only recognised prophets or teachers could proclaim a message from God! Peter reminded the crowd that had gathered of the words of the prophet Joel.

▶ Read **Acts 2.14–21**.

Once again the message was clear – God had called **all** people to proclaim him and **all** could be saved.

Too often Christians have left the work of witnessing for Christ to the so-called professionals. However, today we have begun to awaken to the reality of the ministry of **all** God's people. We all have a gift which can be used by God in his work of proclaiming salvation to the world. Our presence at worship, our loving care of those in trouble, our humble service in the life of the church or community, are all ways in which, through God's Spirit, we can be his witnesses.

✷ *Take my life, and let it be*
 Consecrated, Lord, to thee.   *Frances R Havergal*

Tuesday June 5

Was the Holy Spirit, in some way, the presence of the risen Christ in the world? Jesus had constantly spoken of the Holy Spirit as the One who would reveal and complete the truth of his deeds and words (see for example, John 16.13–14). The Spirit of God had been working throughout Jesus' ministry, producing the evidence that he was God's Messiah. But the Jews, who had been longing for the Messiah, did not recognise this. So Peter, as he continued his powerful preaching on the day of Pentecost, declared that the Messiah had indeed come! He was Jesus of Nazareth – the man who had been crucified just over seven weeks ago!

▶ Read **Acts 2.22–36**.

Peter's sermon declared that Jesus' deeds showed that God was working through him (verse 22). But his ultimate proof that Jesus was the Messiah was the **resurrection**. Peter quoted from two psalms (see verses 25–28 and verses 34–35), which were presumed to have been written by David. However, he interpreted them as words referring not to David, since he was dead, but to the Messiah – the risen Jesus.

What a change had come about in Peter! The man who had denied Jesus (see Mark 14.66–72), now boldly proclaimed that he was the Christ – a proof in itself of the power of the Spirit!

✳ *Lord, fill me with the power of your Spirit so that I, too, may declare your wondrous deeds.*

Wednesday June 6   Acts 2.37–47

Many people who heard Peter's sermon were troubled. 'What must we do?' they asked. Peter told them the way forward – see verse 38. Repentance, baptism and acceptance of Christ would lead to the forgiveness of sins and the gift of the Holy Spirit. That day about three thousand people responded to the gospel and their lives were changed!

Verses 42–47 summarise what the Christian way of life meant in practice for the first Christians. They met together for teaching and prayer; they shared their possessions and cared for those in need; and daily they worshipped God in the temple. They did not turn their backs on their traditional faith, but rather found new life in it.

The first Christians are good examples for us to follow:

- We cannot be vigorous Christians for long on our own; we need others. We must never neglect coming together for worship and fellowship.
- We must also care for the poor – those who are distressed because of unemployment, lack of food and bad housing.
- We must plough our energy into our churches.

✳ *Let us pray for the churches in our neighbourhood and for all those who believe in God, that together we may witness to God in our materialistic world.*

Thursday June 7   Acts 3.1–16

In attending the temple for prayers, Peter showed that Christianity was not opposed to Judaism. He underlined this in two ways:
- The power by which the crippled man was healed was that of none other than the God beloved of all Jews – 'the God of Abraham, Isaac, and Jacob' (verse 13). So why were they surprised at this sign of God's activity?
- Peter reprimanded his fellow Jews for failing to see God at work in Jesus (verses 13–15). His words were a stern accusation, but they were probably said out of love for his people – more in sorrow than in anger.

Peter said that 'the name of Jesus, by awakening faith, has strengthened this man' (verse 16). Here is stated a truth which millions have discovered through their own experience. Sunk in depression, anxiety, guilt, boredom and hopelessness, they have found in the words, deeds and presence of Christ a new reality that has taken away their despair and given them a new impetus for living. They have found a new strength which they never believed possible. They have risen up and walked again!

✳   *Strong in the Lord of hosts,*
           And in his mighty power,
    Who in the strength of Jesus trusts
         Is more than conqueror.   *Charles Wesley*

Friday June 8

For Peter, Christianity was the climax of Judaism – Christ was the fulfilment of the law and the prophets. So he continued preaching in the temple, using the people's knowledge of the law of Moses and the teachings of the prophets to convince them to repent and turn to Christ.

▶ Read **Acts 3.17–26**.

Peter reminded the people that the prophets had foretold a suffering Messiah (see verse 18 and Isaiah 53.3–4), whose life expressed God's ways of justice, mercy and care for the oppressed (see Isaiah 11.1–5). Jesus was this Messiah.

Then, Peter reminded his listeners of their place in God's universal plan of salvation. The prophets had foretold of a time of 'universal restoration' (verse 21). This would be a time when God's loving purposes would be fulfilled in the lives of **all** people – not just in the lives of the Jews (see Isaiah 11.9). All the families on earth would be blessed through the offspring of Abraham – Jesus (see verses 25–26).

However, to acknowledge that Jesus was the Messiah was not enough. Peter's listeners had to respond. He called upon them to turn from their wicked ways to the risen Christ. This still applies to God's people today – if our knowledge of Christ is expressed in all that we do, then God can continue his work of 'universal restoration'.

✳ *Lord, fulfil your purposes in the lives of all people.*

Saturday June 9   **Acts 4.1–12**

The chief priests and Sadducees who opposed the apostles, conveniently ignored that a man had been healed. The Sadducees denied the doctrine of the resurrection, and they were so exasperated because Peter and John had proclaimed the resurrection of Jesus that they put them into prison.

The next day Peter, filled with the Holy Spirit, stood boldly before the Jewish council. He drew attention to the fact that a miracle had been performed by the name of Jesus Christ. Then he used a quotation from Psalm 118.22 – words which avoided the issue of resurrection – to point out to the Jewish leaders the error of their ways. Later we shall see that his bold stance impressed the members of the council.

Often, when Christians are opposed, it is supposedly because of some 'dangerous doctrine' that they are said to proclaim. Like the apostles, the good things that they do are ignored. This suggests that much of the opposition to Christianity is due to people's fear of losing power, or their inability to allow their ideas to be questioned.

We may not be very clever at answering doctrinal questions; but, in the end, the credibility of our answers lies in what Christ has done in our lives.

✳ *Lord, may my actions speak louder than my words.*

For group discussion and personal thought
Read, in **Acts 2.1–13**, how the Holy Spirit came upon the disciples at Pentecost. In what ways were they changed? Consider whether you too have received the Holy Spirit. How has the Spirit changed your life?

Trinity Sunday, June 10   Acts 4.13–22

In view of Peter's well-presented arguments, and the actual presence of the man who had been healed, all that the Jewish council could do was to tell Peter and John to stop speaking in the name of Jesus. However, Peter and John stood their ground. God had commanded them to speak, so the council must judge for themselves as to whom Peter and John owed their first allegiance – to people or to God.

Normally we must respect and obey the laws of our land; but if these seem to be going against the law of God, what then? Men and women have suffered imprisonment, torture and death for the sake of their obedience to Christ; and in following him their faith has overcome all opponents. For decades Christianity was forbidden in China and Russia. However, today, in less restrictive times, it has been discovered that Christians continued to worship and witness insofar as they could – and Christianity has survived!

Have we the confidence and courage to bear our witness in the face of a sceptical world? When we are conscientiously convinced of something, **nothing** – no law or threat – can stop us talking about it.

✳ *Pray for Christians who witness today in difficult circumstances, that they may be enriched by the love of God, the grace of our Lord Jesus Christ and the fellowship of the Holy Spirit.*

Monday June 11   Acts 4.23–31

Once again the apostles were set free with a warning not to

preach in the name of Jesus. On their release they did not go into hiding as they did after Jesus' crucifixion, but went to their friends where they prayed together.

Rather than praying for protection and deliverance from persecution, the apostles and their friends prayed that they would continue to speak with all boldness (verse 29). The Holy Spirit had, indeed brought about a great change in their lives!

Faithful Jews and Christians have always suffered some form of attack because they have been convinced that it is right to obey God rather than people. Sometimes it is hard to continue obeying God. But in those difficult circumstances we can receive a fresh inflowing of God's encouraging and empowering Spirit. Our certainty returns – as it did for those first Christians (verse 31) – and we find that we have the courage to continue our witness no matter what may happen to us.

✳ *Lord God, our Father, when we are opposed or mocked because of our faith, help us not to be ashamed or afraid, but to know that your Spirit is with us at all times, strengthening us and giving us confidence.*

Tuesday June 12   **Acts 4.32 to 5.11**

The first Christians cared for their needy by voluntarily sharing their financial resources with each other. They were not compelled to do so. So why were Ananias and Sapphira dishonest? Were they seeking to be thought well of by the apostles? Did they not realise the seriousness of their hypocrisy? Were they not aware that God required total honesty and commitment – not an outward show? Whatever their motives, the guilt Ananias experienced when he realised that he had lied to God, was sufficient to cause his death.

Today, we who are Christians know that we must show care for those in need. But do we love and trust whole-heartedly? Are we tempted to give because we feel that is what we are expected to do? To give money to a collection for people of a starving country is good. But if our comfortable way of life contributes to their exploitation, are we any less hypocritical than Ananias and Sapphira? It is not enough to hand out charitable gifts. Our commitment needs to extend to developing our understanding of why problems exist and helping to solve those problems in whatever way we can.

* *Lord, help me to recognise and admit when I am selfish and loveless. Save me from pretending to be more loving than I am, and enable me to love with true honesty.*

Wednesday June 13   Acts 5.12–21a

The character and achievements of the first Christians won the respect of the general public – except, of course, the Jewish officials. They were jealous of the apostles and were afraid of losing their power and positions, so once again they arrested them.

One of the reasons for the apostles' popularity was that their activities extended beyond preaching. They also healed the sick, fulfilling Jesus' command to them (see Matthew 10.7–8). The Christian Church has always been deeply involved with healing, and there is a renewed commitment in this area in the Church today.

This does not mean that we are endowed with supernatural gifts which make doctors unnecessary. Healing not only involves curing a physical sickness, it means making people whole and dealing with the underlying causes of illness. Spiritual healing deals with people's inner fears, depressions, anxieties, guilt, loneliness, bitterness and lack of self-worth. But it also involves seeking ways in which to improve social conditions and family relationships.

* *Pray for doctors, medical researchers, nurses, psychotherapists and counsellors in their work of healing wounded bodies, minds and spirits.*

Thursday June 14

The apostles were in prison again; but, during the night, they had been miraculously released. Rather than go into hiding, they had gone straight back to the place of their arrest and continued their teaching. What courage they had!

▶ Now read **Acts 5.21b–32**.

The Jewish leaders finally admitted their reason for not wanting Jesus' name mentioned – they did not want to be held responsible for his death (verse 28). Peter's reply to them was firm and bold. The apostles would continue to 'obey God rather than men' because they and the Holy Spirit were the witnesses of Christ, the Saviour, who would grant repentance and forgiveness to Israel (verses 29–32).

There are times when each of us is called to speak the truth, even if it makes others feel uncomfortable and results in our own suffering. When God's Spirit leads us to do so, he will strengthen us to speak with humble confidence – never with arrogance. However, we must remember that our faith does not deny the reality of suffering, but regards it as a means to resurrection.

✳ *Pray for those who suffer for their faith; and ask that your own faith and confidence in God might grow.*

Friday June 15   Acts 5.33–42

In their preaching, Peter and the other apostles constantly declared that Jesus was the Messiah. A longing for the Messiah was central to the Jewish faith. A thousand years before, David had brought about peace, unity and prosperity in Israel. As time went on, the Jews became subject to powerful nations. They yearned for a return to life as it was in the time of David.

Over the years many had claimed to be the Messiah. They were rebels and terrorists, who wanted to restore Israel's fortunes by force – men like Theudas and Judas the Galilean (verses 36–37). Their promises proved to be empty.

Jesus was not the kind of Messiah the Jews were expecting. However, Gamaliel wisely cautioned the council in case there was truth in the apostles' claim that Jesus was the Messiah. He suggested that they wait and see whether God brought anything out of this new movement (verses 38–39).

Jesus accomplished his purposes without the use of violence. Do we believe that today's injustices can be overcome without the use of force? The first Christians believed that Christ's victory came through the acceptance of suffering. They rejoiced in their suffering. Can we?

✳ *Lord, you gave your back to the smiters and did not hide your face from shame. May we follow your example.*

Saturday June 16   Acts 6.1–7

It was the intention of the first Christian community that none of its members should be in need. So as the Church grew, it became necessary for them to organise their welfare system. By doing this they ensured that the apostles were not overburdened with responsibility and it was also a safeguard against human thoughtlessness, prejudice and selfishness.

In the early Church there were both Jews who had always lived in Judaea and spoke Aramaic, and Jews who had lived in other countries, learned Gentile ways and spoke Greek. It seems that the latter group felt discriminated against. Hence seven people were carefully chosen to be responsible for the daily distribution of goods. It is significant that they all had Greek names (verse 5).

Sadly, there are still people in the Church today who feel discriminated against – some on the grounds of race, others because of their age, sex or cultural background. We must all take care to guard against such signs of lovelessness, recognising that each person has unique gifts and qualities. As we share our lives together and seek to serve each other we will be the living body of Christ, and the word of God will continue to spread more widely.

✳ *Father, by the power of your Spirit you have made us one. Help us to live in love and peace together.*

For group discussion and personal thought
Consider the story of Ananias and Sapphira in **Acts 5.1–10**. What exactly was the sin they were guilty of? In what ways are we in danger of the same sin? Are there times when we say that we want to give our all to God and then reserve a part for ourselves? When, and why, are we most likely to do this?

Sunday June 17   Acts 6.8–15

Stephen, who was one of the seven men we read about yesterday, was a man of great spiritual power. However, when he began to work miracles among the people, he was opposed by other Greek-speaking Jews. They made accusations of blasphemy against him.

Stephen was accused of speaking against the 'holy place' – the temple – and the law of Moses (verse 13), both of which were very precious to the Jews. What exactly Stephen had said we do not know. Perhaps he had spoken out about the temple rituals, saying that sacrifices were no longer needed to atone for people's sin. Concerning the law, he had probably criticised – in the same way as Jesus had done – the rigid way in which the Jewish leaders had interpreted it. But whatever he had said, his words were deliberately misrepresented and twisted by those who witnessed against him to the council.

Many accusations have been laid against what Christians believe and teach. Unfortunately some of these accusations have been true, and we must humbly accept such criticism and learn from it. But more often, criticisms have come from people who are afraid to face the challenge of Christ.

✳ *Lord Christ, help us to understand your teachings and to live by them. As we faithfully bear witness to you, help us to withstand any criticism we may face.*

Monday June 18   Acts 7.1–10

Stephen did not defend himself by contradicting the accusations made against him; nor did he try to explain the meaning of his message. Rather, he began a speech which was a sustained attack on his own Jewish people. Stephen believed that they had been called by God, but had constantly failed to respond to him. Their call was to go out at God's command on a journey – a pilgrimage – and always be attentive to what God wanted for them. So Stephen started by reminding the council of the beginning of their nation.

The call of the Hebrews was to a pilgrimage. It was a call to change – the people were not to remain set in their ways. This is also the call to Christians. We have been called to be a pilgrim people. We are on the march towards the kingdom of God. Our journey is never ended on this earth, 'for here we have no permanent home, but we are seekers after the city which is to come' (Hebrews 13.14).

There are always new things to do for God, new responses to be made. Is your church on the march? Or is it just sitting down, contented with itself, forever repeating its old ways and ideas, unaware of the fresh demands of Christ?

✳ *Lord, may we be prepared to forsake what lies behind us, ever reaching out to that which is before us.*

Tuesday June 19   Acts 7.11–29

Yesterday we reached the point in Stephen's speech where he had recounted the story of Joseph being sold into slavery by his brothers. However, God's hand was on Joseph and through him the children of Israel grew into a nation – a unified group of people. It is interesting to note that the first 'collective sin' that Stephen recounted in the history of Israel was that of jealousy. Jealousy had partly motivated the Jewish leaders to kill Jesus and to persecute the apostles.

Today's reading ends at the point where the children of Israel were suspicious of Moses and rejected him. Stephen was building up a rather unpleasant picture of the forefathers of the Jews – one which showed them to be jealous and suspicious people whose first reaction was to reject their God-chosen leaders. However, history again proved that God's purposes prevailed in spite of the sinfulness of his chosen people.

Sometimes our sinfulness and the tragedies we experience seem to be an overwhelming denial of God's call – even of his very existence. But God will never be beaten! With confidence, we can affirm Paul's words in Romans 8.28 (RSV):

✷ *'We know that in* **everything** *God works for good with those who love him, who are called according to his purpose.'*

Wednesday June 20   Acts 7.30–50

Stephen painstakingly continued to recount the call of Moses – the ruler, liberator and miracle worker (verses 35–36) – who led his people out of slavery in Egypt. And yet the people refused to accept his leadership (verse 39). Stephen reminded his listeners that Moses had promised that God would raise up a prophet, like himself (verse 37). The inference, of course, being that this prophet was none other than Jesus. Again Stephen was reinforcing the point that, like their forefathers who rejected Moses, the Jews were now rejecting Jesus – the Christ.

Stephen was brave to stand up and say these hard things against his own nation and his own leaders – especially considering their deep pride in their national heritage. Are we willing to do the same? Are we willing to stand firm in our faith in Christ when he calls us to speak out against powerful people and institutions who are rejecting the message and ways of Christ? Are we willing to take Christ's stand in the political life of our nation, whatever the consequences?

✷ *Lord, forgive me for the times when I have been afraid to stand firm for what I know to be right. Help me to bear witness to Christ's truth at all times.*

Stephen concluded his speech with a direct attack on the people before whom he stood. His words were filled with passionate anger towards his own people. No wonder the Jewish leaders reacted as they did! He had accused them of opposing God's purposes and messengers throughout their history.

If this seems too harsh a judgement, we must remember that Stephen was driven by his great love for Jesus and also for his people. Perhaps we can also hear an echo of Jesus' words of compassionate anger and pity over Jerusalem (see Luke 13.34–35). This is the anger of love – the anger of God so often portrayed in the Old Testament. It is the anger which parents feel towards their own children when they do wrong, an anger which is far greater than that towards other children. Why? Because they love them more!

Stephen's love for Jesus and his people enabled him to pray for their forgiveness as he suffered death at their hands. He was the first Christian martyr. Indeed he was 'a man full of faith and of the Holy Spirit' (Acts 6.5).

✴ *Lord, fill me with your Spirit, so that like Stephen, I am full of faith and never allow my anger to turn into hatred.*

Stephen's death marked the beginning of severe persecution for the Church. Many of the first Christians were scattered over Judaea and Samaria and so began to fulfil the words of Jesus that they would bear witness for him in these places and to the ends of the earth (see Acts 1.8). Philip, another of the seven (Acts 6.5), appears to have had the most influence in Samaria at this time. The power of his preaching and the miracles he performed were sufficient to lead many people to Christ, including an influential magician called Simon.

Meanwhile, back in Jerusalem, Saul of Tarsus – soon to become the great apostle Paul – was the chief persecutor of the Christians. Was his outrage an expression of the conflict he felt between his strict Pharisaic upbringing and the powerful witness of Stephen's prayer of forgiveness at his martyrdom?

Saint Augustine once said that 'the Church owes Paul to the prayer of Stephen'. But Stephen himself would not have known this as he bravely faced his death.

✽ *Lord Christ, when my faith seems to be doing nothing for others, help me to remember that appearances may hide the truth and that you are at work even in those who seem to oppose it.*

Saturday June 23   Acts 8.14—25

Simon, a pagan magician, envied the way in which Peter and John were able to impart the Holy Spirit to the Samaritans, and so coveted this ability for himself. He imagined that he could buy it to increase his popularity and power. But Peter soon put him straight!

Arising from today's story, there came into the English language the word, 'simony.' It means 'buying or selling of ecclesiastical preferment' – in other words, trying to get into positions of power in the Church through the offering of money. It is a sin because all spiritual gifts are God's gifts to us and cannot be bought.

We cannot buy our way in the kingdom of God. This temptation has come to many people – especially to those who have material wealth and power. They assume that they can dominate the life of their local church. Nor can we obtain God's favour by attempting to bribe him with promises of what we will then do for him. The only way of receiving God's gifts is through faith and giving ourselves to him in humble love.

✽ *Just as I am, without one plea*
   But that thy blood was shed for me,
   And that thou bidd'st me come to thee,
      O Lamb of God, I come!   Charlotte Elliott

For group discussion and personal thought
Study **Acts 7.51–53** and consider the accusations Stephen brought against his own people. Why was he so stern towards his own nation whom he clearly loved? What are some of the accusations which could be brought against God's people today?

Sunday June 24   Acts 8.26—40

Philip had been instrumental in bringing the Samaritans into the Church – the new Israel. Now, led by the Holy Spirit, he continued his work of breaking down barriers between Jews and Gentiles by speaking to an Ethiopian eunuch. The eunuch was probably a black African who lived in the area of present-day Sudan. He was returning home from pilgrimage in Jerusalem which suggests he was a God-fearing Gentile. However, according to the old Jewish law, he would not have been able to become a full proselyte (see Deuteronomy 23.1).

The eunuch's question: 'How can I understand unless someone will give me a clue?' (verse 31), is one frequently asked by people today. Very often they do not understand what Christians believe because they are not familiar with words such as 'salvation', 'repentance' or 'redemption'. Yet they long for these very things. Many are chained by guilt and fear; they want to be free and at peace. But how? If we are sensitive to people's needs, and are prepared to be led by God's Spirit, we shall be given the opportunity to interpret our faith in a way that people can understand. Then they also may discover the joy of following Christ.

✳ *Help us, Lord, to hear the cry for help in people's hearts. Guide us by your Spirit, to help them to find you.*

Monday June 25   Acts 9.1–9

The conversion of Saul is one of the most dramatic incidents in **Acts**. Saul had seen Stephen die and had heard his prayer of forgiveness (see June 22). Since then, this must have been nagging at him unconsciously and undermining his arguments against Christianity. God was preparing him for his meeting with the risen Christ. And now Saul, who had clearly seen a need to eradicate Christianity, was humbled to the ground and blinded! His hatred of Christ was about to be transformed into a love of equal intensity.

Why had Saul's hatred of the Christians and their Christ been so intense? Consider the relationship between love and hate. The opposite of love is not hate – but **indifference**. When we hate something or someone, it is because the object of our hatred touches us deeply and we respond to it with strong feelings. This is also what happens when we love something or someone. Some have even said that hate is often a hidden love unable to admit itself.

Saul's conversion shows us that our deep feelings of hate can be transformed into depths of love by the power of Christ.

* *If you find yourself hating another person, spend some time asking yourself why. Is that person saying something important that you should hear?*

Tuesday June 26   Acts 9.10–22

Ananias was aware of Saul's reputation and may even have known some of the Jewish Christian refugees from Jerusalem whom Saul had set out to arrest. So we can well understand his hesitancy to go to him. However, Ananias was obedient to God's directives – such was the spirit of the early Christians. They knew that it was more important to obey God's call rather than the demands of people, or succumb to their own fears and instincts of self-preservation.

Ananias did not go to Saul grudgingly and prepared to do only what he was asked to do. Rather, Ananias called Saul 'my brother' (verse 17), and so welcomed him into the family of believers. Already the hard saying of Jesus, that his followers must love their enemies and do good to their persecutors (see Luke 6.28), was being put into practice.

The extent to which Ananias and the Christian group in Damascus accepted and cared for Saul must have helped him to grow forceful in his Christian witness. They took the risk of ignoring their natural inclinations and following God – and in so doing countless people were blessed.

* *When you are next faced with a difficult task remember Paul's words in Philippians 4.13: 'I have strength for anything through him (Christ) who gives me power.'*

Wednesday June 27   Acts 9.23–30

Today's reading is a little difficult to reconcile with the account Paul gives in Galatians 1.16–18, of what followed his conversion. There it seems that he went to Arabia for several years before going to Jerusalem. However, both accounts agree on the fact that he was in brief contact with the church at Jerusalem. Not surprisingly the Christians there, at first, distrusted his integrity.

How grateful Saul must have been for the support he received from Barnabas! This is the second time that Barnabas is mentioned in **Acts** (see 4.36–37). He appears to have been generous in his giving of loving support and encouragement as well as in his giving of money. Barnabas saw and encouraged the best in people and did not desert them in their time of failure. This was particularly evident later in his attitude to John Mark (see Acts 15.36–39) – the same Mark whom we presume wrote **Mark's Gospel**. We can never know the extent to which seeds of kindness bear fruit!

However, we do know what a welcome relief it is to receive support in times of crisis and failure. Let us never forget those individuals who have shown us love and trust in our times of need.

✳ *Remember by name and give thanks for people who have stood by you in your times of failure. Pray that you may be ready to do the same for others.*

Thursday June 28 Acts 9.31–43

In writing this history of the early Church, the writer's attention now turns back to Peter and the exciting development of the church in Judaea. He clearly states that the growth and work of the Church was dependent upon the Holy Spirit (verse 31). On a visit to Lydda and Joppa – towns north-west of Jerusalem – Peter performed two miracles, including raising Tabitha from the dead.

The ministry of the early Christian community clearly reflected the ministry of Jesus. These first Christians proclaimed that Jesus was the Messiah, and God confirmed the truth of their claims with practical proof.

This is a challenge to us. We make the claim that Jesus Christ is the Son of God – that he is God revealed in a human life. But are people convinced by what they see in us? What practical proof of Christ's presence is there in our personal lives and in the life of our churches? Jesus healed – are we a healing community? Jesus offered a fresh start to those who had failed – do we help those who have failed and are guilt-laden? Jesus brought hope to the despairing – do we?

✳ *Father, you have called us to be the body of Christ. Help us, as the Church and as individual believers, truly to embody in our lives Christ's qualities of love, healing and forgiveness, so that all people may be drawn to you.*

Friday June 29 Acts 10.1–8

Cornelius was a centurion stationed at Caesarea – a coastal town which was the headquarters of the Roman government for the area, including Judaea and Samaria. He was a generous and deeply religious man who was genuinely seeking the way to God. Probably he had heard about the Christian movement, was deeply impressed and wanted to know more. He had a vision in which he became convinced that a man called Simon Peter would be able to help him.

Notice that it was not Peter who sought out Cornelius, but Cornelius who sought out Peter. However (as we shall read tomorrow), before they met, Peter had to learn a very important lesson about his attitude towards Gentiles.

In the Christian Church we often speak about trying to break into an unbelieving world; but it is salutary to remember that sometimes it is a longing world trying to find a way into a 'closed-shop' Church. A man attended a Boys' Brigade display in a church hall in which his son took part. He was impressed and afterwards said to one of the church members, 'Would I be allowed to come to one of your services here?' That challenged those who belonged to that church to ask why 'outsiders' saw the Church as a closed society where they were not welcome. Does it challenge us?

✳ *Lord, help us, like you, to welcome all who come to us.*

Saturday June 30 Acts 10.9–16

Today's reading tells how Peter was helped to learn his lesson. The discovery that Christ was for all people was one of the most important moments in the whole history of the Church. Imagine the scene: at midday Peter was on a roof-top in Joppa, a town looking out on the blue Mediterranean. He was intending to pray, but he was hungry and possibly sleepy. His surroundings formed the background to a dream. The sheet he saw, filled with all kinds of creatures, was a ship's sail. The voice telling him to eat – and so break the strict Jewish laws about food (see Leviticus 11) – shocked him. What was the meaning of this startling dream? Peter had to unlearn the traditions of a lifetime. In God's sight no creature – and no person – is 'unclean'!

Are we sometimes, like Peter and his fellow Jews, on our guard against people whose race, tribe, culture, language or class differs from ours? This is an especially urgent question for us in today's multi-cultural, multi-racial and multi-faith world. Racism is one of the greatest enemies of the unity of the human family, and Christians must take the lead in conquering it.

✳   *Love, like death, has all destroyed.*
     Rendered all distinctions void;
     Names, and sects, and parties fall:
     Thou, O Christ, art all in all.   *Charles Wesley*

For group discussion and personal thought

Read and study the story of Philip and the Ethiopian in **Acts 8.26–40**. Philip began to proclaim Christ by dealing with the question which was occupying the Ethiopian's mind. What does this say to us about our efforts to proclaim Christ? What are some of the questions people are asking today? Are we dealing with these adequately?

Sunday July 1   **Acts 10.17–33**

It has been said that the kingdom of God is the kingdom of right relationships. When we become aware of God as revealed in Jesus Christ, one of the first things we try to do is to put right any wrong relationships we have with others. We seek to turn enmity into friendship, hatred into love, and fear into trust.

This was what Peter sought to do after he had his dream on the roof-top at Joppa. Traditionally, the Jews considered all Gentiles to be 'unclean' – they would certainly not eat with them or enter their houses. Romans certainly despised Jews. But in today's reading we see how Peter gave hospitality for the night to Cornelius' messengers. Then the next day he went without hesitation to Cornelius' house and entered it. As for Cornelius, he treated Peter with the utmost respect, showing him warmth, gratitude and humility.

The application to us is clearly that we must no longer put people into categories. We must see them all as **persons** – all of equal worth in the sight of God. In doing this we are entering the kingdom of right relationships.

✳ *O God, break down the barriers that exist between us and other people, and bring us together in love.*

Monday July 2   **Acts 10.34–48**

Let us consider three important matters in today's reading:

- First, it tells of the close link between Judaism and Christianity. The Jews have often been depicted as the arch-enemies of Christianity – and this has led to anti-Semitism, one of the ugliest blots on the pages of human history. Peter, in his speech to those gathered in Cornelius' house, made it clear that God sent his word to the Israelites. Judaism was the soil without which Christianity could not have grown. Christians and Jews are to be seen as partners in God's self-revelation.
- Secondly, it gives a succinct account of what is the essence of Christian faith – Jesus' deeds inspired by God's Holy Spirit, and the meaning of his death and resurrection as the supreme revelation of God's love (verses 38–43) – and the growth of a community entrusted to proclaim that faith. This same faith has to be proclaimed by the Church today.
- Thirdly, it tells of the result of the proclamation of the gospel to a group of Gentiles – how the Holy Spirit came upon them. It was like a second Pentecost. Thus we see that **all** who believe in Jesus can receive this gift.

✳ *Thank God that his Spirit is available for all.*

Tuesday July 3   **Acts 11.1–4, 18–21**

The Jewish Christian leaders in Jerusalem questioned Peter about his un-Jewish conduct. When they heard his explanation they were satisfied and gave thanks that the gospel was also for the Gentiles. Now the Church was ready to fulfil Christ's command to witness for him to the ends of the earth (Acts 1.8).

We can see from verse 19 that most of the Christians who had left Jerusalem only shared the gospel with fellow-Jews. They were not yet aware of the message of Peter's vision – that the good news was for all people. However, some Greek-speaking Christians from Cyprus and Cyrene began to speak to Gentiles.

It took time for the first Jewish Christians to overcome their prejudices. We also need time – time to overcome our human fears, doubts and mistaken ideas. Even Jesus, who knew his message was for all people, told his disciples to first of all go to the lost sheep of Israel (Matthew 10.5–6). He knew that they needed a firmer grip of this earth-shattering gospel before they could proclaim it to all nations. New applications of our faith need to be slowly and gently communicated – even to church members. It pays off in the end.

* Lord, teach us how, with patience and gentleness, to lead
   people to a full understanding of your purpose.

Wednesday July 4   Acts 11.22–30

The response of the Christians in Jerusalem to what was
happening in Antioch, indicated their genuine acceptance of
Gentiles into the Church. And later, the breaking down of
barriers was further demonstrated by the Christians at Antioch sending famine-relief to Jerusalem.

Barnabas was certainly a good choice of leader for the
church at Antioch. He was ideally suited to preach to Gentiles
and to promote good relations with them. Not only was he a
Greek-speaking Jew, he was a Cypriot by birth and had
already proved his ability to break down suspicion by his attitude to Saul. Yet again, he showed foresight and generosity.
This time it was by sharing his ministry in Antioch with Saul.
He had recognised the amazing change in Saul's life and
perceived that he would be the best one to help him in his
Gentile mission in Antioch.

We can presume that the Christian mission in Antioch
made a strong impact. It was here that the disciples were first
called 'Christians' (verse 26) which means 'belonging to the
party of Christ'. Perhaps they were seen as a vigorous and
united movement – not just isolated individuals – which was
determined to attack the paganism of Antioch.

* Pray that the ministry of your church will make as powerful
   an impact as did the church in Antioch.

Thursday July 5   Acts 12.1–11

Throughout the entire time of Roman occupation in Judaea,
different members of the Herod family were given authority
over the Jews. The Herod in today's reading was Herod
Agrippa the first, grandson of Herod the Great who ruled at
the time when Jesus was born. He instigated a renewed persecution of church leaders, probably to keep in favour with
the Jewish leaders who hated and feared the Christian movement. James was the first apostle to be killed.

The reference to 'the Jews' in verse 3 did not apply to all
Jewish people but to the orthodox Jewish leaders. Therefore,
it was politically expedient for Herod to arrest Peter.

The story of Peter's release from prison is told as a miracle. We do not know why Peter was spared and James was killed, but we do know that by this time it was dangerous to be a Christian. Immense courage was required. Regardless of the fact that he was awaiting death, Peter appeared to be at peace. Guarded and chained, he could still sleep (verse 6)!

We may fear that we could never have the courage of these first Christians. But, in moments of fear and danger, have we not found a quietness and strength which has amazed us?

✳ *God never forsakes those whose trust is in him.*

Friday July 6   Acts 12.12–17

The house in today's story is that of Mary, the mother of John Mark. This is the first mention of John Mark in **Acts**. Some have thought that he was the young man mentioned in Mark 14.51–52 (see April 6). Perhaps he had followed Jesus to Gethsemane after the Last Supper.

Traditionally, Mary's house is thought to be the house with the upper room where the Last Supper was held. This became the first meeting-place of the disciples and where they experienced the coming of the Holy Spirit at Pentecost. Verses 13–14 tell of a rather amusing scene! Peter knocked, Rhoda hastened to the door and when she recognised Peter's voice was so overjoyed that she forgot to let him in!

Peter came to the house while a prayer meeting was in progress. No doubt they were praying that God would miraculously intervene and save him. But, look at their reaction in verse 16 when they actually saw him! How often we are like this! We earnestly pray for someone or for a particular situation and then act as if God did not hear our prayers. When the answer comes we may even refuse to recognise it.

✳ *Lord, thank you for answering our prayers. Forgive us when so often we are slow to recognise your answers.*

Saturday July 7   Acts 12.18–25

It is not surprising if we detect a slight note of satisfaction in this account of the death of Herod. The Jews and other oppressed people in Europe may have felt the same way when they learned of Hitler's death in 1945. The writer appears to have included the account of Herod's death as a way of rounding off the first section of his history of the early Church. Herod's slow and miserable death stands in stark contrast to the life and growth of the Church. 'Meanwhile,' it is calmly said, 'the word of God continued to grow and spread' (verse 24).

Certainly those who spread the word of God had suffered, but their spirits could not be broken and the message could not be suppressed! This has been the constant message in our readings from **Acts**. It is also the message of Christianity down through the centuries, and even in our own time. Despite today's scepticism, materialism and sometimes persecution, the word of God continues to grow and spread. In the lives of millions – especially the outcasts and the poor – new hope and joy come to birth. And so will it always be. Jesus said, 'In the world you will have trouble. But courage! The victory is mine; I have conquered the world' (John 16.33b).

* *Give thanks for the life and witness of the first Christians. Pray that we, too, might have their spirit in us.*

For group discussion and personal thought

Consider some of the outstanding stories of events and people in **Acts 2–12**. What qualities were revealed by the early Church? Where do we see these same characteristics in the Church today? How can we become more like the first Christians?

For children

- Dated daily Bible readings

- Interesting notes, activities and prayers

- *UK price: £2.00 for 1990*

AMOS

Notes by the Revd Donald Hilton, BA

The notes in this section are based on the New English Bible.

The first half of the eighth century was a period of stability and peace in Israel. The economy flourished. Controlling major trade routes, merchants grew rich quickly. Some were greedy. When small farmers were in difficulty – perhaps because of a bad harvest – they bought their land at low prices and built up big estates and luxurious houses. The poor became virtual slaves.

Amos, a shepherd from Judah, traded in the north and saw the oppression there. Bribery was rife, even in the law-courts. Peasants were oppressed, and traders gave short measure for inflated prices. The big religious services were well-attended but the worship was shallow.

What is the word of God in such a situation? It fell to Amos to wrestle with that question, and then find courage to proclaim God's message.

Suggestions for further reading

Amos and Micah by John Marsh, Torch Bible Paperbacks (SCM Press Ltd)

Amos, Hosea, Micah by Henry McKeating, Cambridge Bible Commentaries on the New English Bible (Cambridge University Press)

Sunday July 8   **Amos 1.1–15**

Amos was a clever communicator. To attract the crowds he first criticised Israel's neighbours. Taking them one by one he recited their sins and told of impending punishment. Northeast of Israel lay Syria with Damascus as its capital city. Amos condemned them for driving their chariots over prostrate prisoners of war. Gaza, capital of Philistia, south-west of Israel was condemned for slavery. Phoenicia, with its capital, Tyre, north of Israel was condemned for selling Israelites into slavery despite a treaty not to do so. Edom and Ammon came under similar criticism.

These were ancient cities but the sins are very modern. In our own century, nations have imprisoned the innocent in concentration camps; used napalm bombs on whole villages; toppled democratically-elected foreign governments; invaded nations pretending it was 'liberation'; and rich nations have exploited poorer nations.

Is any nation guiltless? What can break the cycle of world violence? The clue Amos gives us is his recognition that all nations stand under the judgement of God.

* *For frantic boast and foolish word –*
Thy mercy on thy people, Lord!   *Rudyard Kipling*

Monday July 9   Amos 2.1–8

Moab, lying south-east of Israel came under the hammer next, for an act of sacrilege against the king of Edom. As Amos spoke against these foreign nations so the cheers of the people increased. They grew even louder when he began to condemn Judah, the nation where Amos himself lived.

Southern Judah and northern Israel had separated from each other about 200 years before, but mutual suspicion remained. The northerners, to whom Amos was speaking, would have loved to hear a southerner condemning his own people (verses 4–5) for disobeying the law. They had always said that themselves!

But the tirade was not finished! Amos went on to catalogue the sins of Israel – slavery, oppression, prostitution, and drunkenness (verses 6–8). Hopefully, some of the Israelites, seeing the sins of others, would have then recognised their own. Most did not.

There is a false patriotism which can only see faults in other nations. There is a personal hypocrisy which enjoys seeing other people under the moral spotlight but prefers its own faults kept in the dark.

* *Grant, Lord, that I am never so keen to see the sins of my neighbours that I am blind to the same faults in myself.*

Tuesday July 10   Amos 2.9–16

Amos outlined how God had helped the Israelites to defeat strong enemies and had also given them Nazirites and

prophets to guide Israel (verses 9–12). The Nazirites were a
'puritan' group, calling the nation to live sober lives befitting
a godly people. However, they had been forced into drunkenness and had betrayed their own ideals. Further, the rulers
had prevented the prophets from speaking.

Israel was thus doubly guilty. Creating a corrupt society,
they had then silenced those able to point to better ways.
Although Amos condemned the nation, he portrayed God as
'groaning under the burden' of Israel's sin (verses 13–16). In
describing God thus, one commentator sees this as 'a percep-
tion that truly anticipates the cross'.

Any nation that silences its own idealists puts itself in moral
peril. An early act of the Nazis was to burn any books they
thought critical of their regime. In several nations today,
governments try to silence church leaders and other critics.
Such nations condemn themselves.

✳ *Lord raise up amongst us writers, broadcasters, and speak-
ers who help us see ourselves.*

Wednesday July 11   Amos 3.1–11

'Action and consequence' is the theme of today's reading.
People can only work together on the basis of an agreement,
and birds are caught only if the trap is first set. The act of
blowing the trumpet to sound the alarm has the consequence
of warning the people of danger.

Using these illustrations Amos drew two conclusions:
● **The first was about Israel**. God had a special relationship
  with this nation, above other nations. Out of that action
  came the consequence – Israel had to carry the punishment
  when things went wrong. Privilege brought responsibility.
● **The second was about himself**, and it allows us to see
  his motivation. Like others, Amos was a reluctant prophet.
  He would have preferred a quiet life but God had given him
  a message. The consequence was that Amos must speak.

Both conclusions affect us. We rejoice in the knowledge of
Christ's love but we must also bear its burden. It is a demanding love that calls us to discipleship and service. Similarly,
like Amos, having heard a message we cannot be silent. We
must be prophetic.

✳ *My gracious Lord, I own thy right*
   To every service I can pay.   *Philip Doddridge*

As a shepherd Amos knew what it was to find a young lamb, savaged by a lion, with only an ear or a couple of bones left. Amos foretold a destruction of Israelite society as complete as that! 'But why?' the people might have asked. Amos gave three reasons:

- Their **false religious life** (verse 14). Festivals were well-attended but the worship did not spring from the heart, nor result in action.
- Their **ostentatious luxury** (verse 15). While the poor suffered, the rich built luxurious summer-houses and winter-houses, paid for by exploiting the labourers.
- Their **insensitive greed** (verse 1). Merchant's wives cared only for their luxuries, not for justice. They could have influenced their husbands for good; instead they egged them on to greater excesses of greed.

This is not a complaint about possessions in themselves. It is a condemnation of the greed and injustice which allows the few to prosper while others live in abject poverty.

✳ *What would Amos say to us, living in a world where rich nations still fail to tackle the poverty of poor nations?*

If Amos 2.13 is very close to the New Testament (see notes for July 10), then today's verses are far distant from it. Amos, like many Old Testament writers, believed that God intervenes directly in human affairs sending famine, drought, and plagues as punishment.

Such false ideas still occur today. 'What have I done to deserve this?' people sometimes ask when things go wrong. We can, of course, bring some suffering on ourselves – for example: by overeating, excessive drinking, or rejecting friendship. However, the Christian answer must often be: 'You have done no wrong. Your suffering is a sheer accident.'

The cross of Jesus teaches us that suffering is not God's way of punishing us. Indeed he suffers with us and bears the pain of our wrongdoing. In this way he invites us to friendship and a new way of life.

'Prepare to meet your God,' Amos was saying. If accident and suffering remind us of our weakness and of God's strength, then pain may well help us prepare to meet him. When we do meet him we shall find him to be all-loving.

✶ *God of love, may all life's experiences lead me to you.*

Saturday July 14   **Amos 5.1–15**

The prime message of the prophets was the centrality of God
in all things. Amos was no exception. 'Resort to me, if you
would live' (verse 5). He then carefully analysed places where
God's supremacy must be reaffirmed.

● **In worship** (verses 4–5). 'Don't go to Bethel; come to me
  instead,' was God's message. The Israelites were religious,
  without being spiritual. When worship is formal and
  church-going is an easy habit, then spiritual life is corrupt-
  ed.
● **In human society** (verses 7,10–11). God must be supreme
  in the market, in tax rules, and law-courts. We worship him
  with justice and compassion.

In 1987, Professor Forrester led a Church of Scotland working party which looked at social security in Britain. He found
the gap between rich and poor was increasing and declared
that a nation is under the judgement of God when 'poverty
increases and the poor are not given special care and priority'.

Amos would not give up hope. He urged the people to repent,
and restore a just society, so that God may yet be gracious to
them. This ancient message to governments and individuals
alike loses none of its relevance in our own time.

✶ *In church and home, in shop and factory, God be honoured!*

For group discussion and personal thought
Amos spoke sternly against the social evils of his day (for
example, see **Amos 2.6–8; 4.1; 5.10–13**). What are the social
evils of our day? What can ordinary citizens do to fight against
these and help create a just and fair society?

Sunday July 15   **Amos 5.16–27**

Amos showed communication skills again. He took an idea
which people thought they understood, then gave it a new
meaning. 'What will the day of the Lord mean?' he asked (see
verse 18a). Everybody thought it was the day when God would
defeat all their enemies. But Amos redefined 'the day' as a

time of darkness when Israel would pay for its neglect (verses 18b–20). They did not like the idea, but it made them think.

Injustice and evil always have a price. The lax morals of the Roman empire contributed to its downfall. Oppression in nineteenth-century Russia fed the 1917 revolution. The world faces an uncertain future if the gap between rich and poor increases; and if societies continue to discriminate against people because of their race, violence is almost inevitable. When we sow oppression, we reap violence.

Verses 21–27 can be summarised as God saying: 'Please do not worship me again until you have created a just society.' Camilo Torres, a Roman Catholic priest in Colombia, took that idea seriously. Colombia is divided into the very rich and very poor. He said he would no longer celebrate Mass until the sharing of bread, symbolised by the Mass, could also be seen in society.

✳ *Judge of the nations, spare us yet.*   *Rudyard Kipling*

Monday July 16   Amos 6.1–14

Amos presented a series of pictures to his listeners. Verses 1–2 tell of the cities which had probably fallen to the Assyrian army. The next picture (verses 3–6) portrays complacent Israel sprawling lazily on couches. Could they not see the approaching danger? The third picture (verses 8–11) foretells Israel's deserved destruction in the future. It would be so devastating that out of ten men in one house none would be left. Those who survived the war, would perish in a plague.

The final picture (verses 12–14) comes back to Amos' time, and offers hope. There was still time to repent. Just as it is unnatural for horses to gallop over rocks or for men to try to plough the sea, so the false worship and social injustice were unnatural. Israel had to become its true self.

This is a supremely important insight from Amos. When we sin, we say, 'I'm only human.' But in fact, we are then less than human. The natural thing is to be just and caring. Evils such as racism, injustice, and neglect of the poor are freaks of human behaviour. We are made for better things.

✳ *Lord, help me to become the person you intend me to be.*

Tuesday July 17   Amos 7.1–9

Mercy and judgement are two sides of the same coin in the

currency of God's loving providence. If we over-emphasise
God's mercy we misrepresent his character as being lax. If we
over-emphasise his judgement he seems harsh.

Amos interpreted three visions in a way that balanced God's
mercy and judgement at a critical time in Israelite history.

- **Mercy** (verses 1–3). Locusts attacked the corn in late
  summer. The crops could hardly recover. The farmer would
  lose all. Amos pleaded with God. The locusts departed.
  Then, in verses 4–6, the whole earth was to be destroyed
  by fire. Again a plea for mercy was met by God's forgiveness.

  But mercy and judgement unite. Another picture was
  needed to portray the whole truth.

- **Judgement** (verses 7–9). In the building boom, brought
  about by Israel's new wealth, Amos often saw workmen
  setting a plumb-line against a wall to make sure it was
  upright. It was the perfect picture to redress the balance of
  the other two visions (see verses 1–6). The merciful God
  tests the hearts of his people. Do they measure up to his
  standards?

✳ *Receiving your mercy, O God, we acknowledge your rule,
  and see both mercy and judgement as signs of your eternal
  love.*

Wednesday July 18   Amos 7.10 to 8.3

Church and State united against the trouble-maker, Amos.
Amaziah, the official priest at Bethel, told Amos to go back
south and do his prophesying at home.

- In eighteenth-century Britain, priests needed the bishop's
  permission to preach outside their own parish. John Wesley
  replied, 'The world is my parish.' God's word has no boundaries.

Amaziah reminded Amos that he was preaching on royal
territory, implying that he should modify his message to
suit the king.

- In seventeenth-century Britain, Crown and Church united
  to stop Dissenters forming churches which they believed
  were true to the Bible. 2,000 ministers were imprisoned for
  affirming that God's authority was greater than that of the
  State.

In Britain today, the political authorities often see Bishop
David Jenkins as a trouble-maker, when he criticises government action in the light of the gospel. In South Africa, Arch-

bishop Desmond Tutu and Dr Alan Boesak play similar roles. Before he was assassinated, Archbishop Oscar Romero had the same task in El Salvador. Fearless prophets are still needed today.

✳ *Think about these words spoken by Robert Runcie: 'Life and death for the gospel are still the way Christians are called to change the world.'*

Thursday July 19   Amos 8.4–14

Today's reading begins with an exposure of commercial fraud and ends with a description of spiritual stagnation. The two were related in Amos' mind.

Verses 4–8 picture shopkeepers greedily longing for the Sabbath and festivals to be over so that they could get down to business again. When they did, they used false scales and sold adulterated wheat. Such practices violate society more than they violate personal morality. They are an affront to God: 'Shall not the earth shake for this?' (verse 8a).

Insensitivity to the needs of people leads to insensitivity to God. Amos foretold a time of spiritual poverty when there would be no one to speak of spiritual values (verses 11–12).

The spiritual quality of any society is not only to be judged by listening to people's prayers or counting the numbers in church. It must also be seen in personal honesty, the value placed on individuals, and by the priorities society holds.

✳ *Judge eternal, throned in splendour,*
   Lord of hosts and King of kings,
 With thy living fire of judgement
   Purge this realm of bitter things.   Henry S Holland

Friday July 20   Amos 9.1–10

Amos' final vision concerned the temple. Some commentators think that there was an actual earthquake at the time, and that Amos described what he saw as the temple columns trembled and the porch shook. Amos saw this natural disaster as a sign of God's judgement on the religion of Israel.

National reform will often begin at the 'temple'. God can use the people who worship to challenge the nation – but only if they are fit instruments for God's work. He will not use shoddy worship or hypocritical religion. In order to reform a nation we need a Church that:

- is centred on Jesus Christ;
- gives dignity to all people especially any belittled by the rest of society;
- puts others above self, giving before receiving, and love before prejudice;
- honours the past and believes in the future.

God is not obliged to use the Church. We are not indispensable. It is in his mercy – and for our joy – that he calls us to be partners with him.

✳ *Lord, make us instruments of your purpose.*

Saturday July 21   Amos 9.11–15

Most of **Amos** speaks of impending doom but the final verses promise renewal. Why this change? Some commentators believe that these verses were added later to soften the harsh message. However, there **has** been a thin thread of hope throughout. If God is merciful, renewal is always possible to the penitent.

Throughout the Dark Ages in Europe it seemed that humanity would sink only further into ignorance. Before the Reformation in the sixteenth century the gospel seemed distorted by a corrupt Church. In this century, Christianity was forbidden in communist China for many years and the Church there seemed doomed to extinction. Yet the Renaissance bloomed out of the Dark Ages, a new Church took root at the Reformation, and the underground Church in China came out of its darkness more powerful than ever. Why?

- Because God remains God. He can never be defeated.
- Because the faithful few always remain, nurturing the truth and waiting to make their witness again.

Even in the corrupt gloom that Amos depicted, there must have been small groups meeting in quiet and hopeful prayer. Scattered individuals retained their vision of what their nation could yet be. On such a foundation revival comes.

✳ *God of constancy, stay with your fickle Church!*

For group discussion and personal thought

Study the three visions in **Amos 7.1–9**. What do these tell us about God's mercy and judgement? What do you think is God's 'plumb-line' for society today?

COLOSSIANS; PHILEMON

Notes by the Revd Michael Walker,BD,MTh,PhD

The notes in this section are based on the New English Bible.

These two letters – **Colossians** and **Philemon** – were probably written during the period of Paul's imprisonment in
Rome. The first is addressed to a church wrestling with ideas
that tended to distort the gospel. Paul affirms the centrality
of the risen Lord and the Christian response of obedience in
daily life.

The letter to Philemon gives a vivid example of what it
means to follow in the Christian way. Paul is returning the
runaway slave, Onesimus, to his master, Philemon, urging
that he be forgiven and accepted back as a brother in Christ.
Such a response on Philemon's part would have required great
charity and a brave willingness to depart from the accepted
norms of his time.

Suggestion for further reading

Colossians and Philemon by Ralph P Martin, New Century
Bible Commentaries (Marshall, Morgan & Scott)

Sunday July 22   **Colossians 1.1–8**

Paul is only a few lines into his letter when he introduces his
great trinity of Christian experience – faith, hope and love
(verses 4–5). The **faith** is the faith we hold in Christ and the
love is the love we bear towards God's people. Both are born
out of the **hope** which all Christians share.

Hope keeps faith alive. Sometimes faith is all we have.
Little evidence is given to our eyes that what we believe is
true. Hope provides what sight cannot. We can only see what
is happening now: sight locks us into the present. But hope
carries us beyond the present into the future; it extends the
possibilities of God's purposes into the endless days yet to be.

So faith can go on trusting. If it is dark now, it will not
always be so. If injustice seems to hold the whip hand now, it
will not always do so. If Christ seems absent now, the days to
come will prove that he is not and has never been.

144

Hope also keeps love alive. We do not tire of love when we truly believe in its capacity to change things. The hope of what is yet to be will keep us loving, even in the face of indifference or hostility.

✻ *Lord, you are our hope:*
even in the darkness, you give us faith,
and when the world grows cold, you give us love.

Monday July 23   Colossians 1.9–12

Compared with the Old Testament, the New Testament contains few written prayers. Here and there, however, in verses such as these, we are given some idea of how people prayed for one another in the early Church.

At the heart of Paul's prayer is the desire that his readers should become good people. He asks that their wills may be aligned with God's will; and that this union of the human with the divine will may result 'in active goodness of every kind' (verse 10).

It has been said that there are two ways of looking at the work of the Church. Its first task is that of saving sinners; its second, that of making saints. The first marks the beginning of Christ's work in us, the second is the work of a lifetime.

Paul describes all the resources that God makes available to us. They represent God's commitment to us, to which we reply with our commitment to him. Thus, the pursuit of goodness is the working out of a partnership between God and ourselves. We seek his will, and he fills us with his grace. Becoming a saint may well seem beyond the grasp of most of us. With God's help, however, goodness is within the reach of all of us.

✻ *Lord, may we be open to your will in our lives and become*
the people you want us to be.

Tuesday July 24   Colossians 1.13–20

This is one of those moments in the letters of Paul when he staggers us with the immensity of his vision. He is speaking of Christ, the agent of God's final purposes. We have to remind ourselves that the Christ of whom he speaks is Jesus, the babe of Bethlehem, the carpenter of Nazareth, the Galilean preacher and the man condemned to die on Calvary. This

Christ, says Paul, is the one through whom all created things came into being and through whom all created things will be reconciled to God (verses 16–20).

The immensity of our vision of Christ is matched by the immensity of God's purposes in him. At the end, we shall see that what began on the cross and in the empty tomb embraces the entire universe. The work of Christ does not extend simply to the few, to the Church or any particular part of the Church. Nor does it extend simply to one race, nor even to humankind as a whole. His work extends to the reconciling and uniting of the **whole created order**.

Thus to love Jesus and to serve him is to live towards a great destiny. The Christ who is now known in the intimacy of our hearts is the final healer of all things.

✳ *Lord Jesus Christ, may awe and love mingle together in our worship, our prayers and our service to you.*

Wednesday July 25   Colossians 1.21–27

Sometimes the process of healing requires the willingness to be broken and to suffer. The means by which God reconciles the world to himself is that of the suffering of Christ upon the cross (verse 22).

The suffering does not end there, however. Paul states that, in being called to be a minister of the gospel, he too has been called to a vocation of suffering. Indeed, Jesus continues his suffering and reconciling work through him (verse 24).

We must not allow the greatness of Paul to distance us from the work that we, like him, have been called to do. To be a Christian is to enter into partnership with Christ in his redeeming work. Jesus himself made that clear when he invited men and women to follow him, denying themselves and carrying the cross (see Luke 9.23).

The work of reconciliation is always painful. The same enmity that crucified Christ will be directed at those who witness to the cross as God's way of putting right a torn world. Yet it is those who are willing to stand in the firing line, to suffer with Christ, who release into the world that love which God victoriously revealed at Calvary.

✳ *Lord, help us to accept the cost of sharing your reconciling work. May we know that out of love, suffering is born, and out of suffering, healing.*

146

In today's reading Paul continues the theme of partnership.
The partnership to which we are called is one of union with
Jesus Christ. At the heart of that union is a great mystery of
grace, the mystery of Christ dwelling in us. The key verse
here is verse 29, where Paul talks of 'toiling strenuously', but
with 'the energy and power of Christ at work in me'.

Our partnership with Christ calls for commitment, zeal and
love on our part. This involves every part of our being, heart,
mind and, not least, the will. It would appear to be a commitment that demands all our resources and calls on single-
mindedness and dedication on our part. Yet, when we have
made all our resolutions and summoned up all our energies,
we learn increasingly that we are dependent upon Christ.

It is not our strength that counts, but his strength within
us; not our love, but his indwelling love. This is the mystery
of grace that only those who have actually lived it can fully
understand. I, yet not I, but Christ within me. My love, yet
not my love, but Christ's love in me.

Unlike our resources, the grace of Christ is never exhausted. It is on that grace that we are chiefly dependent if we are
to grow to that maturity which Paul so coveted for his readers
(verse 28).

✳ *Lord, may I daily enter more deeply into you and your grace
into me.*

Our partnership with Christ and our openness to his grace
rest upon our union with him (verse 6). It is a union that is
effected in our baptism, where faith lays claim to the active
resurrection power of God (verse 12). That, in turn, rests upon
the redemptive work which Christ did for us on the cross
(verses 14—15).

Union with Christ is at the heart of the Christian life. A
deeper union with him is our goal. The cross made possible
that union, by reconciling us to God. We share in that reconciliation when we are baptised. In baptism and faith, we
appropriate what Christ has done for us and begin the journey
which takes us ever deeper into him.

Paul speaks of the things which make that possible — being
rooted and built in Christ, consolidated in our faith and our
lives filled with gratitude (verse 7). All these things are gath-

ered up in prayer which is the soil in which faith grows. It is
there that we enter more deeply in Christ and he into us. In
the darkness of prayer, we discern the face of Jesus and grow
more familiar with his features. Prayer, as Richard of
Chichester believed, helps us to see Christ more clearly, love
him more dearly, and follow him more nearly.

✴ *Lord, may my heart, mind and will be open to you, so that
I may grow in you and you may grow in me.*

Saturday July 28   Colossians 2.16–23

In this letter, Paul has presented to us a cosmic vision of
Christ which carries radical consequences for our daily living.
There were those at Colossae, however, who would have dis-
tilled this vision into yet another religion, and have organised
their passionate gratitude into a system of observances.

We have seen that the will is important as the seat of love.
But that is not the same as saying that our faith can be
expressed in terms of, 'Don't do this' or, 'Do that' (verses
16–18).

The Church always faces the danger of putting its own life
and concerns – its rules, its organisation, and even its theological disputes – at the centre of God's redeeming purposes.
The cosmic Christ, however, embraces the world and the
Church exists to serve his loving purposes in the world. Our
Christian life needs to be structured around certain observances. We need to pray regularly, to read the Bible, to share
in the Lord's Supper and to meet with our fellow Christians.
But we do not do these things in order to increase our sense
of self-satisfaction or to multiply our religious achievements.
Rather, everything in our Christian life should serve the pur-
pose of making us more loving people.

✴ *Lord, may our religious practices be a means of faith and
not an end in themselves.*

For group discussion and personal thought
Read and study **Colossians 1.17–22, 27–28**. How can the
Church assist us in our growth to maturity as Christian men
and women? Does it take that process of growth seriously? In
what ways does the Church help or hinder our personal and
spiritual growth?

Sunday July 29   **Colossians 3.1–11**

The theme of fellowship with Christ, mentioned so often in
this letter, is again followed in today's reading. It is the resurrection that makes possible our union with Christ and,
through him, with God the Father. That union creates within
us a deep longing for life in God, a longing that reaches beyond
what we know and experience now (verse 2).

We do not, however, live in two divorced and separated
realms. There is not, on the one hand, our life in Christ and,
on the other, our life in the ordinary world. Life in Christ has
strong ethical and moral implications for our life in the world.
The more we long for a deeper union with Christ, the more
aware we become of all that stands in the way of it.

Paul lists the hurdles that we have to overcome in our quest
for a deeper fellowship with the risen Christ. They are those
commonplace sins that mar our earthly life – 'anger, passion,
malice, cursing, filthy talk' (verse 8). We could perhaps add
others, closer to our own experience, which daily involve us
in closely-engaged battles and in small, unheroic fights, as we
progress to deeper union with the risen Lord.

✷ *Lord, may we not cease from prayer as we struggle with
those sins that keep us from you. May we long to enter ever
more deeply into the mystery of your resurrection.*

Monday July 30   **Colossians 3.12–17**

The barriers to our fellowship with Christ arise out of the real
world of our daily living; and it is in that same world that
the fruits of our union with him are evident. The Christian
community, which Paul so glowingly describes here, exhibits
qualities that are life-transforming and life-enhancing. It is a
community marked by forgiveness, love, peace and gratitude
(verses 13–16).

These qualities are an outworking of the Christian gospel
– the good news. Forgiveness is not simply to be proclaimed;
it has to be lived and experienced. Among Christians sin is
not to be allowed to fester, unrecognised and unforgiven. Just
as God, through forgiveness, has removed the barriers that
exist between him and us, so we are not to allow lack of forgiveness to wound our fellowship with one another.

Forgiveness happens where love is given priority. If we
think of the Church in terms of status or the selfish satisfaction of our own needs, then we will create communities in

which people value their own rights and privileges more than
the duty and concern they owe to one another. But, where love
is put first, forgiveness and peace will follow.

✳ *Lord, may our life together in Christ visibly bear the marks
of the gospel that we proclaim to others.*

Tuesday July 31   Colossians 3.18 to 4.6

We must not side-step the difficulties in this reading. Paul
talks about a network of relationships, between husbands and
wives, fathers and children, and slaves and masters. The last
of these, we would firmly believe, has no place in the twentieth
century. Even when masters are urged to be just and fair to
their slaves (verse 25), and all authority is placed within the
context of Christ's authority, slavery remains an institution
that is totally abhorrent and unacceptable. Nothing can
reduce the innate evil of such a system.

Many of us in the twentieth century find it no easier to
accept Paul's view of the submission of women and his hier-
archical view of the family. Through the centuries, these
views have been the basis of much shameful treatment of
women and children, even in Christian theology and practice.
Instead, we have to work out ways of expressing the equality,
freedom and love which Christ has brought us.

As we consider these verses we have to distinguish between
what belongs to the insights of a certain historical time and
what belongs to the essence of the Christian gospel.

✳ *Pray that Christian family life may be based on mutual love
and respect.*

Wednesday August 1   Colossians 4.7–18

When we read one of Paul's letters, with its profound theological reflection and its inspired insights, we can forget that this
is what it was – a letter. It was addressed to people of greatly
varying abilities and at different stages of Christian development, all of whom were trying to live out their faith in their
daily lives.

We are reminded of that readership when we come to the
last part of this letter where Paul, and those with him, send
greetings to specific individuals. He is surrounded by friends
– from Aristarchus, a fellow prisoner to Luke the doctor; and

he writes to friends – including the congregation at Nympha's house, and Archippus, to whom he sends a special message.

The Christian faith, of which Paul writes so eloquently, is shared by people to whom our lives are closely bound. Our faith is never isolated from life or from the concerns of other people. In the end, even the deepest theological reflections have to do with people and the way they live.

✳ *Still we are centred all in thee,*
  Members, though distant, of one Head:
 In the same family we be,
   By the same faith and Spirit led.   *Richard Baxter*

Thursday August 2   Philemon 1–7

Here Paul is writing the opening sentences of a letter that requires great tact. He is about to send Onesimus, a runaway slave who has become a Christian, back to his Christian master, Philemon. If Philemon is to receive back Onesimus in the Spirit of Christ, then he will have to go against the common practice of his time. There was little mercy for runaway slaves – they could be punished with death itself. Paul is asking Philemon to receive Onesimus as a brother in Christ.

So Paul begins by affirming what is good in Philemon and his fellow Christians. He is 'delighted and encouraged' (verse 7) by the reports he has received of their love; and it is this love to which he appeals as he seeks to reconcile master and slave.

The work of reconciling people and groups who are divided requires tact, patience and hope. It is good to begin as Paul began, not in discussing the contentious issue itself, but in affirming the goodness of the adversaries. If we begin by seeing the good in other people, even our enemies, then the road to reconciliation is made easier. How could Philemon possibly deny the love that was so notably a feature of his life and that of his fellow Christians?

✳ *Let us remember and give thanks for the good we see in the lives of those with whom we have differences.*

Friday August 3   Philemon 8–16

These verses are the heart of the letter. Paul asks Philemon to accept Onesimus back without any recriminations. Indeed,

he asks that the man who had run away as a slave might now
be accepted back as a brother (verse 16). The extent to which
Christian values challenged and reversed those of society
could not be more apparent. Instead of being punished,
Onesimus was to be accepted. Instead of being condemned to
humiliation, he was to be treated as a brother.

In its attitude to slaves, Christianity was indeed a subvers-
ive presence within society. Although not challenging the
institution of slavery itself, the Church created a community
in which slavery had no place. If everyone in Christ was a son
or daughter of God, then all were equal in his sight.

Paul could speak with great moral authority. He was, after
all, in prison himself (verse 10). He was classed among those
who were rejected, the felons of society, the people who did
not conform. If Philemon accepted Paul the prisoner as his
father in God, he could not reject Onesimus the slave as his
brother in Christ.

✸ *Pray for the Church, wherever it stands in solidarity with
those who are rejected or enslaved – that it may witness to
justice, to sisterhood and brotherhood.*

Saturday August 4   Philemon 17–25

Paul here describes a situation in which people are indebted
to one another in various ways. By deserting his post,
Onesimus was debtor to his master Philemon. It was a debt
that Paul was willing to repay on his behalf (verse 18). Philemon, on the other hand, was indebted to Paul with a debt that
was incalculable. Philemon owed to Paul his knowledge of
Christ and his surrender to the gospel (verse 19).

We are all indebted to one another within the complex
framework of our human relationships. Forgiveness is often
a mutual act of grace, since each owes something to the other,
and each may bear some responsibility for the sin that has
been committed. In our service to the Church we can never
make it our debtor, since we have received from it more than
we can measure. We receive the Scriptures and the sacra-
ments, the examples of the apostles, saints, prophets and
martyrs who have gone before us. Our lives have been surrounded by the witness, encouragement and love of countless
Christian people.

In asking Philemon to accept Onesimus back as a brother,
Paul appealed to grace. It is grace that makes all things pos-

sible. Even if Philemon owed nothing, Onesimus was still a fellow human being, a brother in Christ.

✳ *Lord, fill me with the grace of your love and forgiveness.*

For group discussion and personal thought
Consider what Paul's teaching in **Colossians 3.12–15** means for our relationships with one another. To what extent is Paul's view of the family in **Colossians 3.18–21** valid for today? What 'model' for the Christian family do you think is best?

GOD AND THE WORLD
Selected Psalms

Notes by the Revd Lesley Husselbee, MSc, PhD

Lesley Husselbee is minister of the Cores End United Reformed Church, Bourne End, Buckinghamshire. She has previously taught in primary and secondary schools in London, was a senior lecturer at the Roehampton Institute, and held a pastorate in Coventry.

The notes in this section are based on the Good News Bible.

The book of **Psalms** is the hymn-book and prayer-book of the Bible. Like most prayer and hymn-books, it was written by many different authors over a long period of time. The people of Israel used it in their worship and, eventually, it was included in their Scriptures.

A favourite theme in **Psalms** is that of praise to God for his creation. The psalmists frequently used examples from nature to illustrate the character of God. During the first week of this section, we shall consider the ways in which the psalmists praised God through the wonder of creation; how his power and strength is seen through the natural world and through men and women; and the way in which he cares for and protects us. During the second week, we shall look at some of the more destructive forces of nature, and consider how God's love is constant whatever happens.

Suggestion for further reading

Psalms, Volumes I and II by George A Knight, Daily Study Bible (Saint Andrew Press)

GOD AND CREATION

Sunday August 5   **Psalm 8**

This psalm says it all! With great economy, sheer joy and awe we are made aware of the greatness of God as creator of the universe, and, at the other end of the scale, of his love for each one of us.

Have you ever stood on a clear night, and looked up at the sky? Many of the thousands of specks of light are stars, the size of our sun, supporting many planets. And God created it all!

Yet, despite the sheer size of the universe, God cares about every single living thing. In fact, he does even more than this. The poet cries out in awe to God that he has made men and women inferior only to himself and crowned them with glory and honour (see verse 5). The Greek translators of the Old Testament were so shocked to read that we, as human beings, are only one stage lower than God himself that they used the word for 'angels' instead of 'God' – 'For thou hast made him a little lower than the angels'. What can we do in response to God's great love and nearness to us but worship him too?

✳ *Lord of all being, throned afar,*
Thy glory flames from sun and star;
Centre and soul of every sphere,
Yet to each loving heart now near.   *Oliver W Holmes*

Monday August 6   Psalm 104.1–18

What a wonderful world we live in! The psalmist is so thrilled with the magnificence of creation that he cannot seem to stop thinking of examples. However, he is not just praising nature. His praise is for God who created all this splendour. We can never fully understand God; but the wonders of his world are rather like an outer garment which God wears in order to help us begin to understand a little of his nature (verses 1–2). If we can imagine God using the clouds as his chariot and riding on the wind, then we can begin to understand the way in which he is constantly with us. He is ready to rush to our aid, in control of everything that happens and provides for our needs.

It is sometimes tempting to take our world for granted, and even complain about it when it is too hot, too wet or too dry. But this psalm reminds us of God's constant presence, and of the unlimited resources that he has at our disposal to meet with all eventualities – if we can only remember his presence and ask for his help.

✳ *Lord, give me a sense of childlike wonder in your creation. May I never stop being surprised and uplifted by the beauties of your world.*

Tuesday August 7   **Psalm 104.19–35**

If God is so powerful, so much in control of creation, then how
is it that tragedies happen in our world? Why is there death?
Verse 29 suggests that when God takes our breath away, then
we die. But the psalmist does not see this as a bad thing. It is
all a part of God's creative plan. In order for life to renew itself
there needs first of all to be death. A seed needs to fall to the
ground and shrivel and die before a new shoot can grow. Jesus
Christ himself needed to die before there could be resurrection.

God can only give new life to us when we are ready to 'die'
to the things of this world. A minister from Zambia gave this
illustration: 'Imagine a cup that is full. Try as you will, you
can't pour any more water into it without it flowing over. Now
imagine a half-full or empty cup. The more empty it is, the
more room there is to pour in more water.' God can work best
with us when we are ready to empty our lives of our own sense
of self-importance. When we are ready to 'die' for him, when
we are aware of our own dependence upon him, then he can
use us most.

✴ *Lord, help me to be empty for you so that you will be able to
create new life in me.*

Wednesday August 8   **Psalm 1**

Most of British Colombia, in Canada, has a heavy rainfall
and, on the Rocky Mountains, there is much snowfall. But,
tucked away between the coastal ranges and the Rocky Mountains, is the desert area around Kamloops. This area is in the
rain shadow of the westerly winds from the Pacific and so has
very little rain. Farmers go to a great deal of effort to irrigate
the land in order to provide grazing for herds of cattle. They
depend on the Fraser River for water.

Water is mentioned a great deal in the Bible, probably
because Israel is similarly a dry, desert land. It is the symbol
for cleansing, for baptism, for life. Therefore, it is not surprising that the psalmist here compares those whose lives are
rooted in God with trees that grow beside a stream. We, like
the desert farmers, depend on God's water of life so that we
can bear fruit. Without the daily sustenance of prayer and
study of God's word we shall be like the unwatered straw that
blows away in the wind.

* *Lord, help me to spend time with you each day, so that I*
may drink in your presence in everything that I do.

Thursday August 9   **Psalm 136.1–11, 23–26**

This psalm is a litany, and would have been used in public
worship. We can imagine the psalmist choosing well-known
phrases about God from other psalms, which would have been
sung or said by the priest, and then the people would have
responded with the phrase, 'his love is eternal' ('for his stead-
fast love endures for ever', RSV). Just imagine – these words
sung in praise to God down through the centuries. They
remind us of the way in which God has worked through creation, and through events and people of history. In joining in
this psalm, we are one with the people of God through all time.

As we join in, we, too, can thank God for all those people
who have demonstrated his love through history – prophets,
apostles and ministers; doctors, teachers, mothers and
fathers; artists, musicians and writers; and farmers, labourers and clerks – to mention but a few. Most of all, we can
thank God for Jesus Christ and for accepting us as part of that
great band of people; and for calling us and equipping us to
communicate his love to the world.

* *Let us with a gladsome mind*
  Praise the Lord, for he is kind:
      For his mercies aye endure,
      Ever faithful, ever sure.   *John Milton*

Friday August 10

Gladys sat at the table. She anxiously wondered where she
was going to find food to feed her husband and five children.
Gladys is a minister, working in a shanty-town settlement in
one of the large towns in Africa, and the stipend that she
receives each month is not enough to feed her family. Then,
as Gladys prayed for food, there was a knock on the door. A
lady from the church stood there with some maize and eggs.
'I had a strong feeling that I should bring these to you – that
you would need them,' she said. Gladys praised God. She
knew how much she depended on God, and he never let her
down.

In the West, harvest is often taken for granted. Shops are
overflowing with food from all over the world. Some families

do find it hard to feed themselves, but for many it is not something they think about much, let alone thank God for. The psalmist, on the other hand, is fully aware whom to thank for fertile land, abundant rain and overflowing crops.

▶ Read **Psalm 65**.

✳ *To thee, O Lord, our hearts we raise*
  In hymns of adoration;
 To thee bring sacrifice of praise
  With shouts of exultation;
 Bright robes of gold the fields adorn,
  The hills with joy are ringing,
 The valleys stand so thick with corn
  That even they are singing.   *William C Dix*

Saturday August 11

Fire can be very destructive. A careless match dropped in an armchair can destroy a house and kill the people in it. A lighted cigarette can trigger an explosion in a chemical tanker. A spark can eradicate a forest. We might be tempted, therefore, to say that fire is just too dangerous to be used. Fire, however, is one of the most valuable elements of God's creation, if used in the right way. It keeps us warm, cooks our food, kills bacteria, sterilises, and creates useful substances from chemical reactions.

▶ Read **Psalm 97**.

When this psalm was written, the people of Israel had just returned from exile in Babylon. They had no king, and it seemed as if God had left them too. They had experienced the 'fire' of exile and destruction. But with that destruction had come a cleansing and purifying of the nation. The psalmist teaches us that we cannot always judge by appearances. Whenever we feel stifling pressures around us, we need not be afraid, because God is still there protecting and helping us.

✳ *Lord, support those, who in darkness, despair and anxiety*
 feel that you have abandoned them. Assure them, and us,
 of your ever constant love and care.

For group discussion and personal thought

Look at **Psalm 104.10–30**. In what ways do the beauties of creation help us to come closer to God? How far must we be personally responsible for safeguarding creation – ensuring that the resources of the world are not exploited? To what extent does our way of life lead to exploitation of the earth and of other people?

GOD PROTECTS AND HELPS

Sunday August 12   **Psalm 95**

It is appropriate that we read this psalm on a Sunday, because, traditionally, it is read or sung in many churches as a call to worship. We come to worship because God is a great God, a loving God, and because he always kept his covenant to our forefathers, even when they rebelled against him.

Perhaps there have been times when you have not felt much like worshipping God. Maybe you were tired or had other interesting things to do; or maybe you were just bored. The psalmist, however, urges us to worship God whatever our feelings, because he has made us and he loves and cares for us.

A mother does not say to her child, 'I don't feel like looking after you today, so I won't.' Because she helped create that child, she usually wants to care for that child whatever happens. God is the best kind of parent there can be. He created us, and he cares for us like a good shepherd does for his sheep. So 'Come, let us praise the Lord!' (verse 1).

✴ *Help me, Lord to respond to your love for me with gratitude and thanks – especially in the times when you seem far away. Go on nudging me and challenging me.*

Monday August 13   **Psalm 89.1–14**

Here we have a picture of a strong and powerful God, who controls the raging forces of nature, and whose faithfulness is as permanent as the sky (verse 2). If we look at the sky we find it ever-changing – sometimes it is clear and sunny, sometimes cloudy, sometimes dark and seemingly impenetrable – but it is always reassuringly there.

The psalmist continues to depict God's strength and faithfulness to us in his crushing of the legendary sea-monster, Rahab (verse 10), which represented the forces of chaos and evil. To those of us who look for a loving, caring God, this may seem excessively warlike and ruthless. However, the psalmist is using examples of creation to symbolise the evil forces in the world which need to be defeated so that God's kingdom of righteousness and justice (verse 14) will be victorious.

We, too, must do all that we can, with God's help, to rid the world of evil – injustice, exploitation and self-interest. And to do that we need all the strength that God can give us.

✳ *Be our strength in hours of weakness,*
In our wanderings be our guide;
Through endeavour, failure, danger,
Father, be thou at our side.   *Love M Willis*

Tuesday August 14

From time to time, disaster strikes. Months of drought can create famine; earthquakes can suddenly bury whole towns under tons of rubble; volcanoes can engulf hundreds of people under clouds of ash overnight. How are we to understand such events? Do they represent the wrath of God? Geologists tell us that volcanoes and earthquakes are the means by which the earth is constantly being formed.

So doesn't God care for the people who suffer because of such natural disasters? Are they expendable? Today's psalm assures us that they are not.

▶ Read **Psalm 18.1–16**.

God cares for all of us. In this psalm the writer uses picture language based on the natural world to describe the troubles that we go through. He then goes on to assure us that God, in fact, saves us and pulls us out of the trouble that we get into. This does not mean that we are freed from tragedy and suffering. However, they are not planned by God as a punishment. He suffers with us when things go wrong, and, above all, he cares.

✳ *Lord, be with those who have suffered through natural disasters. May they be assured of your love and care.*

Wednesday August 15

Occasionally, events happen in people's lives which completely change their way of life. For example: a life-long partner dies; or a man or woman who has worked all their life in a seemingly secure job, is suddenly made redundant. Sometimes whole communities are suddenly engulfed in a tragedy like a train crash, a fire or a natural disaster; and from time to time, the outbreak of war. Similar catastrophes were known to the writer of today's psalm.

▶ Read **Psalm 46**.

The people of Israel were constantly threatened by invasion from surrounding nations, and were, indeed, taken off into exile. And yet the writer of this psalm can say with supreme confidence that it does not matter what happens to us in life. Whatever happens – war, natural disaster, and if he lived in this century, he might have added nuclear annihilation – God is still 'our shelter and strength' (verse 1). He is always aware of our problems and fears. His eternal plan is not cancelled out by the whims of men and women or the freakish accidents of nature. Through all the turmoil of our lives we can hear God saying to us:

✳ *'Be still, and know that I am God' (verse 10, RSV).*

Thursday August 16   **Psalm 107.1–3, 23–38**

This psalm recounts the adventures of the people of Israel as they returned home from exile in Babylon, and also comments on what happened to those who stayed at home. Some wandered across desert lands (verses 4–9). Others travelled by sea; and on their voyage home they experienced a severe storm. The sailors were at their wit's end but when they cried out to the Lord in their trouble, he calmed the storm (verses 23–32).

Those who stayed at home were not immune from troubles. We are told that God made rivers dry up, and the land become a salty wilderness; which sounds very unlike God the creator. However, if we look further we see that these conditions had been caused by the wickedness of those who lived in Israel. Erosion is common in our world today, because we have over-cropped and cut down trees in a desire to use the land as much as we can.

How often do we live blissfully unaware of God's protecting presence, until we get into difficulty? How often do we take our present resources for granted, greedily taking what we can from the world without thought for succeeding generations? How often do we experience the protecting and saving love of God without feeling the need to tell others about it?

✻ *Lord, help us to use the world's resources responsibly.*

Friday August 17   Psalm 121

Some people find that they are closest to God when they are walking alone in the countryside. This is often especially true when they walk in mountainous country, perhaps because there seems to be a stability and splendour in the peaks reaching up towards the sky. Many people say that they gain inspiration from the mountains and hills. But is it the mountains themselves which help them, or their creator?

Imagine that you are among the people of Israel going up to Jerusalem three times a year to one of the great festivals. As you made the climb up to the temple at the top of the hill in Jerusalem, you might ask whether your help came from the hill itself. After all it was the custom to make sacrifices to Baal on high places. And then you would be given the answer: 'No!' The answer to all our problems and needs comes from God himself. His concern for us is constant; he protects and shades us from all the forces of evil, which, whether we like it or not, are about in our world.

✻ *Rock of ages, cleft for me,*
  Let me hide myself in thee.   *Augustus M Toplady*

Saturday August 18   Psalm 96

What exuberance! What unaffected joy and praise to God! The psalmist is so grateful to God, for his goodness, that he calls on everything in the world – people, earth, sky and all living things to worship him.

This psalm is also recorded in 1 Chronicles 16.23–33 and was sung when the ark of the covenant was taken to Jerusalem by King David. Yet the psalmist urges us to sing a new song to the Lord. In doing this he is recognising that God is continually doing new things in the world. God goes on creating, so there is always new life. We, too, can sing a new song every day. Indeed, our response to God helps to form God's new creation. He needs us to enable his work to be done.

There is nothing that we can think of that has not been created by God: even the things which have been fashioned from men's and women's minds and hands – like aircraft,

rockets, computers, art, architecture, music and literature –
they all come from God. So let us celebrate God now, today!

✳ *Let all the world in every corner sing*
        My God and King!   *George Herbert*

For group discussion and personal thought
'God has never promised us a trouble-free life; but he does
promise to help us when we are troubled' (Robert Draycott).
What troubles people most in today's world? Meditate on
Psalm 46. How does God bring help to a troubled world?

A selection from the NCEC catalogue

AT HOME series

A welcome new series of studies, specially written for
use within house groups and Bible study groups. Each
individual study is based on an everyday object – for
example, loaf, fruit – in order to provide a visual and
symbolic focus for Bible study, discussion, reflection and
prayer.

Book 1 FOOD FOR THOUGHT
Book 2 NATURAL RESOURCES

TALKING TOGETHER series

A series of six books of introductory and background
material for house groups and Bible study groups.

RAW MATERIALS OF FAITH by Donald Hilton
RESOURCES FOR FAITH by Simon Oxley
RELATIONSHIPS IN FAITH by David Owen
RISKS OF FAITH by Donald Hilton
RESULTS OF FAITH by Donald Hilton
RESPONSE IN FAITH by Simon Oxley

*For further details about these books
and all NCEC publications, write to
Robert Denholm House, Nutfield,
Redhill, Surrey, RH1 4HW, England.*

REVELATION

Notes by Revd John H Atkinson, MA

John Atkinson is a Methodist minister in Leicestershire. He has been a college tutor in the West Indies. In Britain, he has served as a circuit minister, a District Chairman and as General Secretary of the Methodist Division of Social Responsibility.

The notes in this section are based on the Jerusalem Bible.

The book of **Revelation** was written to strengthen the faith and courage of Christians who had to face persecution. It is full of symbolism, much of which comes from the Old Testament and other Jewish sources. There have been many different interpretations of these symbols and therefore of the meaning of the book. Sometimes these have been expounded in bizarre ways, far removed from the picture of Jesus in the Gospels.

The main theme of **Revelation** is, however, quite clear. Evil will in the end be conquered by God through Jesus. The Lamb who was slain will become Lord of lords. Those who remain faithful to him will share in the new heaven and the new earth over which he will reign for ever.

Suggestions for further reading

The Revelation of John, Volumes 1 and 2 by William Barclay, Daily Study Bible (Saint Andrew Press)
Revelation by G R Beasley-Murray, New Century Bible Commentaries (Marshall, Morgan & Scott)
The Revelation of Saint John the Divine by G B Caird, New Testament Commentaries (A & C Black)

Sunday August 19   **Revelation 1.1–8**

As John greets the seven churches of Asia, he reminds them of the greatness of Jesus by the titles he gives him and the way in which he tells of what he does. In verses 5–8, John describes Jesus as:

- **the Christ** – that is, the Messiah, God's long-promised anointed one.
- **the faithful witness** to the truth about God's nature and his will.
- **the first-born from the dead** – he was dead and is alive again, sharing his victory over death with all his people.
- **the ruler of the kings of the earth** – his dominion and power will never end.
- **loving us** – great though he is in power and majesty, he is greater still in mercy and love.
- **cleansing us** and freeing us from our sin – he is the Saviour by whose dying love we are made clean and new.
- **calling us** to service and glory – we shall be kings and priests if we are willing to serve God faithfully.
- **the constant Lord of all**, the Alpha and the Omega, the beginning and the end, the same in every age.

✳ *Thank Jesus for each of these truths about him.*

Monday August 20   **Revelation 1.9–20**

John's first vision was of the risen and ascended Jesus (verses 12–16). It was a vision filled with light. The face of Christ was like the sun in its glory. He had seven stars in his hand and seven golden lamp-stands at his feet. The lamps represent the churches on earth – specifically the seven to which the message of the **Revelation** is addressed. The stars represent 'the angels of the seven churches' (verse 20). This is a difficult phrase. It could mean simply the guardian angels of the churches. However, it is more likely to represent the heavenly equivalent or ideal of the churches – the splendour which they will have when they have been transformed by Christ's glory and power.

There are two great messages in this picture:
- **Jesus is in his Church**. Despite his great majesty, he walks among the lamp-stands; he is present with his people.
- Although the churches (and we who belong to them) are like flickering lamps, Jesus means to transform them (and us) into the eternal, glorious lights of heaven itself.

✳ *Lord, I am only a flickering lamp. May I see the bright glory of your majesty; and, by your mercy, grant that one day my lamp may become a star.*

Tuesday August 21

Revelation 2 and **3** are fairly straightforward. These two chapters consist of seven letters to the main churches in western Asia Minor (now Turkey). The first letter was to the church in **Ephesus**, the greatest city of the region, a major port, and a centre of Greek, Roman and Jewish religion as well as of magic. It was also a very important Christian centre in which Paul had spent three years. It had the reputation of being a happy and harmonious church. It deserved praise – but it also needed a challenge.

▶ Read **Revelation 2.1–7**.

No one knows precisely what the Nicolaitans believed. It seems that they lived indulgent and immoral lives. Perhaps they felt that the law did not matter because they lived under the grace of God – whatever they did, God would forgive them, and so they could do what they liked.

The church in Ephesus firmly rejected such teaching and remained faithful and orthodox. Unfortunately, it was a less loving church than it had been in the past. Orthodoxy can have this effect. We must, of course, hold fast to our faith and reject false teaching. But we must also be warm in our love to God and our neighbour.

✳ *Lord, help me to love the truth and to be truly loving.*

Wednesday August 22

Smyrna was a beautiful city and a centre of trade. For about four centuries, from 600 BC onwards, it had lain in ruins. However, it had risen gloriously from ruin and death. The letter to the Christians there reminded them of One, greater than any city, who had been dead and was alive forever.

▶ Read **Revelation 2.8–11**.

The church at Smyrna was weak. It had to face persecution and poverty, and many of its members were probably slaves. But it was spiritually rich (verse 9) and full of faith. The Christians there were not told to have faith but to keep faithful in suffering (verse 10).

Being a Christian calls for courage, stamina and determination. It is like being a runner in a marathon. Perhaps it is significant that the city of Smyrna had games, like the Olympic games, in which those who won races were garlanded with a crown of an evergreen plant – the laurel. Maybe that is why the Christians there were told that those who run the race of life to its end will receive a far greater, everlasting 'crown of life' (verse 10). The Christians at Smyrna lived up to this challenge – of the seven cities to which the letters were sent, theirs was the only one in which Christianity has never died out. May we, too, be always faithful.

* *Lord, keep me faithful so that even I may receive the crown of life.*

Thursday August 23

Pergamum (also called Pergamos) was an impressive city, built on a mountainside. For nearly four centuries it had been the capital of its province. It was a great cultural centre, and was also a centre of the worship of the Roman emperors and of Asclepius, the god of healing. Christians might easily have felt overawed by such a place.

▶ Read **Revelation 2.12–17**.

In the letters to Ephesus and Smyrna, Christ says that he knows all about the work and trials of the Christians there. The phrase in the Pergamum letter is different: 'I know where you live' (verse 13). Christ knows and understands the setting and the circumstances in which his people have to live out their faith. One of the Pergamum Christians, Antipas, had already been murdered for his faith. Not surprisingly some had wavered in their faith, compromising with the pressures and influences of the city. Some had even accepted the heresy of the Nicolaitans (or followers of Balaam – see the notes on August 21 about this sect).

Whatever the pressures, however brutal the persecution, Christians must never compromise with evil.

* *Lord, help me to recognise when I am being tempted to compromise and give me the strength to refuse.*

Friday August 24

The letter to **Thyatira** is the longest of the seven. Yet Thyatira was the least important of the seven cities. It did, however, lie on an important road and prospered commercially. There were many trade guilds in the city – potters, textile workers, dyers, tanners and significantly, bronze (brass) workers (see verse 18).

▶ Read **Revelation 2.18–29**.

The Christians at Thyatira were not given any new 'special duty' (verse 24). They already lived by the right pattern. This pattern, described in verse 19, consists of:

- **love** (they are 'charitable') – whatever else Christians are, first and foremost they must be loving people.
- **faith** – the church must hold firmly to Christ and reject the voice of sin, here symbolised by 'Jezebel'.
- **service** ('devotion') – Christians, like their Lord, are to be the servants of all.
- **endurance** – faith needs to have the patience to live in trustfulness and the courage to bear hardship.
- **progress** – faith which is alive must grow.

✳ *Pray that you may have each of these Christian graces.*

Saturday August 25

Sardis was a city whose glories lay in the past. Once the capital of the province of Lydia, it had fallen to the level of a second-rate town. An earthquake in AD 17 had accelerated its decline. The Christians in Sardis were rather like their town – not as good as they had been. There was another parallel between the city and its Christians. Sardis had a citadel which had been thought to be impregnable. But twice it had fallen in a night attack because its defenders were too complacent. Christians also need to wake up lest they lose their most precious possession – their faith.

▶ Read **Revelation 3.1–6**.

Christians should have a faith which is wideawake and eager, not complacent and half-dead. How keen a Christian are you? How alert are you to the danger that temptation or complacency might fatally undermine your faith?

Isaac Watts put these questions into a hymn:

> And shall we then for ever live
>   At this poor dying rate?
> Our love so faint, so cold to thee,
>   And thine to us so great!

✳ *Lord, help me to keep my faith eager and wideawake.*

For group discussion and personal thought

Read the five letters in **Revelation 2.1 to 3.6**. What good
qualities in these churches are praised? What criticisms of
them are made? How can we develop the former and avoid the
latter?

Sunday August 26

Philadelphia was the most recently built of the seven cities
to which the **Revelation** letters went. Its main purpose was
to act as a centre of Greek culture – a 'shop-window' for the
Greek way of life, and a gateway through which it could
spread far afield.

▶ Read **Revelation 3.7–13**.

The church in Philadelphia was not strong (verse 8), but it
stood with an open door before it. The door was open to provide
many opportunities. It was the door:

● **into God's presence**. The Philadelphians were assured of
Christ's love for them because they had kept his commandments and honoured his name (verses 8–9, 11a). It has
even been suggested that this door was Jesus, himself. He
had referred to himself as 'the door' (see John 10.7, 9, RSV).

● **into the heavenly city**. Christ has opened the kingdom of
heaven to all believers.

● **of evangelism** – of missionary opportunity. Philadelphia
was on the road of the imperial postal service. Armies travelled this road and so did caravans of merchants. Now it
was beckoning the missionaries of Christ.

✳ *Thank Jesus that all these doors are open to you, too.*

Monday August 27

Laodicea was a prosperous commercial city. The Christians
there belonged to a church in an affluent society. Like their
counterparts in the more prosperous parts of today's world,
they often allowed themselves to be influenced by the surrounding wealth and luxury. In fact, the risen Christ could
not find a single good word to say about the Christians in
Laodicea.

▶ Read **Revelation 3.14–22**.

Once again a door becomes a striking symbol (see verse 20). Unlike the 'open door' in the letter to Philadelphia, this door is not the door of opportunity through which Christians enter the presence of God, the kingdom of heaven or the field of evangelism. Rather, it is the door of their own hearts which they must open to Christ. He stands outside that door knocking for admission. He does not tap timidly, but with the firm knock of one who has the right to enter; he does not batter down the door or force its lock, but waits for us to open it. If we do, he will come and be our guest, 'side by side' with us (verse 20). The lukewarm, self-satisfied Laodiceans were keeping the door shut against him. Are you?

✳ *Lord, my heart's door is open to you. Come in and stay by my side forever.*

Tuesday August 28   Revelation 4.1–11

After transmitting the letters to the seven churches, John begins to describe the visions which came to him. The letters were addressed to the struggling churches on earth; while the visions depict the glory and triumph of heaven.

When John looked through heaven's open door, the first thing he saw was a **throne** (verse 2). This is a symbol that God reigns, for he is the One who sits on the throne (a favourite phrase of John's). He is King of kings, and the light of his glory is like the flashing of jewels (verse 3).

But God is not only great in majesty. He is merciful, too. There is a **rainbow** circling his throne, recalling the sign of his covenant-love promised to Noah (see Genesis 9.8–17).

As the vision developed, John saw four creatures (see verse 7). These may well represent all created things; and their unceasing song means that all creation shall sing the praises of God. The words of their song (verse 8) are a summary of God's glory – he is holy, almighty and eternal. Like them, we should praise God, too.

✳ *Holy, holy, holy, Lord God Almighty!*
   All thy works shall praise thy name in earth and sky
      and sea.   Reginald Heber

Wednesday August 29   Revelation 5.1–14

Two great pictures are brought together in this reading – the conquering Lion and the slaughtered Lamb. John saw a Lamb (verse 6), but he heard about a Lion (verse 5). What John saw was the **outward appearance**; what he heard about was the **inner reality**. The Lamb is what Jesus **appears to be** – weak and wounded; the Lion represents what he **really is** – strong and triumphant.

The conquering 'Lion of Judah' in the Old Testament and especially in the period between the Old and New Testaments was a symbol of God's Messiah who would come and conquer.

John's vision joins this triumphal image to the apparently pathetic picture of a Lamb covered with the wounds of its slaughter – obviously a symbol of the crucified Jesus.

When the two pictures are brought together, a basic theme of the book of **Revelation** and of all Christian devotion is made clear. The Saviour who gave himself up to suffer a cruel death on the cross is for that very reason raised up by God and made the eternal Victor who will rule over all.

✳ *Rejoice and be glad! For the Lamb that was slain,*
   O'er death is triumphant, and liveth again.
   Rejoice and be glad! For our King is on high;
   He pleadeth for us on his throne in the sky.

                                                    Horatius Bonar

Thursday August 30   Revelation 7.9–17

In ancient, as well as in modern times, victorious troops have paraded through their capital city, with their leader given pride of place in the procession. In today's reading, John is describing the victory parade of heaven. The 'troops' are the faithful host of Christ's people. They salute God and the Lamb – their leader (verse 10). They not only shout a victory cry, they also carry palms – the symbols of victory – and wear white clothes. White was the colour of triumph; Roman generals wore white in their victory parades.

However, white has another significance – it is the sign of purity. The white robes of the heavenly host have been 'washed . . . in the blood of the Lamb' (verse 14). They – and we – have no virtue or purity of our own. It is the mercy of Jesus which cleanses us and sets us on the path to purity.

Perhaps, therefore, it is not an accident that the same Hebrew word which means 'victory' also means 'salvation'. The victory Jesus has won is salvation for all who will accept him. The only victory we shall ever know is the one which is ours when we turn to him.

✳ *Use verse 12 **slowly** as a prayer of adoration and thanks.*

This is perhaps the strangest chapter in the whole of **Revelation**. Although it is almost impossible to unravel all its symbolism, the basic pattern is clear.

The dragon is the personification of evil at war with God and humankind – the word 'Satan' originally meant 'adversary'. The child must be the Messiah – the Christ – because he is destined to rule the nations (verse 5). The woman, however, is not his mother, Mary, but a symbol for the whole community of God's people – the new Israel, the Church.

The dragon – evil – tries to destroy the child Messiah, but fails. This not only reminds us of Herod's attempt to kill the new-born Christ but all the devil's other attacks on Jesus from the wilderness (Luke 4.1–13) to the cross (Luke 23.35–39).

Having failed to kill the child, the dragon fights the angels but is again defeated. So he turns instead on the earthly followers of Jesus (verse 12).

Christians must therefore expect to have their faith attacked. The method will vary – temptation, doubt, rejection, suffering. But Christ has conquered all evil and he can help us, also, to overcome its power.

✳ *Lord Jesus, conqueror of evil, help me to conquer evil, too.*

Usually the word 'new' means 'fresh', 'different', or 'just discovered'. But, often in the Bible, it has another significance – it is a **salvation** word.
- The **new man** of whom the New Testament speaks is a person saved by Christ.
- The **new city** about which we shall read later in **Revelation** is the eternal kingdom of the redeemed.
- The **new song** or hymn in verse 3 is a song of salvation, and can only be learned by the redeemed.

Christ makes all things new because he is the Saviour of all. Those who have been redeemed by Christ are fundamentally and eternally changed. They are also devoted to Jesus. That is why they are described as 'the ones who have kept their virginity and have not been defiled with women' (verse 4). Sexual defilement is often used in the Bible as a picture word for religious unfaithfulness. Here the term 'not defiled' is used in a spiritual, not a sexual, sense, and refers to those who are utterly faithful to God. They bear his name (erse 1) and show the constancy which marks his saints (verse 12) – a constancy which is lifelong (verse 13).

✱ *O Lord, you have saved me and made me new,*
May my love for you be ever constant and true.

For group discussion and personal thought

Laodicea was a church in an affluent society (see **Revelation 3.14-22**). How typical are its faults of modern churches in prosperous communities? What other faults may such churches have?

Sunday September 2 **Revelation 15.1–8**

Most of us think of the sea as something which is pleasant and good. We enjoy walking beside it, swimming in it, and sailing upon it. It is pleasant to look at, sparkling in sunshine or gleaming in moonlight. In the Bible, however, the sea is neither good, nor pleasant. It is the place where God's enemies – the forces of evil and chaos – dwell. That is why in heaven, 'there was no longer any sea' (Revelation 21.1). Evil and chaos have no place in the eternal city.

This helps us to understand the significance of the 'glass lake' or 'sea' in today's reading (verse 2). It is the reservoir of evil which the redeemed must overcome if they are to reach heaven. And it is the sign of the great distance which separates God and sinful people. But the glass lake is 'suffused with fire' (verse 2).

This is God's fire, intervening with judgement and redemption, consuming evil and refining what is good.

Those who were conquerors by God's grace, stood on the heavenly shore of the lake singing his praise. Their song was 'the hymn of Moses' (verses 3–4) because Moses had led the Israelites through the perils of the Red Sea, just as God had led these people through the dangers of the glass lake.

✱ *Lord, deliver me from the place where evil dwells and bring me at last in safety to the heavenly shore.*

Monday September 3 **Revelation 19.1–10**

There are two vivid pictures in today's reading. The first is that of 'the famous prostitute', who like Babylon (see Revelation 17.5), was a symbol of evil and persecution. She represented the forces of destruction, but now that God has triumphed, destruction itself is destroyed (verse 3).

The second picture is that of the approaching marriage feast of heaven. The idea that God's people are his 'bride' runs through the Bible. In the Old Testament, God's bride is Israel (for example, see Hosea 2.19–20). Jesus also used this picture in his parables (see Matthew 22.1–14).

Marriage is meant to be a joyous, loving, intimate relationship based on an endless covenant of faithfulness. Wedding feasts celebrate that bond. So the heavenly banquet celebrates the joyous, faithful bond of love between Christ and his people. Their wedding garments have been washed in the blood of the Lamb (Revelation 7.14), and they are radiant with the good deeds of the saints (verse 8).

The invitation to the wedding feast is still open. It is for all those who know Jesus as their Saviour and who live faithfully in a joyous, loving closeness to him.

✻ *Lord, help me to live faithfully and joyfully, loving you always.*

Tuesday September 4   Revelation 19.11–21

Jesus now takes centre stage in this divine drama. He appears as the rider on a white horse who comes finally to destroy the forces of evil. John's vision spells out his greatness (verses 11–13). Ponder these details:

- He is called 'Faithful and True' – his love is constant, his truth eternal, his kingdom endless.
- He is 'a warrior for justice' – he comes to vindicate goodness and righteousness.
- His eyes are 'flames of fire' – searching heart and mind, and destroying evil.
- On his head are 'many coronets' – one is not enough, for his splendour far outshines any earthly sovereignty.
- His cloak is 'soaked in blood' – his own blood, poured out on the cross, and that of the saints spilled in martyrdom.
- He is the 'Word of God' – through him God is revealed and through him the almighty power of God is released.

Some of this vision is violent and lurid, but at heart it pictures the Lord who conquers because he is the life-giving redeemer. The victory he wins is the destruction of all that is evil.

✳ *Praise Christ, the redeemer, the conqueror of evil.*

Wednesday September 5　　　　　　**Revelation 21.1–8**

John sees that in the end God will make a new heaven and a new earth. The distinction between the two will in fact disappear, because God will live among his people, making his home with them (verse 3). Wherever that happens, it is heaven. Everything which belongs to our state of sin and death will be destroyed. We will be made new – recreated.

But God goes further. The **whole of creation** is to be remade – not destroyed (verse 5). The world of created things may be imperfect, but it is not hopelessly evil. After all, God made it. Now he remakes it to become part of the new heaven-and-earth.

In order to share in this joy, we must:
- **be thirsty** – seeking and longing – for the life which only Jesus can give us.
- **be faithful** – never falling into any of the categories listed in verse 8, but remaining faithful to the One who is himself faithful and true.

✳ *Lord Jesus, you make all things new,*
　All people, all creation.
　In seeking and in following you
　I share that great salvation.

Thursday September 6　　　　**Revelation 21.9–14, 22–27**

In this majestic vision of the heavenly city, it is striking to note that it does **not** have a temple or any 'natural' light (verses 22–23).

When we remember what the earthly temple was, we can immediately see why heaven does not need one. The temple was:
- the sign of God's presence, his 'dwelling-place'. But in heaven God is ever-present and no building is needed to symbolise that presence.
- a place where constant sacrifice was made to cleanse God's people from their sins. However, heaven is filled with those who have washed their robes in the blood of the Lamb and need no further cleansing.

a place where earthly and holy things were separated. But God has remade all creation and the old distinction no longer applies.

It is even easier to see why the 'new Jerusalem' does not need any created light. It is made radiant with the glory of God and of the Lamb. The one who said, 'I am the light of the world' (John 8.12) has become the eternal light of the heavenly city.

✳ *We thank you, Lord, that we can have a foretaste of heaven because here and now we can know your presence, receive your cleansing and walk in your light.*

Friday September 7   Revelation 22.1–7

The final chapter of the Bible begins with a marvellous picture of paradise restored. Already, John's visions have proclaimed Jesus as the beginning and the end, the Lord of creation's dawn and the King of the heavenly city. We have also seen how in the new heaven-and-earth, not only humankind, but **all** creation, is remade. Now, as **Revelation** moves to its final climax, the first joy of Eden is restored.

In the original paradise, a river flowed to water the garden (Genesis 2.10). In heaven, there is a river whose source is God who gives life to all.

In the first Eden, there were trees – supremely the tree of the knowledge of good and evil. It was by disobeying God and eating the fruit of this tree that rebellious sin first showed itself. In heaven, too, there are trees, but their leaves now are for 'the healing of the nations' (verse 2, RSV).

In paradise, Adam and Eve lived in God's presence and saw him face to face. That same direct experience of God returns in heaven (verse 4).

✳ *Grant, Lord, that though I share in the sin that lost the first paradise, I may through Christ come to that place where paradise is restored.*

Saturday September 8   Revelation 22.8–20

These closing verses of **Revelation** contain:
- **a great title for Jesus** – 'the bright star of the morning' (verse 16). The morning star is the brightest of all stars and it heralds the coming of full day. Jesus is supreme and he ends forever the night of sin and death.

- **a great invitation from Jesus** – 'Come' (verse 17). Great though his glory is, he bids us come and share it. Great though our sin is, he offers us the water of life freely.
- **a final promise from Jesus** – 'I shall indeed be with you soon' (verse 20). However close or distant his final victory may be, Jesus will come to any of us now if we open our hearts to let him in.
- **a final response to Jesus** – 'Amen; come, Lord Jesus' (verse 20). Use this last prayer in the Bible as an affirmation of your faith that Christ will indeed come in glory!

✳ *Yea, amen, let all adore thee,*
    High on thine eternal throne;
  Saviour, take the power and glory,
    Claim the kingdom for thine own:
      Come, Lord Jesus!
      Everlasting God, come down!   Charles Wesley

For group discussion and personal thought
Read **Revelation 21.1–11, 22–27** and **22.1–7**. How does this vision of heaven help us in our lives **now** on earth?

177

INTERNATIONAL APPEAL

Lesotho

Guatemala

Mozambique

Peru

Zaire

Ghana

Kiribati

Nigeria

Samoa

No, not the roll-call for a meeting at the United Nations! Just some of the countries, large and small, where local Christians receive help from the IBRA International Fund.

To make the best use of its money, the IBRA International Fund works through churches and Christian groups in the countries concerned. These are some of the ways we are able to help people around the world read the Bible regularly and with understanding.

Bible reading cards produced in Spanish and Portugese for distribution in Africa, Central and South America.

Paper, covers and film supplied so that printing can be done locally.

Grants given towards costs of producing local translations of IBRA material.

Books like this one sent free of charge so that they can be sold at subsidised prices. Money earned locally is then used to cover distribution costs and fund further IBRA work.

THE ONLY MONEY WE HAVE TO SEND IS THE MONEY YOU GIVE!

Please respond with generosity. *Place your gift in the envelope provided and give it to your church representative OR send it direct to IBRA International Appeal, Robert Denholm House, Nutfield, Redhill, Surrey, RH1 4HW, UK.*

DEUTERONOMY

Notes by Adrian G Hudson, MA

Adrian Hudson is a Methodist local preacher living in North Devon. He has worked as a probation officer in various parts of England; and, for ten years prior to his retirement, was Deputy Chief Probation Officer for West Yorkshire.

The notes in this section are based on the New International Version.

Deuteronomy presents three speeches (chapters 1–4, 5–28 and 29–33) delivered by Moses to the assembled people who were then on the east side of the River Jordan poised for their entry into the promised land. The first is an account of God's dealings with the children of Israel; the second is mostly a code of law which was to apply to the people in the promised land; while the third is an exhortation to accept God's law and live by it. Our readings from **Deuteronomy** will cut across these three parts as we look first at **people and the law**, then at **the law and the land**, and finally at **choosing and keeping faith**.

The word *'Deuteronomy'*, literally meaning 'second law', is a mistranslation of the Hebrew title of this book which means 'a copy'. Much of it can also be found in **Exodus** and **Numbers**. Some scholars think that **Deuteronomy** was put together in its present form in the time of King Josiah when some manuscripts of the law were rediscovered in the temple.

Suggestions for further reading

Deuteronomy by David F Payne, Daily Study Bible (Saint Andrew Press)

Deuteronomy by J A Thompson, Old Testament Commentaries (Inter-Varsity Press)

PEOPLE AND THE LAW

Sunday September 9

Throughout history many a conquering nation has subsequently lost its identity as its occupying troops have been absorbed into the nation they have conquered. For example, many of the ancient Romans who came to Britain settled down, married local women and never returned home. The dangers of fraternising with the enemy have always been recognised.

▶ Read **Deuteronomy 7.6–9**.

The children of Israel were to remain distinct from other peoples because they had a special relationship with God. They might have been insignificant in comparison with the great nations of the day, but God had chosen them. Note how God's love dominates these verses. Because of God's love the Israelites were a redeemed people. The same description fits the Church today. We, too, must be distinct from the non-Christian world – we are in it, but not of it.

▶ Now read **Deuteronomy 7.17–24**.

The God who brought the Israelites out of Egypt was easily able to take care of them in the struggle to possess the land they were about to enter. The same God can take care of his Church today as it engages in spiritual warfare to repossess the world for him.

✴ *Lord, give us courage to claim our country for you.*

Monday September 10   **Deuteronomy 5.1, 6–21**

Some churches have the ten commandments inscribed in gold on wooden panels fixed to the walls where the whole congregation can see them. Obviously earlier generations valued them highly. It was expected that children would learn them off by heart. Now the gold lettering is often faded and the words can be very difficult to read. This seems to reflect the position that the ten commandments now occupy in our society. Most people know that there are ten commandments but few can say accurately what they are.

Probably the last five are the best known (verses 17–21). Perhaps this is because those forbidding murder, stealing and false testimony, have been included in the laws of almost every country. Other parts of the ten commandments, like the law forbidding adultery, have become more a matter for the individual's conscience. Covetousness is a sin of the mind and would be difficult to enforce. Yet this perhaps comes nearest to Jesus' teaching that sin starts in the mind (see Matthew 5.21–30). Paul also referred to some of the ten commandments, and concluded that they may be summed up in one rule, 'Love your neighbour as yourself' (Romans 13.9).

✳ *Father, may our rules of life be such that we express your love to our neighbours.*

Tuesday September 11   Deuteronomy 6.1–12

It was from today's reading that Jesus quoted when he was asked which was the most important of all the commandments (see Mark 12.29–30). For him love came even before obedience. It is love that will make us **want** to do God's will. Love is a much better motivation than fear. So love will make us want to impress God's commandments on our children (verse 7).

Nevertheless it is so easy to forget this, especially when all is going well and life is comfortable. A land flowing with milk and honey is not the easiest place to remember one's indebtedness to God. No wonder Moses warned the people to be careful not to forget the Lord (verse 12), because their prosperity as a nation depended on their obedience to God's commands.

Today, strict Jews still try to obey Moses' instructions literally, by wearing little boxes (phylacteries) containing portions of the law on their arms or foreheads. However, God has promised to write his law on our hearts – a much better place to carry the law of love (see Jeremiah 31.33).

✳ *Lord have mercy upon us, and inscribe your laws on our hearts, we pray.*

Wednesday September 12

One of the problems which we all face is that of family responsibilities. All over the world, people are concerned to maintain the family line. Land, particularly, is often entailed so that it is not lost to the family. In the past, widowed mothers usually lived with their sons. Many great estates have a dower house for this reason.

▶ Read **Deuteronomy 25.5–10**.

Here we read of a way of providing for the widow who did not have a son to look after her. Today we would not regard this as a very effective way of doing it, and even in Moses' time there were many snags. We can imagine some of them. The brother-in-law might already be married and have more than enough family responsibilities already. A way out for the man who simply did not want to fulfil this duty to his sister-in-law involved a peculiar ritual if the elders failed to persuade him. In Ruth 4.1–12 we can read an account of the actual application of this law at a later time.

We may have got rid of ancient and peculiar ceremonies, but do we do any better at actually caring for widows in our modern societies? Some of our economic structures and rules may actually put widows at a disadvantage.

✷ *Pray for the work of organisations caring for widows.*

Thursday September 13   Deuteronomy 15.1–11

When a people are richly blessed as the children of Israel were, there should be no poor among them (verse 4). We are assured today that the world has the resources to provide enough for all its people, but there is still the problem of distribution. When Jesus said, 'The poor you will always have with you' (Mark 14.7), he was probably quoting verse 11. Therefore, his hearers would have been aware of the remainder of the verse – the command to be generous to their brothers, the poor and needy.

Some international organisations today are proposing an idea similar to the periodical remission of debts in verse 1, as a means of solving the problems of many countries carrying debts which they cannot repay. So far banks have only rescheduled their repayments, but this merely postpones the problem. Moses saw that hard-hearted people might look after their own interests by not lending when the seventh (or Jubilee) year was imminent. Such tight-fistedness is a sin (verse 9). See how Jesus made the same point in his parable of the two servants (Matthew 18.23–35).

✷ *O God our Father, may we not have grudging hearts. Let your Spirit order the affairs of nations so that the poor may be released from their chains of debt.*

Friday September 14

Even today there are parts of the world where people can be sold into slavery in payment of their debts. In the time of Moses slavery was general and an alternative to hired service, but the principle of release after seven years was also to be applied to slaves.

▶ Read **Deuteronomy 15.12–18**.

Jesus often came into conflict with the Pharisees because they attended to the letter of the law but not the spirit of it. The spirit of this law about releasing slaves is to be found in God's dealing with his people. They had been slaves in Egypt. When the time came for their final release from that land, God saw to it that they had plenty to take with them, heaped on them by the Egyptians themselves (see Exodus 12.35–36). So the master releasing his slave was to ensure that he had the means to make a good start in his independence.

However, not all masters were bad and not all slaves wanted to leave. Christians, too, are freed men and women, who choose to serve God because they have learned to love him.

✳ *Lord God, our redeemer, may we so love you that we are glad to be your servants for life.*

Saturday September 15

Whatever system of government we have, it is vital to get the right people to hold office. Two offices are described in today's reading. The first is that of **judge**.

▶ Read **Deuteronomy 16.18–20**.

The reason for having judges and officials in every town was so that everyone might have access to justice. For the same reason judges were not to accept bribes. All attempts to pervert justice were against God's will and had to be resisted. This is equally true today.

The second office described is that of **king**. The nations surrounding Israel had kings over them. So, as the time would come when Israel would want a king of their own, God set out the qualities necessary for a king.

▶ Read **Deuteronomy 17.14–20**.

The qualities necessary for a king of God's choosing were that he must not be a foreigner, nor go in for self-aggrandisement; but he was to make the law of God his guide in all things.

Jesus was born as one of the people. He possessed nothing of his own and was obedient to his Father. In all things he met these requirements perfectly.

✳ *King of glory, King of peace,*
   I will love thee.   George Herbert

For group discussion and personal thought

What are the different types of laws we need in society today?
How do laws benefit us? To what extent do some laws disadvantage certain groups of people? Look at **Deuteronomy
5.6–21** and **6.1–9.** How does the teaching of these verses
relate to your country in 1990?

THE LAW AND THE LAND

Sunday September 16　　　　　　**Deuteronomy 8.1–10**

In today's reading the children of Israel are on the verge of
entering the land which God had promised to them. Moses
reminded them that the long and hard way by which they had
come to this point was a humbling experience designed to
teach them their dependency on God. Some of us have had to
spend many years of our lives getting to where we are now –
years of study, work and gaining experience. As we look back
we can see that God's hand was in it for us. Only after the
discipline of hard work and overcoming difficulties can we
really be trusted to handle prosperity correctly.

If we need to remember the past in order to appreciate what
God has done for us, we also need to appreciate the present.
The description of the promised land emphasised God's
bounty to the children of Israel. Their only adequate response
was not just satisfaction, but thanksgiving.

The land in which we live may not be as bountiful as the
promised land. However, the gift of life itself is always rich
with possibilities. For this, and all of God's gifts to us, let us
always give him thanks and praise.

✳ *We thank you, Lord, that you do not always lead us by an
easy way, but train us so that we are fit for your kingdom.*

Monday September 17　　　　　　**Deuteronomy 11.10–21**

Recent floods and droughts in various parts of the world
remind us that one of the things over which there is no human
control is the weather. However, the children of Israel may
not have realised this while they were in Egypt. There, they
had an endless supply of water which had to be lifted out of

the Nile to fill the irrigation ditches and water the fertile land.
They had to work hard, but they were not knowingly dependent on the rain.

Things were going to be different for them in the mountainous country above the Jordan valley, where rain was necessary for life and growth. They would be more dependent on the
gifts of God than on their own hard work. If God was to be
expected to be faithful in giving the rain, should not the people
be faithful in keeping his commands?

Today, many nations are becoming more aware of the
importance of the weather in maintaining the delicate balance
of nature. As we strive to get more and more out of the land,
we are having to re-learn about the responsible use of all of
God's gifts to us. We need to obey his commandments to love
each other so that all peoples are able to eat and be satisfied
(verse 15).

✳ *Lord, thank you for the land. Teach us to use it wisely and*
remind us of our dependence on seasonable weather.

Tuesday September 18

People in small businesses often have a problem with getting
their accounts settled promptly. Sometimes large firms keep
them waiting when the money is needed to buy materials for
further manufacturing. These firms may not be dishonest but
they are inconsiderate.

▶ Read **Deuteronomy 24.10–22**.

Verses 10–13 show us how to be considerate when making
a loan. Too often our attitude is that if someone wants our
money they must do things our way. Paying a wage should
also be done with consideration – especially to poor people
(verses 14–15). They have to live from day to day and need
prompt payment. Those who receive state benefits, count on
them coming on time. Postal workers, counter clerks and
others in the civil service, who strike in pursuit of their own
rights, need to consider the poor.

The principle of concern for the poor in Israel extended to
foreigners, orphans and widows. One way of helping them
was to leave the missed sheaves of grain, and fruit, for them
(verses 19–21). If we live in the caring way that God shows
us, then there will be enough for everyone.

✳ *Lord, teach us to think first of the needs of others.*

185

Wednesday September 19

Each year the Israelites celebrated three special feasts. The
first was the Feast of the Passover. The second and third were
agricultural festivals. These were a reminder to the people
of their need for God's help, and an opportunity for them to
celebrate the fruits of their labours. All the people were to
participate totally in these feasts by bringing offerings to God
and joyfully celebrating God's provision for them.

▶ Read **Deuteronomy 16.9–17**.

The Feast of Weeks (verses 9–10) corresponded to the
beginning of the harvest, and later became known as the Feast
of Pentecost. The third feast, the Feast of Tabernacles (verses
13–15), was celebrated when the harvest was completed and
processed – when the grain was threshed, the grapes and
olives pressed, and the wine and oil stored.

In many countries today, the majority of the population
does not produce food. Supermarkets, freezers and refriger-
ators detract from our awareness that we – and the whole
world – are dependent on successful harvests. However, in
appreciation of the provision of our daily needs, we need to
find new ways of celebrating the wonders of nature and thank-
ing God for the ability of those who work to feed us.

✳ *Think about ways in which you can celebrate and show your*
appreciation to God for the harvest.

Thursday September 20   Deuteronomy 26.1–11

In some harvest celebrations, children are encouraged to
bring a basket of fruit and other produce and hand it to the
minister who places it among the harvest gifts. This personal-
ises the harvest ceremony for the children and gives them
each a small part in it. Today's reading gives us an account of
a personal ceremony for individuals or families, in which they
could have their own offering received by the priest and make
their own thanksgiving. There was no set time for this ceremony. The only thing specified about the offering was that it
should be some of the first-fruits.

We are invited to bring some of our 'first-fruits' to God – the
first signs that our labours are rewarded. The first-fruits are
usually of the highest quality. It is right that we should offer
our best to God. If, later, there is some disaster, the first-
fruits may be the only fruits for some time. In bringing God
the first, we are showing that he comes first with us, even

before ourselves. First-fruits are gifts of enthusiasm, given cheerfully. We do not have to wait for the harvest before we bring our first-fruits to God.

✳ *Meditate on the theme of first-fruits and think what you should have in your 'basket' to place before the Lord.*

Friday September 21

The word 'tithe' is generally taken to mean one-tenth. Some practise tithing today in their giving to the Church, but it is no longer a practice that is generally observed. But tithing was not only a religious practice – in times when the Church and state in Britain were not so clearly separated, it seems to have been as much a form of local taxation as an offering to God.

▶ Read **Deuteronomy 14.22–29**.

This is not the only account of tithing in the Bible and it would seem that the practice varied at different times and in different circumstances. The main element was the setting aside of one-tenth of the produce for religious purposes. It may come as a surprise, therefore, to find that some of the produce was to be eaten at a feast in the presence of the Lord. Only one year in three were the tithes to be used for what we might call 'church purposes'. These included the maintenance of the ministry – for the Levites who had no land of their own; and provision for aliens, orphans and widows who also had no means of their own.

Although in most countries the State usually helps those without means of support today, we still need to give regularly and generously not only to the Church but also to organisations which help the needy.

✳ *Think and pray about what you have and what you give.*

Saturday September 22   Deuteronomy 28.1–6, 9–14

Today's reading is an assurance to the children of Israel that God will bless the **whole** of their lives if they will diligently obey all his commandments. All their labours would be productive (verses 3–6). They would enjoy financial success and they would always be 'at the top' (verse 13).

The prosperity that God promised was more than a reward for good behaviour. As a holy people (verse 9) the children of

187

Israel were to be a living witness of the righteousness of God to all the other nations. Those at the top had the responsibility of leadership and setting an example. Other nations would receive God's benefits through Israel.

This has happened. Many of the laws God gave in **Deuteronomy** have found a place in modern countries as the basis for policies for public health, justice and care for the poor.

The policy of living in a relationship of love with God and with one's neighbour will never be out of date and will fulfil the deepest needs of all peoples.

✱ *Pray that the legal systems of your country may provide protection and justice for all.*

For group discussion and personal thought
Look at this week's readings and see how they emphasise the relationship between God's provision for us and what he requires from us. Read **Deuteronomy 14.22–29**. Is tithing an adequate response to God? In what other ways can we give to God; and with what attitude should we give?

CHOOSING AND KEEPING THE FAITH

Sunday September 23   **Deuteronomy 4.1–14**

Most of us retain only about thirty percent of what we hear. It just seems to go in one ear and out the other! Parents and teachers are well aquainted with this problem. We retain more of something when we both hear and see it; and if we can also experience something for ourselves, we are most likely to remember it.

Prior to entering the promised land, a thorough knowledge of God's laws was most important for the children of Israel. They could not afford to forget them because these laws would not only be the foundation upon which their society was to be founded, but they were also to become an example to other nations (verse 6). So Moses reminded the people of the occasion on which they received God's commandments – it was one of **hearing, seeing and experiencing** the evidence of God's presence with them (see verses 10–13).

Moses told the people to put what they had learned into practice, and to teach the laws to their children. Nothing will better fix God's commandments in our minds than acting on them – allowing them to be a part of our own experience.

✳ *My heart is fixed, eternal God,*
       Fixed on thee.   *Richard Dukes*

Monday September 24   Deuteronomy 5.22 to 6.3

There would be little point in leaders giving commands unless they could expect them to be acted upon. In today's reading there are three keywords which help us to understand more about obedience.

- **Do** (verse 32). To do something requires an act of the will. We can make the choice to do what God commands.
- **Keep** (verse 2) – obey (GNB). This implies a state of permanent willingness. When we hold the spirit of the law in our hearts, specific commands for each and every situation should not be needed. Instead of being like an unwilling servant, we respond to God like a willing child.
- **Fear** (verse 29) – honour (GNB). Fear is often thought of in negative terms but not all fears are bad. At the early stages of our moral development it is the fear of punishment that makes us obedient. However, this immature fear can grow into a healthy respect for rules and an awe of God.

God no longer issues his laws to us through mountaintop smoke and fire. Instead, he has written them on our hearts (Jeremiah 31.33). As we mature in our faith our love for God deepens, and like the psalmist, we can say:

✳ *I delight to do your will, O my God;*
    your law is within my heart.   *(Psalm 40.8)*

Tuesday September 25   Deuteronomy 30.1–10

The people of Israel had everything in their favour. They were assured of God's blessings if they obeyed his commandments. However, the Old Testament shows that time and time again they preferred to go their own way, and their disobedience resulted in them being taken captive by foreign nations.

Deportation was a terrible fate for the Israelites. In an alien land they felt that God had abandoned them. However, God's purpose for his people was redemption – he offered them more than simple justice. He punished them only with the purpose of securing their repentance. Once the people returned to him, they would be restored to their former prosperity in the promised land (verse 3).

Separation from God is also the worst fate that can befall us. However, God recognises the weakness of our human nature, and does not reject us but offers us the chance of forgiveness and a fresh start when we repent. There is a warm description of God's restoration of his people in verses 9–10 which reminds us of Jesus' teaching about the joy in heaven over one sinner who repents (see Luke 15.7).

✳ *Father, however far I stray, let me hear you calling and so turn back to your everlasting mercy.*

Wednesday September 26

Making choices is not a new problem appearing for the first time in a world bewildered by new technology, the consequences of which cannot be clearly foreseen. Choosing how to use rightly the facilities and blessings we have, has always been a God-given responsibility.

▶ Read **Deuteronomy 30.11–20**.

Moses set two alternatives clearly before the people – choose life and prosperity or death and destruction. We do not always like choices to be put so bluntly, but prefer to see very complicated issues with many pros and cons to be considered. Sometimes, in that way, we are able to put off making any decisions because of all our 'ifs and buts'.

The Christian life, however, is all about making choices. We **choose** whether or not to be a Christian in the first place; but the choices do not end there. Each day we are confronted with various situations in which we have to choose whether or not to follow the way of Christ. Will we respond to the needs we see around us, or will we 'turn a blind eye'? God never forces us to love and follow him, but he does promise us the reward of riches in his kingdom.

✳ *'Choose life, so that you and your children may live.'*
(verse 19)

Thursday September 27

It is usually easier to remember words when they are sung. That is the reason for so many advertising jingles. In the Old Testament, songs were an important medium through which the people recounted their history (for example, see Psalm 106). Today's reading is a fine example of this.

▶ Read **Deuteronomy 32.1–12**.

The main theme of these verses from the song of Moses is the **faithfulness of God** (verse 4). This faithfulness is contrasted with that of an unresponsive people (verses 5–6). In superb poetry Moses goes on to set out the love and care through which God showed his faithfulness.

Today, song is still one of the best ways of extolling God's faithfulness and unfailing love for us. Most hymn-books contain a substantial number of hymns on this theme. It helps us to learn these, so that we can sing them to refresh ourselves and strengthen our faith in time of distress.

Paul also knew the value of singing hymns. When he was in prison, he wrote, 'Let the word of Christ dwell in you richly . . . as you sing psalms, hymns and spiritual songs with gratitude in your hearts to God' (Colossians 3.16).

✳ *Lord, fill my heart and mind with songs of praise for your continuing faithfulness.*

Friday September 28   Deuteronomy 32.13–18, 28–33

In his song, Moses strongly warned the people of the dangers of prosperity – the dangers of growing 'heavy and sleek' (verse 15). This is a warning Christians must take to heart. While we may not enjoy personal wealth, many of us live in a prosperous nation and it would seem that the more prosperous a nation becomes, the less time it has for God. When this happens and when people forget God, human greed can have disastrous consequences. For example, the desire to increase profits, regardless of the cost to the environment, has led to severe pollution of water supplies and the atmosphere.

When we are prosperous we fall into the trap of following other 'gods' – gods of pleasure, profit-making, and the cares of this world. How easy it is to forget God and lose the sense of where we are going! Forgetfulness is a common human failing which has serious consequences. Sometimes we wonder how many disasters it will take for us to learn the simplest of lessons. Verse 28 might well apply to us!

Moses did not issue this warning in order to condemn the people, but to ensure that they would live long in the land they were about to possess (see Deuteronomy 32.47). Likewise, God only reminds us of our need of him because he loves us.

✴ *O God, give us the sense to heed your warnings, and never to forget you.*

Saturday September 29

It was, and often still is, expected that when a man is about to die his family should gather about him to receive his blessing and hear his last words. In a sense, Moses was father of his people and so, knowing that he would not lead them into the promised land, his last act was to pronounce his blessing on the tribes as they gathered before him.

▶ Read **Deuteronomy 33.1–5, 26–29.** (*Jeshuran* (verses 5,26) means 'the upright one', and was a way of speaking of a faithful Israel.)

These blessings are in poetic form and are intended to be repeated and remembered. The people were not blessed just because Moses blessed them. Verse 1 reminds us that Moses was a man of God. He spoke with God's authority and he blessed with God's blessing. We need to recognise this same note of authority in our churches today. God has his human agents in the pulpits and at the reading desks. His are the pastors who visit us. Men and women may speak the words of blessing but the blessing that we receive is from God himself and what can be better than that?

✴ *May the blessing of God almighty, the Father, the Son and the Holy Spirit be with us and remain with us always.*

For group discussion and personal thought

The Israelites were offered the choice of living the kind of life which no one else had ever enjoyed. Study and discuss **Deuteronomy 30.15–20.** When we refer to God's kingdom we often talk in purely spiritual terms. What can we learn from **Deuteronomy's** down-to-earth approach to life?

● Have you remembered to send your gift in response to the **International Appeal** (see page 178)?

THE CHARACTER OF GOD'S KINGDOM

Notes by the Revd Michael Walker, BD, MTh, PhD

The notes in this section are based on the New English Bible.

The kingdom of God is central to the teaching of Jesus. Although unseen and intangible, its impact is enormous. Jesus often spoke of it in terms of:

- **hidden-ness,** like the treasure in the ground;
- **influence,** like the yeast in the dough;
- its **revelation of God's presence,** like the city set upon the hill.

God's kingdom is more than the Church – it is the total activity of God within the world. In this three-week section we shall be looking at some of its characteristics – **light** and **truth**; **hope** and **peace**; **thanksgiving** and **joy.**

Suggestion for further reading

Soul Making: the Desert Way of Spirituality by Alan W Jones (SCM Press)

Sunday September 30   **Psalm 27.1–4; 119.25–32**

GOD – OUR LIGHT AND TRUTH

Truth is a way of life – it is a path and a course to be run. Truth is accompanied by light, a light that streams from nothing less than the being of God himself.

Light is important because it reveals God in a way that we can see him. None of us sees God in the fullness of his glory, but the light draws us and reveals where he is to be found. Our hazy, half-discerned perceptions are clarified and sharpened through prayer.

This 'vision of God' is central to our attempt to do the truth in the world. It throws light on the path ahead of us. Living out the Christian life requires us to be wise, to know where we are going and why we do what we are doing.

In prayer, we commit our way to God who is light; we then follow where he leads, more certain of the truth because it is his light that goes before us.

✳ *Lord, let your light shine before me and make me long to follow where you lead.*

Monday October 1   John 1.1–9, 14–18

THE INCARNATE LIGHT

During the hours of daylight, we do not normally see the stars, although they are there in the sky above us. It is only when darkness falls that we see their spangled brightness.

Since the beginning of all things, Christ has been present to the world. It was through him that God brought the world into being, and through his life that we received life. Yet, it was only in the incarnation – when Christ came in our human flesh and blood and entered into our darkest experiences – that we at last saw him. For there, in the midst of human life, he was as a light shining in the darkness.

We all fear the darkness to some extent. We do not know what it conceals or where our path lies. We think of experiences of change, illness, separation or bereavement, as times of darkness. The darkness, however, is a place where we may discover the light. There we see what cannot be seen in the brightness of the day. Martin Luther sometimes talked of Jesus as 'the hidden God' – a God hidden in the cross and all those human experiences that resemble it.

✳ *Lord, in every darkness, come to us, that the night may become as the day.*

Tuesday October 2   Matthew 5.14–20

THE CHRISTIAN LIGHT

In this reading, Jesus tells us that Christians are to be light in the world. He then goes on to speak of the law and the authority that law is to continue to hold in our lives.

The law, or *Torah* as it is known among the Jews, provides a spiritual and ethical pattern to which people's lives are to conform. As Jesus interpreted it in the Sermon on the Mount, the *Torah* is a searching code, a guide not simply to outward actions but an instruction book on the way we are to handle our deepest feelings, from anger to religious aspiration.

The call to be light and to live in obedience to Christ's teaching belong together. Light issues from a quality of life which comes from self-discipline and commitment to an ethical way

in which we believe. What we are cannot be separated from
what we believe, nor can it be separated from what we do.
Our actions either serve to increase light in the world around
us or to deepen its darkness.

We can live this life of light and obedience only in union
with Jesus Christ. If obedience is not to degenerate into legalism then it must be lived out in loving fellowship with Jesus
and openness to his indwelling spirit.

❊ *Lord, write your law in our hearts that we may love it and
learn obedience to it.*

Wednesday October 3   **John 3.1–3, 9–21**

THE LIGHT OF JUDGEMENT

In the night-time, when Nicodemus came to him, Jesus spoke
of the searching light of judgement (see verses 18–21). It is a
light that uncovers things we would rather conceal. It is a
penetrating light that requires courage and honesty if we are
to expose the inner places of our souls.

In verse 16, we have the classic statement of God's love to
us in Jesus Christ. We sometimes see a conflict between that
love and the judgement of which Jesus goes on to speak. Love,
so we imagine, is to be welcomed, but judgement is to feared.
Judgement, however, is a function of love. The light of God
does not search us in order to destroy, but to heal us. It is the
hidden, unrecognised and unresolved sins that most threaten
to destroy us. If they are to be forgiven, and we are to be fully
healed, then they must be uncovered.

It is not always easy to be honest with ourselves. We do not
simply hide our follies from others, we refuse to admit them
even to ourselves. Our sins grow familiar and we learn to live
with them, no longer recognising them as sin. By compelling
us to face up to them, the light of Christ's judgement points
us in the direction of God's everlasting mercy.

❊ *Lord, may I not hide from your light. May it show me myself
and lead me to your mercy.*

Thursday October 4   **John 8.12–19**

THE LIGHT OF TRUTH

The Christian faith embraces the whole world. It claims that
the life and work of Jesus, who was born in a particular place

and time, has significance for the whole human race. Christianity began with the particular and ends with the universal.

This claim for universality is made by Jesus himself in verse 12. In him is a light that transcends all national divisions and all eras of historical time. He speaks to everyone, in every generation and in every place.

Our experience of the Christian faith is personal to each one of us, and shared with others in the Church. It is a very intimate experience and known only by that small minority who comprise the Christian Church. There is always the danger that we shall see Christ's influence running no further than this comparatively small group.

Truth, however, cannot be personalised and particularised in that way – it is universal. Christ's light shines everywhere and is for everyone.

* *Light of the world, undimming and unsetting,*
O shine each mist away!
Banish the fear, the falsehood, and the fretting;
Be our unchanging day.   *Horatius Bonar*

Friday October 5   **John 13.31 to 14.6**

THE WAY OF TRUTH

When Jesus spoke to his disciples in the Upper Room, he was very close to the place and time of his death. Yet he spoke like a man on a journey – he spoke of going and of coming, of places where others could not follow, and of a way.

To be a Christian is to be 'in Christ'. No matter how far we have to travel or how near to our destination we may be, we are people on the way with him. Christianity is a constant pilgrimage, a journey of faith. The important things on any journey are the route, the destination and the resources needed for its successful completion. For us, Christ is all these.

The route we must follow is that of obedience to his word. In today's reading this is quite simply described as keeping his 'new commandment' (see verse 34). The destination is that place where Christ has gone before us – it is our home and destiny, 'the Father's house' (verse 2). And our resources are Christ himself, his life lived in us and our lives lived in him. Our journey does not cease until we come at last to the Father's house.

Jesus is the **way**; he is the **truth** to which the way leads; he is the **life** of those who travel on the way.

✳ *Lord, may we keep our eyes on the way; trust in the truth;
and live the life with joy.*

Saturday October 6   **1 John 2.1–11**

LIVING IN THE WAY OF LIGHT AND TRUTH

The Christian life is lived within the context of forgiveness
(see verses 1–2). As the writer of **1 John** goes on to speak of
commandments and our obedience to them, it is important
that we remember this. All life is lived within the context of
grace. Within that loving, forgiving environment, we are
called to live as Christ lived, in obedience to the commandment to love God and our neighbour. Obedience or disobedience to that commandment is as different as light is from
darkness (see verses 9–11).

The light is a place of truth. There can be no deception in
the light. In it, we are seen to be what we are. To live in the
darkness is to hide what we are and to cover our deeds. It may
seem that life is not as simple as that. Yet, the only evidence
that we are committed to Christ's commandment to love
others, is the way we treat them and the actions that charac-
terise our lives. It is a style of living that is visible, it is out in
the open, it is in the light.

Light and truth do not belong together simply as abstrac-
tions. They have to do with the real world in which we live
and the sort of people that we strive to become.

✳ *Lord, may we remain committed to your way of love and
not run to the shelter of darkness in order to escape from it.*

For group discussion and personal thought

'Truth is a path and a course to run' (Michael Walker). Our
Christian life is often spoken of as a pilgrimage: how do we
gauge what progress we are making? In our modern 'pilgrim's
progress', what perils do we face? Which of life's experiences
would you describe as 'dark' experiences? How do we discover
God's light through them?

Sunday October 7   **Psalm 146.5–10; 29.7–11**

GOD – OUR HOPE AND PEACE

A good deal of the Old Testament, like the New Testament, is written out of situations of suffering and injustice. Men and women were aware of the contradiction of faith as they lived in a world that seemed to 'writhe in travail' (Psalm 29.8).

Today's readings hold out hope for a future marked by peace (Psalm 29.11) and justice (Psalm 146.7), both of which were missing in the turbulence and the oppression of those times. The longing of the psalmist reaches us across the centuries, for both peace and justice are central to the agenda of human and Christian concerns in the contemporary world.

It seems as if full-scale wars have been replaced by local wars that drag on for years. In other places, military confrontation is replaced by the covert operations of terrorists with their subversion of normal civilian life. In some countries governments persecute their own citizens, setting justice and law on one side. Minorities are harassed, dissidents imprisoned or worse, and opposition silenced.

Our prayer for peace and justice is both a prayer of hope for the future and statement of faith about the present. That which we long for, and which we believe to be possible in the future, we try to attain here and now.

✳ *Pray for countries where people's lives are disrupted by terrorism or threatened by oppression.*

Monday October 8   Luke 1.68–79

A SONG OF HOPE

Before and during the birth of Jesus, there was a good deal of singing. Mary sang her glorious *Magnificat*, the angels sang over the fields of Bethlehem and, in today's reading, Zechariah sang a song of greeting to his son, John. John was to be the forerunner of Jesus, the 'Prophet of the Highest', the one who came 'to prepare his way' (verse 76).

John is thought of as the last of the prophets – that long line of men who had kept hope alive, even in the darkest times and places. It was an austere vocation to which John was to be called, and one that he would finally pay for with his life. John was born in the grey light that preceded the dawn. The one whom he would proclaim was to be 'the morning sun from heaven' (verse 78).

Wherever Jesus comes, he brings the light of his presence. All of us, as Christians, are called to witness to the possibility of Christ's coming in every human situation. There is no time in which he does not come to us and no place beyond his reach.

In our day-to-day living, in our own lives and in sharing the lives of other people, there is always hope, always the assurance of Christ's presence. That is why there were songs at his coming and there have been songs ever since.

✳ *Lord, may we look with joy for your coming in every human situation.*

Tuesday October 9   Luke 24.13–32
THE RESURRECTION HOPE

The travellers on the road to Emmaus were walking away from a situation that had left them devastated. They had witnessed a terrible cruelty and so many of their hopes had died with the death of Jesus. The world was a place of confusion, rumour and uncertainty. Three things changed their despair to hope – not suddenly, but gradually:

● The first was the **presence of Jesus**. He was unrecognised, but he was there, making the journey with them, walking at their side.
● The second was **a growing understanding of the Scriptures**. As Jesus revealed its meaning to them, they came to understand more deeply what had happened.
● The third was **the breaking of bread**. In this loved and familiar action they, at last, recognised Jesus.

These are still the ways in which hope is restored to us: Christ's presence is with us; the promises of the Scriptures affirm God's loving purposes in our lives and assure us of the final triumph of divine live; and the Lord's Supper is the place where faith, hope and love are renewed and strengthened.

✳ *Lord, be the unseen traveller on all our journeys. May we hear your voice speaking to us in the Scriptures and share in your risen life in the Lord's Supper.*

Wednesday October 10   Luke 8.42b–48
PEACE THROUGH HEALING

Jesus' final words to the woman healed of her haemorrhage were, 'Go in peace'. Her illness had been a disturbing experience, one that induced in her a sense of shame and a desire to hide from others. Whatever the physical symptoms of her disease, they were matched by her soul's inner struggle.

Healing is always a process that involves heart and mind, as well as the body. Beyond the bodily wounds that others can see, there lies an inner turmoil that we want to conceal from their gaze. Perhaps a sense of shame prompts our secrecy. We may feel guilt for our illness, believing it to be, in some way, our own fault. There may lie within us the memories of unforgiven sins, unresolved situations or painful failures.

Whatever we may wish to conceal from others, we can conceal none of these things from Christ. To touch him in faith and to open our lives to his healing power, is to deal with the deeper hurts of the heart, as well as those of the body. Without such healing in depth, we cannot know wholeness, and without wholeness we cannot be at peace with ourselves.

Today, let us reach out to Christ and ask for his healing power in our whole life.

✳ *Lord, when you pass by, may I not miss the opportunity for wholeness that you bring. In faith I touch you and ask that I may be whole and at peace.*

Thursday October 11   John 14.15–29
THE PEACE OF JESUS

Evelyn Waugh, in his novel *Brideshead Revisited*, describes a moment of parting as one of 'broken sentences'. There is always a feeling of incompleteness when we part from people. There are things that have been left unsaid, promises that have not been kept, plans unfulfilled, longings unsatisfied.

John 14–17 are poignant chapters which recall the words of Jesus to his disciples on the night when he parted from them. In the few hours that remained, he had much to say to them. Above all, he needed to reassure them that the future was secure, even though they were soon to see the world collapsing about their ears. Beyond the darkness, there was to be light; beyond loss, immeasurable gain.

As is appropriate at a time of parting, Jesus gave his disciples a gift – the gift of peace. Jesus alone holds the key that unlocks the door of the tomb of death and darkness. He sets us free from the power of the grave which destroys all our dreams and brings to an untimely end all our loves. He is the source of our peace. Even when we are faced with the most calamitous times of parting in our lives, Jesus assures us that nothing is taken away from us that will not be returned a hundred times over.

✳ *Lord, thank you for your parting gift. May peace be ours at every crossroads and every separating of the ways.*

THE PEACE OF THE SPIRIT

In these verses, the risen Christ greeted his disciples with the
traditional greeting of *shalom*, which is the Hebrew word for
peace. He then breathed his Holy Spirit into them, giving
them the awesome power to absolve human sin.

The image of the Spirit's coming that most readily springs
to our minds is that of Pentecost (see Acts 2.1–4). The mighty
wind, the tongues of fire, the reversal of the apostle's timidity
and fear, all seem dramatic evidence of the Spirit's presence.
However, his coming can also be as gentle as breathing. He
may come, not as a turbulent presence in a turbulent world,
but as the bringer of peace.

The two ways of Christ's coming are not at variance. The
rushing wind, the fire that ignites our passion, the tongues of
ecstasy which proclaim Christ, all serve the purpose of bringing peace into the world. A gospel that is able to absolve men
and women from their sins is a gospel that breaks down barriers and effects reconciliation between God and humankind,
and between people divided by enmity and suspicion.

✳ *Breathe through the heats of our desire*
　　Thy coolness and thy balm;
　Let sense be dumb, let flesh retire;
　Speak through the earthquake, wind, and fire,
　　O still small voice of calm!　　*John Greenleaf Whittier*

HOPE AND PEACE FOR ALL

The longing for peace is one that is shared by people of many
different persuasions and in all parts of the world. Yet the
world continues to be split by factions. Communities can be
torn apart by divisions, in some cases inherited from previous
generations. Ideologies compete with one another and deeply
held convictions divide people into opposing camps.

'Eyeball to eyeball' confrontations often marked the
relationship between Jews and Gentiles in the world of New
Testament times. But not always, for some Gentiles were
drawn towards the Jewish faith and all that it stood for. However, differences could smoulder and sometimes ignite into
fierce confrontations.

Paul believed that, in the cross, Christ had provided the
means of reconciling the two sharply divided cultures. The

broken, divided body of Jesus in his death is the means by
which enmities are reconciled and divisions healed. Thus the
cross is a sign of both peace and hope. Because it holds out
the possibility of bringing together the most hostile of adversaries, it means that we do not have to resign ourselves to
despair in the face of the world's divisions. Because there is a
way to peace, life can be lived in hope.

✳ *Lord, grant us your peace in our hearts that we may be
peacemakers in our daily lives.*

For group discussion and personal thought

As Christians our hope is for a future filled with peace. What
do this week's readings tell us about the way in which we can
attain this hope? How do we sustain the experience of an inner
peace when our lives are stressful, when we are anxious, or
when we are very busy?

Sunday October 14   Psalm 100.1–5; 30.1–5
REJOICING IN GOD

Psalm 100 describes how we are to approach God when we
come before him in worship. We are to come 'in gladness',
'with songs of exultation', entering his house 'with thanksgiving' and 'praise' (verses 2,4). So to enter God's presence is
to come, not unwillingly, but eagerly; not with fear, but with
confidence.

Eagerness and confidence arise from what we believe about
God. If we are uncertain of him and feel we cannot trust him,
then we will come to him reluctantly. If we believe that his
greatness, his glory and his eternal mystery conceal a nature
that is vengeful and hostile to us, then we will come in fear.
Our thanksgiving is founded on our belief, and confirmed in
the experience of Israel and God's revelation in Christ, that
he is utterly to be trusted and that his nature is love.

It is that same conviction that makes it possible for us to
bear the darkness, believing that 'joy comes in the morning'
(Psalm 30.5). There will be experiences, when 'tears . . .
linger at nightfall' (verse 5), which will make thanksgiving
difficult. It is not easy to give thanks for pain and adversity.
However, belief in God's trustworthiness will sustain us. As

surely as tomorrow's sun will rise, joy will be given back to us.

✳ *Lord, may I live my life gratefully and trusting in your good purposes for all creation.*

Monday October 15   **Luke 17.11–19**

THE GRACE OF GRATITUDE

The failure of the nine lepers to return in order to show their gratitude for what had happened was a failure at two levels:

- First, at the level of **human instinct**. It should have been natural for them to respond to something as liberating as what Christ had done for them. The ordinary human reaction would be one of gratitude.
- Secondly, at the level of **culture and religion**. They were Jews of whom Jesus might have expected some gesture of gratitude. Their Scriptures, their liturgy and their experience of God should have taught them the high priority of thanksgiving.

It was a Samaritan who returned to give thanks. In the eyes of some Jews he would have been someone from whom normal, decent human behaviour was not to be expected – a man without true religion, under no constraints to act in a religious way.

We must resist within ourselves any world-weariness or indifference which is put to shame by other people's spontaneous gestures of thanks. Our Christian faith has gratitude at its very heart. The blessings of heaven should never find us thankless and ungrateful.

✳ *Lord, may we never lose our sense of gratitude for all you have given us in our lives and through Christ.*

Tuesday October 16   **Luke 15.1–10**

THE JOY OF DISCOVERY

In these two parables, the finding of a lost sheep and a lost coin are likened to the finding of a lost person. Both parables are placed within the context of Christ's concern for social outcasts (verses 1–2).

The experience of being **lost** is always an unhappy one. When we lose our way in unfamiliar countryside we may lose all sense of direction. In a strange town, the streets and high buildings close in on us. There is no long-distance perspective to tell us that we are going the right way, so we find ourselves travelling in circles and coming back to the place where we began. 'Lostness' is an experience of disorientation, of uncertainty, sometimes of fear.

The lost sheep was found, and the shepherd rejoiced as he brought it back home to the flock. The lost coin rested in a hand where it was valued and cherished, and the owner looked at it with joy. There is always joy when Christ finds us. It is like a home-coming; our lives are no longer adrift and uncertain. We become part of a community that is given its strength and direction from the Christ who goes before us like the shepherd who leads the flock. We know our lives to be held in his hand. When Christ finds us, he looks at us with joy.

✳ *Lord, we thank you for the joy of coming home, of being found and of finding you.*

Wednesday October 17   John 15.5–17
JOYOUS UNION WITH CHRIST

The theme of union with Christ is one that recurs throughout the New Testament. Here it is described in the image of the vine and branches. Elsewhere, our union with him is compared to being a member, a part, of a body – a union in which we share Christ's death, burial and resurrection.

The Christian life is a journey in which we travel ever deeper into Christ and he enters more deeply into us. This journey, that cannot be hurried, follows the path of obedience and advances by the steps we take in prayer. It is a journey into love in which we realise how much love embraces us and what it means for us to love in response (verses 9–10).

Out of our union with Christ there comes a joy which reaches its completion in us (verse 11). This is not a momentary enthusiasm, a transient feeling of well-being or a brief interlude of happiness, but a state which survives the shadows and which emerges even from sorrow.

Joy is knowing Christ in us and our lives in Christ. It is a growing awareness of the destination towards which we travel – that fullness of Christ where there is no more pain, injustice or grief. It has no earthly equivalent.

✳ *Lord, through discipleship and prayer, may I grow in you and your joy grow in me.*

204

Thursday October 18   **John 16.16–24**

JOY OUT OF PAIN

The picture of the woman in labour (verse 21) is a powerful
one. Here is pain that has a basic purpose – that of bringing
a child into the world. It is pain that is quickly forgotten once
that purpose has been served and the child has been born. In
that sublime moment there is only joy.

It could be argued that not all our pain is like that. There
is pain that serves no purpose. There is also pain, either our
own or what we witness in other people, that is never forgotten. Pain like that demands faith if we are to bear it, believing
that good will come from it.

Jesus was speaking only hours before the ordeal of the
cross. The disciples were about to be plunged into grief, and
made to be witnesses of a pain that in no way resembled the
pains of labour. The cross would seem to be pain to no purpose
– a cruel ending to dreams and hopes and prayers. Yet, the
cross would change the world and the resurrection would
bring a joy unforeseen and boundless.

We must not lose heart when we cannot see the point of
what is happening to us. The cross points the way to a joy that
will one day come from the greatest grief.

✴ *Lord, may I trust you even in what seems meaningless, looking to your cross, and awaiting the joy of resurrection.*

Friday October 19   **Luke 10.1–7, 17–24**

THE JOY OF SHARING

In sending out the seventy-two (seventy in some versions),
Jesus was sharing the fruits of his mission with a wider group
of people. It was a mission that carried a message of peace
and cast out the powers of evil. The disciples returned from
this mission 'jubilant' (verse 17), and Jesus 'exulted' (verse
21), rejoicing in what had been achieved through them.

Since the beginning of his ministry, Jesus has called people
to share with him the task of spreading the news of the kingdom. First there were the twelve, beyond them the seventy-
two and, through the succeeding centuries, countless witnesses have followed in their footsteps.

As the story of Christian mission is recounted, there is evidence of the joy and power of the kingdom in people's lives.
In a torn world, the word of peace is being proclaimed, and
diseases that have long haunted people in some places are

now being cured. Even in those places where the Church has
been locked in conflict with tyranny and the evil abuse of
power, there are signs that love and goodness have prevailed.

We are all of us part of Christ's mission, and we are all
called to share in its joy.

✴ *Father, we thank you for the joy of witnessing to the risen
and ascended Lord.*

Saturday October 20   Philippians 1.1–6; 4.4–7
THANKS IN ALL THINGS

From his prison cell, Paul gave thanks to God for the people
to whom he was writing. Later, he told those same readers
that every part of life is to be embraced in 'prayer and petition
with thanksgiving' (4.6).

In prayer we give thanks for others – for the people who, in
various ways, share our lives. In their very familiarity they
merge into the landscape of our daily lives. We forget how
much we owe to them and the contribution that they make to
our happiness. In his prison experience, Paul had cause to
be deeply aware of his debt to the Philippians (see 4.10). It
sometimes takes extraordinary circumstances to remind us of
how much we owe to others.

Thanksgiving also plays its part in the way we see the
world. The very fact that we have to offer prayers and pet-
itions is a sign of the world's imperfection. Our awareness of
its divisions and its pain can make us resentful of the world
or deeply pessimistic about its prospects. Paul counsels us to
offer all our prayers in a spirit of thanksgiving, one that looks
at the world with hope and compassion.

Living gratefully is to live acceptingly with all things.

✴ *Lord, thank you for the people who share my life, returning
love for love; thank you that, in all our circumstances, we
are held in your eternal love to us all.*

For group discussion and personal thought
What is 'true joy' (see **October 17**)? What are the chief sources
of joy in our lives? How do we express our gratitude for them?

BUILDING IN FAITH
Selections from Ezra; Nehemiah; Haggai

Notes by the Revd Howard Rady, BA

Howard Rady is minister of Christchurch United Reformed Church at Walton-on-the-Hill, Surrey, England. He has previously served at churches in North London, and is a retired teacher and headmaster.

The notes in this section are based on the Revised Standard Version.

The books of **Ezra**, **Nehemiah**, and **Haggai** belong together. The first two were originally one integrated history designed to be read as a sequel to the events recorded in **1, 2 Chronicles** – hence their position in the Old Testament. Then, in **Haggai**, we hear the living voice of one of the prophets in this crucial period of Israel's spiritual development.

The story that unfolds in these books tells how some Jews began to return to the ruined city of Jerusalem about seventy years after they had been forced to leave it (see 2 Chronicles 36.17–21). There is plenty of drama as, first the temple, and then the city walls are rebuilt under the leadership of these three men of vision.

This part of Jewish history is essentially about the triumph of faith over adversity and so this section of readings has much to say to today's Church. All Christians who are anxious to see the building up of God's people will find help in these books.

Suggestions for further reading

Ezra, Nehemiah and Esther by J G McConville, Daily Study Bible (Saint Andrew Press)
Ezra and Nehemiah by Derek Kidner, Old Testament Commentaries (Inter-Varsity Press)

Sunday October 21   **Ezra 1.1–11**

What prompted Cyrus to take such a far-reaching course of action? If we accept the inscription on the 'Cyrus cylinder' (now in the British Museum), Cyrus wished to show respect

to the deities of conquered peoples by permitting the reno-
vation of their holy places. And in any case, such a popular
move was bound to reduce the dangers of revolt among his
subjects. But, whatever the motivation, there is no doubt that
the Jews believed that it was God who had moved Cyrus to
make his remarkable proclamation. Indeed, this is one of the
constant themes of the Bible – that, without depriving individuals of their power to choose, God was able to use their
choices to forward his own purposes.

How many of the exiles welcomed the relaxing of their 'cap-
tivity' when it came? No doubt many had been praying fer-
vently for it, yet not all of these were 'moved' to return when
the opportunity arose. Age and infirmity would have excluded
a proportion, and no doubt there was a limit to the size of
the party permitted to undertake the journey. But how many
found it more comfortable to remain where they were and
leave the hard work to others?

It is sometimes easier to give generously to a noble cause
than to take part! And sometimes it is easier to sing about
being a pilgrim than to be one!

Prayer to use during the Week of Prayer for World Peace – One World Week (October 21–28)

*Lord God, you have created us to share the blessings
of one world. Yet often we destroy the precious
resources of the earth by living as if no one else mattered. Save us from this foolishness and make us
realise just how much we depend on each other. In this
way may harmony grow between peoples and nations,
and the search for peace be pursued in sincerity and
truth. We ask this in the name of the One who is our
peace – Jesus Christ our Lord.*

Monday October 22

It is sad how many worthwhile projects undertaken by Christians come to nothing. Sometimes the vision fades; sometimes
the necessary dedication is lacking; and sometimes there is
simply insufficient planning and attention to worship.

▶ Read **Ezra 3.1–13**.

The returned exiles' sense of priorities and their attention to practical detail is an object lesson to all who would work for God.

- They established daily worship as soon as it was feasible.
- They made no attempt to exploit the services of the craftsmen who had travelled with them and saw they were properly rewarded for their work.
- They traded fairly with the timber-producing nation of Lebanon.
- They made sure all the work was carefully supervised.
- They knew when to cease working and give time to celebration
- They were not deterred by the knowledge that there were many who had known the first temple and did not share their enthusiasm for the new building.

* *The altar was a reminder of God's presence and a visible symbol of his promises to Israel. How significant are religious symbols to our faith today?*

Tuesday October 23   Ezra 4.1–16

This reading can be very confusing unless we realise that, beginning at verse 6, the writer gives a 'flash forward' to the reigns of two future kings – a preview that lasts until the end of verse 23. This was to show that the harassment of the Jews was not for a limited period but lasted for some hundred years.

Why were the Jewish leaders so uncompromising in their attitude towards the help offered by those who claimed to worship the same God? These would-be helpers were the descendants of displaced persons who had been settled by the king of Assyria in and around Samaria over one and a half centuries earlier. A racially mixed people, these 'Samaritans' had received a rudimentary instruction in 'the law of the god of the land', but they had also continued 'to serve their own gods' (see 2 Kings 17.24–34). As such, their religious outlook was totally out of keeping with the Jewish idea of one God.

In some parts of the world today, 'inter-faith services' occasionally take place. Some Christians consider that such acts of worship compromise their witness to the uniqueness of Christ. Others believe this attitude actually displays a lack of confidence in the Christian message. Both viewpoints are worth thinking about.

* *How confident am I that Jesus is 'the way, and the truth, and the life' (John 14.6)?*

Wednesday October 24

The letter, written by Rehum and his associates about the rebuilding of the walls and foundations of Jerusalem, in yesterday's reading (see Ezra 4.11–16) had been deliberately intended to play upon the Persian fears of rebellion. Like other poison–pen letters, it was selective in its use of the facts.

▶ Now read **Ezra 4.17–24**.

Although a knowledge of the past has a part to play in assessing any current situation, it is never wise to rely too heavily on 'the verdict of history'. Not only may facts have been used selectively, but it is also dangerous to view the present almost solely in terms of the past. For this presupposes that history must somehow always repeat itself and does not allow sufficiently for the possibility of changed attitudes and responses.

The 'flash forward' to the reign of Artaxerxes ends at verse 23. The story then returns to a period of some sixteen years during which no substantial work was done on the temple. The fear of harassment by the local population was uppermost in the builders' minds and prevented them from getting on with the work.

✴ *Pray for historians and those who interpret history; that they may always seek the truth in as far as it can be discovered by their research.*

Thursday October 25

Faced with persistent set-backs, most of us begin to lose heart and often look for new outlets for our energies. This is what happened to the temple builders in Jerusalem. Confronted by a determined opposition, they lost interest in building a house for God and began to build houses for themselves!

▶ Read **Haggai 1.1–15**.

The inertia that springs out of disappointed hopes is all too common in church life. 'It's been tried before and doesn't work' may often sound like realism, but frequently it is the cry of Christians suffering from a loss of nerve. Haggai's call to the people of his day could hardly have been more direct. He said to them:

● You are too cosy in your well-furnished houses to finish the job you came to do.

210

- Because you have neglected the primary task, your whole way of life is blighted.
- A ruined house of God is a sure sign that you are not putting first things first.

Haggai's over-simplified connection between obedience and prosperity needs the correction of Matthew 5.45b. Even so, in the long run, spiritual attitudes are bound to affect the health and efficiency of any community.

* *My God, my Father, make me strong,*
   When tasks of life seem hard and long.   *Frederick Mann*

Friday October 26

It is always sad to see a noble place of worship being pulled down for redevelopment while its congregation has to re-establish itself in some lesser building in a side-street. At such times we may even catch ourselves thinking that the scaling down of the architecture somehow diminishes the greatness of God! How easily we forget that the true splendour of any sanctuary does not depend on its externals but on the self-offering of those who worship there!

▶ Read **Haggai 2.1–9**.

The reduced scale of the new temple that was being built affected the enthusiasm of some of the builders. To combat their mood of pessimism, Haggai reminded the people and their leaders of the marvel of the exodus from Egypt. What God had done then, he could do again. His new 'earth-shaking' miracle would be the opening of the temple to the worship of Gentile nations.

Although this prophecy was not fulfilled literally, the vision has been partly realised in the universal Church. Meanwhile, we still await the fullness of the people of God as visualised by Haggai (see Revelation 7.9–11).

* *Let every kindred, every tribe*
   On this terrestrial ball,
   To him all majesty ascribe,
   And crown him Lord of all.   *Edward Perronet*

Saturday October 27   Haggai 2.10–23

If you put a rotten apple in a box of sound apples, some of the good ones will soon go bad. The good fruit will not change the

211

bad fruit. Corruption is contagious in a way that goodness is not. This was the thought that lay behind Haggai's questions to the priests about ceremonial holiness and uncleanness. Goodness is not automatically infectious.

It is one of the continuing errors of some educationalists that they suppose that beautiful surroundings produce beautiful characters. Surround children, they say, with beauty and truth and they will grow up into good people. But goodness is not acquired solely through good external agencies. The disposition of the heart has to be changed – there has to be a definite hungering and thirsting after goodness.

This was precisely what Haggai was calling for through the reiterated phrase 'from this day onward' (verses 15, 18–19). He wanted the people to begin living as those who had just laid the foundation of a building dedicated to the glory of God. Only those committed to living as God's people could be truly good.

❋ *O Jesus Christ, grow thou in me,*
   And all things else recede;
  My heart be daily nearer thee,
    From sin be daily freed.   *Johann C Lavater*

For group discussion and personal thought

Read and study **Haggai 1.1–15**. What difficulties did the people of Judah have to face in rebuilding the temple on their return from exile? The temple symbolised God's presence. How does the Church symbolise God's presence today? In what ways does the Church need 'rebuilding', and what hinders this from happening?

Sunday October 28   Ezra 5.3–5; 6.1–12

The stirring words of Haggai – and another prophet, Zechariah – had helped the builders overcome their fear of reprisal. Then a different kind of threat arose – that of officialdom. Questions were asked, reports written, documents passed between departments and time-consuming searches made. In some ways the resulting sense of frustration was worse than when the builders had been targets of open hostility.

It is one of the facts of present-day church life that much

time is spent in dealing with official bodies. In many parts of the world, buildings can only be erected or altered with planning consent. Sometimes processions cannot be held without police permission. And, where churches are in receipt of grants towards social work, there are numerous forms to be completed annually. No wonder church officers are over-burdened and congregations feel unnecessarily hindered.

Doing things 'decently and in order' (1 Corinthians 14.40) is nevertheless part of Christian stewardship. Moreover, it was because of an unknown scribe's 'memorandum' (verse 2, NEB) that the builders were eventually able to proceed unmolested.

✱ *Pray for those who work in the service of your country, that they may be fair and honest in all they do. Pray, too, for those who work in the service of the Church, that they may be efficient, patient and courteous.*

Monday October 29   Ezra 6.13–22

The temple was completed four and a half years after Haggai's first call to action – a truly magnificent achievement. The dedication festival that followed was undoubtedly a joyous time and, as far as we can tell, free from excessive self-con-gratulation. Too often similar occasions are marred by those who, as one cynic has remarked, 'are willing to give God the glory provided they get the credit'. If there was nothing like that at the dedication festival it was because the central act of worship was made on behalf of the **whole** of Israel (verse 17). The focus of attention was thus directed away from the returned exiles towards those who were unable to join with them in worship. Countless Israelites, scattered throughout the Middle East, had longed for the privilege now granted to the builders.

True worship always involves a sense of privilege and the recognition that the praise we offer is on behalf of others pre-vented from being with us. Indeed, at its best, worship is an invitation to the whole of the created world to join in the worship offered by the heavenly host:

✱ *'Therefore with angels and archangels, and with all the company of heaven, we laud and magnify thy glorious name; evermore praising thee, and saying, Holy, holy, holy, Lord God of hosts, heaven and earth are full of thy glory.'*
(from the 'Sursum Corda')

At last we come to the man after whom the book is named.
And from now on it is Ezra who dominates this part of the
story. Others have undoubtedly played an honourable part in
the restoration of the religious life of the returned exiles, but
it is Ezra who most interested the compilers of the book. He
is introduced as someone possessing a threefold authority:

- He had an impressive pedigree and religious background
  (verses 1–6).
- He had an unquestioned knowledge of all the intricacies of
  Jewish religious law (verse 6).
- He knew something of the secret of spiritual power – the
  hand of God was upon him (see verses 6, 9).

There can be no doubt that Ezra used his authority to
redirect the religious enthusiasm of the restored community.
He recognised that zeal for the temple and its worship were
insufficient in themselves; instruction in the ways of God was
also needed. Thus it was largely through him that the Jewish
nation became 'a people of the book'. However, it is also possible
to argue that the excessive legalism of later generations owed
a great deal to Ezra's devotion to the letter of the law.

✳ *Lord, I have set my heart to study the teaching of the Bible.
As I discover your will for me, may I do it.*

Wednesday October 31

It seems likely that Ezra had been called upon to advise Artaxerxes on ways of stabilising the Jewish community in Jerusalem. If so, he was probably the one who advocated the
sending of a commision to reassert the proper place of the law
among the settlers. In the event, he was given the task of
implementing just such a policy (see Ezra 7.14).

▶ Read **Ezra 8.15–23**.

During the period of exile in Babylon, those classed as
Levites and temple servants had not been subordinated to the
priests. Thus, when the call to return to Jerusalem came,
perhaps they were reluctant to take up the rigid discipline of
temple worship which contrasted with their softer and more
prosperous life in Babylon. They were not numbered among
those who volunteered to return to Jerusalem with Ezra.
Unfortunately, their story is a familiar one in many churches,
when those with the necessary training and skill opt out of
the work for which they are ideally suited.

Ezra's reluctance to ask for military protection (verse 22) raises the question of whether he was acting in a foolhardy fashion. When Hudson Taylor was sailing for China in 1853 he decided he had faith enough not to purchase a lifebelt. Then he became aware that he was collecting various floatable objects in his cabin! Later he decided that to use the means provided does not deny faith.

✳ *Lord, help me to serve you without reserve and with no delay.*

Thursday November 1

The journey from Babylon to Jerusalem took four months, an indication of the scale of the undertaking. It must have been with considerable joy that Ezra and his companions celebrated their safe arrival and handed over the commissions (document) and treasures they had brought with them (see Ezra 8.31–36). But almost at once Ezra was faced with a critical problem:

▶ Read **Ezra 9.1–5**.

Ezra was determined to ensure the continued existence of the returned exiles as a distinct people. This, however, was not so much an attempt to preserve the identity of the race as the purity of the Jewish religion. Syncretism – mixing of religions – of any sort would surely damage the people's witness to the uniqueness of Israel's God. This had to be resisted at all costs.

▶ Read **Ezra 10.1–12**.

These verses make unhappy reading; but, as far as Ezra was concerned, desperate times needed desperate remedies. Could anything else have been done? Paul's answer to the problem of mixed marriages was different. He believed that even when only one partner in a marriage had become a Christian, there was no need to dissolve the bond. By preserving the marriage, it might be possible to win the unbelieving partner to faith. (See 1 Corinthians 7.12–16.)

✳ *Pray for those who are experiencing tensions within their marriage.*

Friday November 2

The temple had been rededicated and Ezra had begun his task

of making the restored community 'a people of the book'. But the walls and gates of Jerusalem were still in ruins. To many this was an affront to God and also left the community vulnerable to attack from hostile neighbours. A new building initiative was required, but who would undertake it? The old spirit of inertia was once more affecting the returned exiles.

▶ Now read **Nehemiah 1.1–11**.

Nehemiah, soon to be seen as the dynamic man of action, is shown here as essentially a man of prayer. This was the secret of his venturing faith. He did not rely upon his own wisdom or strength of purpose, but upon God. The actual prayer he used is instructive:

- First, he recalled some of the great attributes of God.
- Next, he identified himself with the sins of the people.
- Then, he claimed the blessings that follow true repentance.
- Finally, he accepted that he himself might be instrumental in answering his own prayer.

If looking into our own lives is a necessary part of repentance, then looking back to what God has already done and promised is part of faith.

✳ *Except the house be built by thee*
 In vain the builders' toil must be;
 O strengthen our infirmity! *Henry C Shuttleworth*

Saturday November 3 Nehemiah 2.1–10

It is a wonderful thing to find oneself the right person in the right place at the right time. It must have seemed to Nehemiah that everything in his past life had been preparing him for his critical meeting with the king. Nevertheless, he still had to choose the right words when the split-second opportunity arose. If ever he needed the wisdom of God, it was at this moment. There was only time for an 'arrow' prayer (verse 4) before he gave his reply – but it was enough.

We should never think of 'arrow' prayers as a substitute for the regular times we set aside for private devotion. Rather, they are the cries of those who already have an established relationship with God. But need we reserve these brief, simple times of turning to God for emergencies only? The seventeenth-century monk, Brother Lawrence, urged Christians to become aware of the presence of God by continually conversing with him. This was probably what Paul meant when he recommended his readers to 'pray constantly' (see 1 Thessalonians 5.17).

> ✻ *Prayer is the burden of a sigh,*
> *The falling of a tear,*
> *The upward glancing of an eye*
> *When none but God is near.*   James Montgomery

For group discussion and personal thought

Read **Ezra 7.6–10**. In what ways do you find it difficult to study and understand the Bible? Consider what would help you to understand the teaching of the Bible more clearly and so enable you to put it into practice. What opportunities do you have to share your knowledge of the Bible with others?

Sunday November 4   **Nehemiah 2.11–20**

Nehemiah was a man of faith and prayer, but this did not excuse him from hard thinking and detailed planning. His reconnaisance of the walls was a necessary preliminary to formulating his plans – but why go by night? In this way he drew the minimum of attention to himself and could be one step ahead of those who would soon be saying, 'It can't be done.'

Recent archaeological work suggests that Nehemiah's plan was not to repair all that remained of the old wall – far too great a task – but to reconstruct a shorter line of defence. It was vital to secure Jerusalem's borders without overburdening those willing to help.

An experienced Christian leader said: 'Pray as if everything depended upon God; plan as if everything depended on you.' Nehemiah would have agreed. The visiting preacher at a special service arrived an hour late and only two minutes before he was due to speak. He claimed that God had got him to the church on time. Later, it transpired that he had spent an hour looking for the venue because he had not troubled to enquire its location beforehand! Nehemiah was careful not to leave anything to chance!

✻ *'Faith is never fanatical . . . never careless . . . and therefore is cautious in its obedience.' (George C Morgan)*

217

Monday November 5   **Nehemiah 4.1–14**

The restored Jewish community was surrounded by various
racial groups who had vested interests in preventing Nehemiah's rebuilding programme from going forward. Among
these the Samaritans were dominant. They were the descendants of various peoples who had been resettled round Samaria
and Jerusalem over the previous 250 years. To some extent
they were still seeking a national identity and envious of the
sense of continuity the Jews had with their past. Sanballat,
for his part, was fiercely patriotic and saw the new settlers as
interlopers. He tried various tactics to drive them out:

● First, he tried ridicule, a powerful weapon when the mock-
  ing words come near to expressing the truth.
● Then, he resorted to 'putting the frighteners' on the builders
  and their labourers. Men carrying loads of debris are easy
  targets for attack, so it was hardly surprising that some of
  the workers began to desert.

Nehemiah's readiness to try to remedy the problem as
quickly as possible reminds us how vital it is not to leave any
church worker exposed to unjust criticism. Nor should any
Christian be left to feel more isolated than is absolutely necessary.

✳ *Help us to help each other, Lord,*
     Each other's cross to bear,
   Let each his friendly aid afford,
   And feel his brother's care.   *Charles Wesley*

Tuesday November 6   **Nehemiah 5.1–13**

Although today's reading interrupts the story of the rebuilding, it is not a digression. Perhaps it illustrates the sacrifices
made by some of the builders by telling us what happened
to them. In particular we are referred to the plight of the
smallholders who neglected their fields in order to do building
work. The inevitable happened. In order to keep going, some
mortgaged their title-deeds, while others resorted to money-
lenders or sold their children into slavery. It was an appalling
situation.

Nehemiah's solution was to face the problem head on and
shame the 'profiteers' into treating their compatriots as true
brothers. But just in case some were tempted to go back on
their word, he applied a solemn religious sanction (verses
12–13). On the surface, one per cent interest (verse 11) does

not seem exhorbitant by any standards, but this may well have been the monthly amount – a very different matter.

Whenever a group of Christians is called upon to make sacrifices in order to forward the work of the kingdom, it is right that the burden should be spread as evenly as possible. No one should stand idly by while another's livelihood or health is severely jeopardised.

✳ *Pray for those who run into debt either through lack of forethought or the lure of easy credit. Pray that banks and finance houses may act responsibly and caringly.*

Wednesday November 7

Sanballat was persistent in his attempts to prevent the completion of the walls. In today's reading we shall read about two more of his ploys.

▶ First read **Nehemiah 6.1–4**.

Why did such a responsible person as Nehemiah reject the invitation to talk things over? No doubt the siting of the proposed meeting at some distance from Jerusalem made him highly suspicious. But in any case, Nehemiah would never allow anything to deflect him from his primary purpose. Such resolve was the secret of his success; it is the person with no sense of priorities who gets nowhere.

▶ Now read **Nehemiah 6.5–9**.

The crude tactic of the 'open letter' – perhaps written on a piece of pottery – was an attempt to get Nehemiah discredited among both his followers and the Persian authorities. In this way Sanballat still hoped to force him to come to the meeting. Open allegations sent in this way are not how slander and libel are spread nowadays, but the sinister practice continues just the same. Rumours are 'leaked'; reputations smeared; inaccuracies multiplied – often under the guise of investigative journalism. In most circumstances the best defence is a clear conscience and firm denial.

▶ Finally, read **Nehemiah 6.15–16**.

✳ *Lord, help me to finish the work you have given me to do.*

Thursday November 8   Nehemiah 7.73 to 8.8

In most countries today it is possible to pass on information to large groups of people very quickly. For example, through newspapers, radios and television, a whole population is able to receive the same piece of information at the same time. These means of mass communication were not available during Ezra's time. His method to ensure that everyone heard and understood God's laws was different. He had a 'read-in'.

Men, women and older children (those who could hear with understanding' – verse 2) were assembled and the whole of the law of Moses was read to them. To ensure that the more difficult passages were clearly understood, Ezra paused every so often to allow time for the Levites to explain the meaning of what was being read to smaller groups of people (verses 7–8). The whole event was wonderfully organised and set within the context of worship.

How important it is to **understand** God's word! An elderly lady, recently widowed, turned for comfort to a Bible she had been given years before. But she had no idea how to use it and soon became confused. Then, a visiting minister discovered her problem, provided her with a guided plan of reading and explanatory notes. Understanding began to dawn and with it a new sense of peace came to her.

✳ *Pray for those who help others to understand the Bible, including the IBRA.*

Friday November 9

Nehemiah had been governor of Jerusalem for some twelve years. During that time he had probably been recalled to Babylon several times to report to the king. During one such absence, without his strong hand, the administration in Jerusalem had grown lax.

▶ Read **Nehemiah 13.4–9**.

Tobiah, though an Ammonite, had married into one of the leading Jewish families (See Nehemiah 6.18) and was also 'hand in glove' with the high priest Eliashib. Thus he was in a position to pull off an audacious coup. He obtained the exclusive use of one of the most sacred rooms in the temple – presumably as 'adviser on religious and cultural affairs' to the high priest! Nehemiah's fierce anger is a reminder that some aspects of religion are not negotiable.

▶ Now read **Nehemiah 13.10–14**.

If the priests were ready to pay a high price for good relations with Tobiah, many in the community wanted their religion on the cheap. People often do. But to under-fund the ministry is often a sign of a devaluing of the treasure of the gospel.

These two incidents are sometimes strangely linked in contemporary church life. It is, after all, not unknown for a congregation to let its premises to unworthy causes simply in order to meet its financial obligations to the ministry.

✳ *Lord, may we not misuse your house or your servants.*

Saturday November 10

A few years ago attempts were made in parliament and elsewhere to liberalise further the Sunday trading laws in Britain. Churches, trade unions and many private individuals opposed the proposed new legislation. Eventually the parliamentary bill was defeated. In the course of the national debate the bill's opponents were sometimes called 'sabbatarians' – those who demand the legal enforcement of Sunday as a day of worship and rest. However, most of the Christians involved were not concerned to impose the fourth commandment on others. They only wanted to ensure that freedom of worship was not eroded by the interests of commerce.

▶ Read **Nehemiah 13.15–22**.

Nehemiah's decisive action may appear strongly legalistic, but he also believed history was on his side. The reference in verse 18 is to Jeremiah's warnings against putting the selling of merchandise before the true welfare of the people (see Jeremiah 17.19–27). Not to make time in daily life to pause and ponder the greatness and love of God is perhaps the most obvious sign of a society drifting away from God. By keeping one day in seven special, we affect our attitude towards the other six.

✳ *The setting apart of the first day of the week is an essential part of the Christian's witness to the resurrection.*

For group discussion and personal thought

Consider the problems outlined in **Nehemiah 5.1–13** and **13.4–22**. What are the difficulties facing your society or church at the present time? How has your study of **Nehemiah** suggested ways in which these difficulties might be resolved?

PROVERBS

Notes by the Revd David M Owen, BA, BD, ThD

David Owen is minister of Reigate Park United Reformed Church in Surrey, England. He has also held pastorates in Bournemouth and South Wales.

The notes in this section are based on the New English Bible.

The book of **Proverbs** is a collection of wise sayings relating to many aspects of life. These sayings were mainly used in the instruction of the young, and impressed upon them the truism that a healthy individual and social life depended upon high standards in honesty and self-discipline.

The central theme of **Proverbs** is **wisdom**. In many verses it seems to say that God is Wisdom and Wisdom is God.

Although it is likely that Solomon wrote some of **Proverbs**, he did not write the entire collection as the opening verse implies. Rather, the book consists of sayings from many authors, written over a long period of time.

Suggestion for further reading

Proverbs by Kenneth T Aitken, Daily Study Bible (Saint Andrew Press)

Sunday November 11   **Proverbs 1.1–9**

Above the entrance of a college I attended as a youth was inscribed a timely reminder of an important truth: 'The fear of the Lord is the beginning of knowledge.' We may regard this statement from verse 7 as the objective of **Proverbs**. The writer begins with a varied list of virtues necessary for integrity and wholeness of character – wisdom, instruction, understanding, intelligence, justice, righteousness, probity, shrewdness, knowledge, prudence, learning, skill. It is possible for these to be practised by people with little or no religious faith, but to 'fear God' is to set life on its proper course, and to put all other virtues into perspective.

To **fear God** does not mean to be afraid of him in the way that we might fear an accident or illness, or as primitive people stood in dread of their deity. Rather, it is to be in awe of him as One who is holy and all-glorious, but in whom we delight because of his faithfulness and love.

In **Proverbs**, wisdom is a general expression for knowledge of all that is good. It is the fool who says there is no God (see Psalm 14.1), whereas the wise person trusts in God and is open to every truth that he reveals.

✳ *Prayer for Remembrance Sunday*

Holy and Almighty God, lead the nations of the world in your ways of wisdom, peace and love.

Monday November 12

I recall as a schoolboy learning in English grammar about 'clauses of condition' – **if** we do this or that, **then** certain results will follow. In life, if we wish to achieve career success, then we must be diligent throughout its many stages of training and qualification. For example, behind the skill of a brain surgeon lies countless hours of dedicated toil and work experience. So, too, with spiritual achievement.

▶ Read **Proverbs 2.1–11**.

Notice how 'if' and 'then' occur in these verses. In this advice to a young man, the goal set before him is knowledge of God (verse 5). The idea of knowing God and understanding his ways appears many times in the Bible. Jeremiah saw understanding and knowledge of God as humankind's greatest boast (Jeremiah 9.23–24a), and Paul believed knowledge of God to be an essential mark of Christian discipleship (Colossians 1.10).

Wisdom is seen as the key to this attainment. If we heed it and treasure it above all other gain, then we shall acquire such knowledge. And what is more, wisdom itself is **given** by God (verse 6) – a gift which enables us to keep on the right path and is our joy and protector (verses 9–11).

✳   *Then, O my soul, if faithful now,*
    The crown of life awaits thy brow.   *William Wright*

Tuesday November 13   Proverbs 3.5–20

Some years ago wall plaques displaying Bible texts were a feature in people's homes. Two popular ones from today's reading were: 'Trust in the Lord with all thine heart' (verse

5a, AV) and 'In all thy ways acknowledge him, and he shall
direct thy paths' (verse 6, AV). It is impossible to say what
impact they had on the family and visitors to the home, but
their message was there for attention, not least by the young.
These two verses, calling us to trust in God as he guides us
through life, are among the loveliest in **Proverbs**.

To be wise to this teaching, and especially in the light of
Jesus' claim to be 'the way' (John 14.6), is to be wise indeed.
However, we must take care that even in this we remain spiri-
tually humble, as verse 7 suggests.

With our heightened wisdom we shall see that the material
side of life – our wealth and earnings (verse 9), silver and gold
(verse 14) – are directed in God's way and not used for selfish
ends. We know that life requires spiritual discipline and that
our reward for good living is infinitely more than worldly prosperity.

✱   *Whether losing, whether winning,*
     Trust in God, and do the right.   *Norman Macleod*

Wednesday November 14   Proverbs 6.6–11,
                                    20–21, 23–24

The common ant is a wise and enterprising little creature.
Ants live in colonies for which they work long and hard without a break or a supervisor to keep them at it. They help the
needy and injured, and busily store up food in the summer
season, mainly for the next generation, for their own lives are
quite short.

We, humans, often contrast with the ant, putting personal
wants above the welfare of others. We are slothful. Work is
sometimes a chore we do because we have to, and too often we
lack a sense of community service. So the ant can teach us a
lesson in industriousness and community living, the wisdom
of which is obvious but often forgotten.

But whatever truths we learn from the ant, no lessons compare with those 'home truths' we get from good parents whose
wise advice and sound judgements guide us like a light in the
dark and alert us to moral dangers.

In the Bible the 'heart' symbolises a person's whole personality and drive, and the centre of their moral and religious
life. So to take all good instruction to heart – which is what
the writer means in verse 21 – is to be truly wise.

✱ *Lord, make us diligent, wise and caring in all we do.*

Works of art are sometimes sold today for vast sums of money. In today's reading, we are invited by Wisdom herself to consider her inestimable worth. No jewels, fine gold or pure silver can match her, she has power, riches, honour and boundless wealth. Priceless and inexhaustible, she is however compassionate and generous, rewarding in kind those who love and search for her.

We are to think of Wisdom making herself available to those who wish to live by high moral standards. It is better that people possess her than material wealth, and follow her leading along the right paths than fall prey to evil influences.

Wisdom also asserts the important truth that good government depends on whether or not rulers possess her. In the difficult, far-reaching decisions that statesmen and politicians have to make it is not enough to possess facts and figures. They need wisdom for the timing and working out of their judgements.

The high claims made by Wisdom in today's reading become more meaningful to us when we think of God as supreme Wisdom, beyond human estimate, yet merciful and generous.

✳   *Everywhere his glory shineth;*
     God is wisdom, God is love.   *John Bowring*

In today's reading, in contrasting verses, Wisdom and Folly, each personalised, issue invitations to passers-by to a feast in their homes.

Wisdom's invitation (verses 1–6) comes after the building of her house, an indication that she is prepared to entertain regularly and graciously any who come to her. She is ready at all times to keep open house and provide lavish food and drink. Her guests are not the morally upright who need no further guidance, nor the deliberately evil who are too far gone to change; but they are the simple who lack understanding and can benefit from wisdom's instruction.

Folly's invitation (verses 13–18) contrasts sharply with Wisdom's in its brashness and impropriety. She sits at her door haughtily offering cheap and stolen pleasures to the unsuspecting and gullible. Little do they know how these can lead to their downfall and even death.

We must learn how to make the right choice. Wisdom or folly, rectitude or depravity, invite us in a variety of ways and we need to be alert to what is on offer.

✳ *'Be most careful then how you conduct yourselves, like sensible men, not like simpletons. Try to understand what the will of the Lord is.' (Ephesians 5.15,17b)*

Saturday November 17

▶ First read **Proverbs 23.22–25**.

It used to be customary for sons to enter their father's profession. Young people now have many more job opportunities and the freedom to choose their own careers, but there are other parental 'legacies' that ought to be remembered.

The **gift of life** itself – conception and birth – is the greatest of all miracles and provisions, and the reason for our deepest gratitude. We must not forget that a mother who has now grown old and feeble once made that miracle possible. In parts of Africa, old age is spoken of as 'the golden age', and regarded as an attainment that brings its own dignity.

When to the gift of life is added a **sound teaching** and **upbringing** – 'wisdom, instruction and understanding' (verse 23b) – then we know ourselves to be well-endowed.

▶ Now read **Proverbs 24.3–7**.

Jesus stressed the importance of good foundations in house building (see Matthew 7.24–27). He was, of course, illustrating life-building, with which **Proverbs** is so much concerned. To the wisdom of building well, we must add the supreme wisdom and the greatest strength of individuals and nations, as expressed in the psalmist's words:

✳ *Unless the Lord builds the house*
 its builders will have toiled in vain.   (Psalm 127.1)

For group discussion and personal thought
What are the differences between the wisdom of this world and the wisdom **Proverbs** speaks about? How can we obtain God's wisdom (see, for example, **Proverbs 9.10** and **James 1.5**)? In what ways are people tempted to be unwise, and how can they be helped to find true wisdom?

1, 2 THESSALONIANS

Notes by the Revd H Graham Fisher, BA

Graham Fisher is a Baptist minister living in Worthing, England. He has spent many years as a lecturer at colleges of further education.

The notes in this section are based on the New English Bible.

It seems that people today react to Bible teaching concerned with the return of Jesus in two different ways. They either disregard it, or else they dwell upon it almost to the point of obsession. Whatever our reaction is, we should not obscure the truth that the 'Day of the Lord' is an essential element of Christian teaching. It is clearly based on the teaching of Jesus himself (for example, see Luke 12.35–40).

The early Christians, including the apostle Paul, were convinced that the Day of the Lord was imminent. In his letters to the Christians at Thessalonica, Paul stresses that this cosmic event will bring terror and calamity to the godless, but deliverance and glory to every true believer. This message is equally valid for our generation.

Suggestions for further reading

The Letters to the Philippians, Colossians and Thessalonians by William Barclay, Daily Study Bible (Saint Andrew Press)
Epistles of Paul to the Thessalonians by Leon Morris, New Testament Commentaries (Inter-Varsity Press)

Sunday November 18   **1 Thessalonians 1.1–10**

The account of Paul's visit to Thessalonica in Acts 17.1–4 indicates the numbers of those affected by the gospel message. In today's reading, the apostle is more concerned with the quality of the response.

Faith, love and hope were created in a community which, for the first time, had heard the gospel. Solid evidence of those qualities had cheered the missionaries – faith expressed in action, love in laborious toil, and hope in fortitude (verse 3).

It is easy to agree with Paul that 'there are three things that last for ever: faith, hope and love' (1 Corinthians 13.13).

227

The acid test is whether these qualities are evident in actual living – action, hard work and perseverance. We see outstanding examples of faith, love and hope in the workers for famine or flood relief, in those who care tirelessly for the sick and handicapped, and in the remarkable courage of those who are confined in prisons and labour camps because of their beliefs. Living out the life of faith, hope and love is a costly business.

✷ *Go, labour on, spend and be spent,*
  Thy joy to do the Father's will.   *Horatius Bonar*

Monday November 19   1 Thessalonians 2.1–9

At Philippi, Paul and Silas had been humiliated, beaten and imprisoned. Miraculously, they had escaped, and, in the process, won their jailer and his family for Christ. (See Acts 16.19–34.)

In Thessalonica, the reception they received was more friendly. Many were affected by their ministry, including 'a great number of godfearing Gentiles and a good many influential women' (Acts 17.4). However, some people had accused Paul and his companions of seeking their own interests and of trying to 'curry favour' (verse 4). Paul replies that they have sought only to please God and to proclaim the good news.

For all who preach the gospel or engage in any kind of Christian service, there will come temptations to work for the wrong motives – for example: this piece of work may improve my standing with others . . . further my prospects of advancement . . . bring financial reward!

Paul suggests, in verse 4, the antidote to such base motives: 'we seek only the favour of God, who is continually testing our hearts'. If we are willing, the Holy Spirit will examine our motives and keep our work sincere.

✷ *Lord, keep me genuine in your service;*
  help me to seek only your glory.

Tuesday November 20   1 Thessalonians 2.10–16

One of the saddest aspects of the Christian story is that those who reject God's message often torment the messenger. During his service in Burma, Adoniram Judson, a nineteenth-century missionary, was made to endure prison and hardship, even though he wished only to proclaim Jesus and his love.

228

Despite persecution, the believers in Thessalonica had received the good news as the 'very word of God', and were seeking to share it. Regrettably, the work of the Church can easily fall from this high standard. The words of men and women may very quickly become more important and more influential than the word of God. What someone thinks or wants – sometimes expressed without much love or grace – may soon obscure our heavenly vision.

If our work for Jesus is to be truly effective, we must sometimes stop talking and listen to the 'still small voice'. This is the 'very word of God at work' (verse 13) – the Holy Spirit, who 'will guide (us) into all the truth' (John 16.13).

✳ *Lord, thy word abideth,*
And our footsteps guideth;
Who its truth believeth
Light and joy receiveth.   Henry W Baker

Wednesday November 21   1 Thessalonians 2.17 to 3.5

It is cheering to witness someone's delight in another's success. It may be the joy of parents at the graduation of their child, a teacher's pride in a student's high performance, or the happiness of a minister when a church member is accepted for missionary work. Such delight usually reflects a high degree of unselfish support on the part of the person who is delighted.

In the same way, when Paul speaks of his friends in Thessalonica as 'our glory and our joy' (verse 20), he reveals the warmth and intensity of his love. Certainly, they had done well, but it was largely because of his unselfish work on their behalf.

Everyone entering the service of Jesus Christ is called upon to nurture a 'pastoral heart'. The commission of Jesus to Simon Peter teaches this. Peter was to take care of the young and not-so-young, and help them grow in their faith (see John 21.15–17). The catch-phrase, 'living to make the other person great', has real meaning when true greatness is understood to be a growing friendship with Jesus.

✳ *Lord, help me to grow in love for those entrusted to my care.*

Thursday November 22   1 Thessalonians 3.6–13

Great waves of love flood today's reading – Paul's love for his friends and their love for him. The apostle also urges that their love should 'overflow towards one another and towards all' (verse 12).

The love-letters of an army chaplain and the lady he later married were published a couple of years ago. This minister and his wife told their story on breakfast-time television. Separated for long periods during the Second World War, they had written to each other every day – sometimes twice. Eventually, they had been able to marry, and now declared they were as much in love as ever!

Asked how this great love affair fitted into his vocation as a Christian minister, he said that his life's mission was to love everybody, to spread love wherever he went. Within this love for people of every race, class and kind, the love between his wife and himself was entirely natural.

Does my life overflow with love?

✴ *O fill me with thy fullness, Lord,*
Until my very heart o'erflow
In kindling thought and glowing word,
Thy love to tell, thy praise to show.   *F R Havergal*

Friday November 23   1 Thessalonians 4.1–12

We may wish to dissociate ourselves from part of this reading. Yes, we may say, it was necessary to address such words to the residents of a city like Thessalonica. Gross immorality was rife there, at a time when even the highest pagan ethic fell far short of the Jewish and Christian standard. Yet we must avoid adopting an attitude of moral superiority. In our own day, when promiscuity, infidelity and perversion are widespread, the Christian standard of purity (see especially Matthew 5.27–28) presents a challenge which many – even among believers – cannot accept.

Paul regards holiness as the antidote to impurity. The answer to lax morality is not a rigid puritanical stance, which, inevitably, is censorious and forbidding. It is a life made clean through the atoning work of Jesus, and filled with the love of God. A life suffused with the beauty of holiness has power to attract people from the sordidness of moral depravity to the purity of the splendour of God.

✴ *'Don't copy the behaviour and customs of this world, but be a new and different person with a fresh newness in all you do and think.' (Romans 12.2a, LB)*

The early Christians believed that Christ would soon return – probably in their own lifetime. They awaited the event in joyful anticipation, but some were troubled about those who had already died. Would they share the rapture of reunion with their Lord? Paul gives the confident assurance that they, too, will share the joys of a future life with Christ.

Many, today, do not believe in a future life. Yet, the gospel assures us of the life to come (see, for example, Luke 18.30 and 20.35; John 14.1–2). Paul has been urging his readers to practise greater love. This he regards as the way to attain the 'firm hearts' which will ensure a place in the heavenly kingdom (3.12–13).

The poet, Sir Walter Scott, wrote that 'love is heaven, and heaven is love'. Friendship with Jesus is an encounter with heaven as well as with love. Since 'nothing . . . can separate us from the love of God in Christ' (Romans 8.39), we may believe that the glimpse of heaven we gain in our fellowship with Jesus on earth will lead to the full vision of his eternal glory.

✳ *'No mere man has ever seen, heard or even imagined what wonderful things God has ready for those who love the Lord.' (1 Corinthians 2.9, LB)*

For group discussion and personal thought
Read **1 Thessalonians 2.1–9**. Paul said, 'We have never sought honour from men' (verse 6, NEB). Is this an impossible ideal? How many Christians can honestly say this in regard to their work for the Lord? Can **we**? How can we progress towards the perfect state of seeking honour from God alone?

In the prophetic books of the Old Testament, we find a number of references to the Day of the Lord (for example, Joel 1.15). It is to be a terrible day for those who do not fear God, but for those who love him, it will be a day of deliverance and rejoicing (Malachi 4.1–2).

Paul takes up the idea, leaving no doubt that there will be a time of reckoning when the bad and good of this life will receive their just reward. Jesus taught that this Day will come suddenly and unexpectedly (see Luke 12.40), but Paul assures those who are 'children of light' that they have nothing to fear.

We, who live in the modern world, should take seriously the apostle's warning – and his assurance – regarding the future. In some parts of the world where cyclones are frequent, people must keep their houses in good repair and so be prepared for the test when the storm comes.

Similarly, if our lives are in good condition – with sins forgiven and spirits daily illuminated by Jesus, the light of the world – we, too, will be ready for that penetrating Day of the Lord.

✸ *Walk in the light; pursue thy way*
  Till faith be turned to sight.   *Bernard Barton*

Monday November 26   **1 Thessalonians 5.12–28**

Paul's concluding words in this letter amount to a counsel of perfection; the standard he sets is daunting! His instructions, faithfully followed, would create not only individual saints, but churches that would astonish the world! Yet this is the Christian ideal (Matthew 5.48). The most realistic thing we can do is to examine a few of these splendid precepts, and ask ourselves some pertinent questions. This should certainly bring us down to earth!

● **'You must live at peace among yourselves'** (verse 14). Are there any with whom I am not at peace? What should I do – pray for them; have a talk with them; make a suitable apology; discuss the situation with an understanding friend? I must realise that I may be wrong.
● **'Always aim at doing the best you can for each other and for all men'** (verse 15). Do I? Is there anyone I avoid, would rather not help, or even seek to hurt? How can I change my attitude? Maybe I can't, but God can.
● **'Pray continually; give thanks whatever happens'** (verses 17–18a). Do I talk with God about everything, and thank him always?

✸ *Lord, help me to make all my relationships more loving.*

Tuesday November 27   **2 Thessalonians 1.1–12**

In his second letter, Paul tells his friends at Thessalonica not to panic at the prospect of Christ's return (2.2) but to 'stand firm' (2.15) in the things they had already learnt. Today's reading is full of warm encouragement. The expected Day of the Lord should not terrify them, but provide an incentive towards the fulfilment of all their good purposes.

For every Christian, Paul's words are a stimulus to keep on striving for the goal of completeness and perfection (compare with Philippians 3.12–14). When we viewed the Olympic Games in 1988 on television, the value of perseverance was constantly seen. The races or contests were often won, not by those who at first seemed to do well, but by competitors who maintained their courage and effort to the very end.

For winners in the Games came the glory of a gold medal and the plaudits of a cheering stadium. For the victorious Christian, there will be the glory of 'the presence of the Lord' (verse 9), and the Master's 'Well done!' (Matthew 25.21).

* *And for thy sake to win renown,*
  And then to take my victor's crown,
  And at thy feet to cast it down;
     O Master, Lord, I come.   *Marianne Farningham*

Wednesday November 28   2 Thessalonians 2.1–12

There are some problems in this reading. For instance: what is meant by 'the man doomed to perdition' (verse 3), and who or what is 'the Restrainer' (verse 7)? Paul's words suggest that, just as the creative power of God 'became flesh' and 'came to dwell among us' (John 1.14), so the destructive power of evil will, at some time, take human form. 'The Restrainer' may have denoted the Roman empire, or even governments in general, which have the power to bridle the forces of evil, and so ward off complete chaos.

What is perfectly clear, both in history and in personal experience, is that an intense conflict between good and evil rages in the universe – a conflict centred in every human heart. Paul points the path to victory in this personal and cosmic struggle. For those who 'open their minds to love of the truth' (verse 10), there will be deliverance and salvation.

The closed mind is dangerous. We need to be guided by 'the Spirit of truth . . . into all truth' (John 16.13).

* *Holy Spirit, truth divine,*
  Dawn upon this soul of mine;
  Word of God, and inward light,
  Wake my spirit, clear my sight.   *Samuel Longfellow*

It was after his dream of the ladder, in the well-known Old Testament story (Genesis 28.10–22), that Jacob had a conversion experience. Although he had been well-informed about the God of Abraham and Isaac, it was only at this point that Jacob himself became aware of the presence of God.

Paul knew the necessity of such an experience in a person's Christian pilgrimage. The faith of others, however impressive and inspiring, must give place to a personal encounter with Jesus. Every believer should possess for his or her own self 'the splendour of our Lord Jesus Christ' (verse 14).

A seventeenth-century Christian, John Gratton, recounting his experience at a Quaker meeting, wrote: 'There was little said in that meeting, but I sat still in it and was bowed in spirit before the Lord, and felt him with me and with friends . . . I was sensible that they felt and tasted of the Lord's goodness, as at that time I did . . . and the presence of the Lord was in the midst of us.'

✳　*I see thee not, I hear thee not,*
　　Yet art thou oft with me;
　And earth hath ne'er so dear a spot
　　As where I meet with thee.　　　　　　　*Ray Palmer*

Human wisdom, with all its brilliance, has failed to rid the world of hatred, disease and misery. In the speeches of our politicians, millions of words are spoken – many of them undoubtedly good and true – but rarely are we led to consider the real answer to our problems.

Our faith teaches that only 'wisdom from above' (James 3.17) can so change the hearts of people and nations that love, health and abundance may be shared by everyone. For this reason, Paul is concerned that the word of the Lord should 'spread rapidly and triumph wherever it goes' (verse 1,LB). He cares deeply that his friends in Thessalonica, and, indeed, everywhere, should turn to God for the strength and direction that they need.

'May the Lord direct your hearts towards God's love and the steadfastness of Christ' (verse 5) is not a pious utterance. It indicates the way the Thessalonians must go for their own highest good. It is also the way our modern world must take, if it is to find true peace, freedom and happiness.

* O love of God, our strength and stay
  Through all the perils of our way;
  Eternal love, in thee we rest,
  For ever safe, for ever blest.   Horatius Bonar

Saturday December 1   2 Thessalonians 3.6–18

William Barclay, in a translation of this reading, used the term 'truants from work' for 'idlers'. Today, there are 'truants from work' – those who run away from the demands of making a contribution to the running of the world. Especially unacceptable are those who not only refuse to work, but also sponge on family and friends. This, of course, does not refer in any way to the unfortunate people who, through no fault of their own, cannot find work.

Christians, like other people, should contribute their knowledge and skills for the benefit of the community. Yet, more is expected of them. Jesus said, 'You can detect them by the way they act, just as you can identify a tree by its fruit' (Matthew 7.16, LB). In this case he was speaking of false teachers, but it is a test which may be suitably applied to every Christian. Although faith, love and prayer are essential, it is the **work** done by Christians that people see – the way that they act.

Certainly, we should do our share of the world's work. We should also take note of other New Testament words: 'Faith that doesn't show itself by good works is no faith at all – it is dead and useless' (James 2.17b, LB).

* Lord, help me to work well in everything I do.

For group discussion and personal thought
Read and study **1 Thessalonians 5.1–11**. There is clear scriptural authority for belief in the return of Christ – the Day of the Lord. In what various ways do you think this might happen? In our Christian teaching today, how should we present the return of Christ?

A REMINDER

● Don't forget to order your copy of **Notes on Bible Readings** for **1991!** You will find the year's scheme on page 256.

ISAIAH 1 – 35

Notes by the Revd David Cornick, MA, BD, PhD

David Cornick is Director of Training in the South-Western Province of the United Reformed Church in England. Previously he was Chaplain of Robinson College, Cambridge. He has also ministered as a University Chaplain in London and in two churches in Hertfordshire.

The notes in this section are based on the New International Version.

Isaiah's ministry as a prophet covered over forty years in Jerusalem, the capital of the southern kingdom of Judah. He was married to a 'prophetess' and had two sons (Isaiah 7.3; 8.3). Amos and Hosea were contemporaries of Isaiah, but they prophesied in the northern kingdom of Israel. Throughout Isaiah's lifetime, Judah was threatened by the expanding power of the Assyrian empire.

Isaiah lived through three distinct political crises: the pressure on Israel to join in the coalition against Assyria in 734/3 BC; the overthrow of the neighbouring kingdom of Israel in 722 BC; the eventual attack on Jerusalem which followed Hezekiah's attempts at rebellion in 701 BC.

Isaiah's ministry shows his instinctive awareness of God's power and holiness. The main points of his message are:

- God's people must behave righteously. Religion without morality is empty gesturing.
- God will inevitably triumph through a Davidic king, and then the peace of Jerusalem will embrace the whole world.

Suggestions for further reading

Isaiah I by John F A Sawyer, Daily Study Bible (Saint Andrew Press)
Isaiah 1–39 by Ronald E Clements, New Century Bible Commentaries (Marshall, Morgan & Scott)

Advent Sunday, December 2

Today, on Advent Sunday, hope is born again as we prepare once more to journey in imagination to Bethlehem, tracing

236

anew the history of God's love for humanity. For many this season with candles, Advent hymns and carol singing is the loveliest of the Christian year. As waiting and preparation give way to celebration, we must take care lest we forget the real meaning of Christ's coming.

▶ Read **Isaiah 1.10–20**.

The prophets of the eighth century BC all warned the people of God of the wide gap between their behaviour and their worship (for example, see Amos 5.21–24). Religion is dangerous when it hides God's holy demands behind a veil of ritual. Isaiah made the remarkable claim that the divorce between observance and intent had made Israel no better than her pagan neighbours in God's eyes. The Hebrew word translated 'detestable' (verse 13) was a technical word for pagan practices which were specifically forbidden in the law (see Leviticus 18.22).

God measures true worship, true holiness, true Advent celebration, by its moral and social results (verse 17).

✳ *O come, O come Immanuel,*
   And ransom captive Israel.   translated by John M Neale

Monday December 3   **Isaiah 2.1–5, 12–18**

Heaven and earth touched in the temple at Jerusalem, for it was thought to be God's 'earthly palace'. Jerusalem has therefore been the focus of devotion and hope for Jews through the centuries and in the midst of grievous tribulation. The political strife, division, and violence, which have surrounded Jerusalem recently, add more meaning to Isaiah's vision of a world at peace. He foresaw a day when the worship of God in his temple would have a place high above all else, and all the nations would walk in God's way (verse 2).

That beautiful vision of what could be contrasted sharply with the way things were; for Judah, in her fascination with wealth, prosperity and foreign ideologies, had forgotten God. However, God's holy majesty would sweep like a violent storm through a world caught up in its own selfish preoccupations (verses 12, 17).

Many years later, these thoughts were echoed in Mary's song of her God who 'has brought down rulers from their thrones but has lifted up the humble' (Luke 1.52). Isaiah's God worked a revolution in Mary's life; her Son turned the world upside down.

✱ *O come, thou rod of Jesse, free*
   Thine own from Satan's tyranny.   *tr John M Neale*

Tuesday December 4

▶ First read **Isaiah 3.1–5**.

What we experience can affect the way we think about God.
Oppression and the threat of invasion were everyday realities
for Isaiah, and so his graphic picture of the judgement of godless Judah echoed the dreadful misery of the aftermath of
invasion. It was Assyrian policy to remove key people from
conquered countries so that anarchy would render resistance
impossible.

▶ Now read **Isaiah 4.2–6**.

These verses – which may well have been written in the
fifth or fourth centuries BC, after the destruction of Jerusalem
– are full of pictures of hope for Jerusalem. The Messiah is
spoken of as a 'Branch' (verse 2). His presence there will transform the land. God's saving, liberating activity in the city will
be like a new exodus (compare verse 5 with Exodus 13.21–22),
providing his people with protection from all that assails
them.

Because God is the God we know, in Jesus Christ, salvation
and judgement are opposite sides of the same coin. Hope
springs continually from the heart of despair.

✱ *O come, thou day-spring, come and cheer*
   Our hearts by thine advent here.   *tr John M Neale*

Wednesday December 5   Isaiah 5.1–7

In these verses Isaiah invites us to share a remarkable piece
of street theatre. We are to imagine a singer, perhaps in a
busy Jerusalem market-place, suddenly capturing our attention with a song. It is about a friend's vineyard. As he sings
the verses 1b–2 in a sad, slow rhythm, we wonder if this is to
be a song of unrequited love, for we know other poems where
the vineyard is an image of a lover (for example, Song of Songs
8.12).

Successful vine cultivation is demanding and time-consuming, so we are not surprised to hear of the devotion and hard
work involved (verse 2), and we share the bewilderment and
sadness of a disappointing harvest. The singer now takes the

238

part of his friend and addresses us directly. He does what we would do if we had a vineyard that failed – he destroys it (verses 3–6).

The song finishes. The singer turns towards us and speaks the words of verse 7. We realise now that **we** are the vineyard, creators of bloodshed (*mishpak*) instead of justice (*mishpat*), and we pray:

✳   *O come, O come, thou Lord of might . . .*
    In cloud, and majesty, and awe.   tr John M Neale

Thursday December 6   Isaiah 6.1–8

During Uzziah's long and prosperous reign Isaiah had denounced the nation for its decadent complacency and faithlessness. His death in 736 BC signalled a change in Judah's political fortunes as the Assyrian threat became all too real. In a year of great danger for Judah, Isaiah came close to God who was working his purposes out through the history of the nations.

Isaiah was overwhelmed by God's holiness and majesty and struggled to convey something of the awesomeness of his experience. Unlike Ezekiel, who also had a vision of God (see Ezekiel 1.26–28), Isaiah made no attempt to describe God. His majesty was such that even the 'train of his robe' filled the temple (verse 1). The seraphs, although heavenly creatures, had to hide their eyes from his holiness (verse 2), and their song of praise made the very foundations of the temple shake.

Yet it was this God, holy and completely other, beyond our imaginings, who came to earth and took the form of a helpless baby born to a humble peasant girl. If we could but catch a glimpse of the magnitude of God's graciousness to us, our lives – like Isaiah's – will be turned about and we will pray:

✳   *O come, thou key of David, come,*
    And open wide our heavenly home.   tr John M Neale

Friday December 7

Ahaz came to power in 736 BC and tried to make an alliance with the Assyrians (see 2 Kings 16.7–9). Archaeological evidence shows that Judah was the only nation in that area not to join an anti-Assyrian coalition. In 733 BC that coalition laid siege to Jerusalem. Isaiah confronted Ahaz with a message from God which implied that there was no need for Ahaz to make an alliance with either Assyria or the coalition. God would be with Judah.

▶ Read **Isaiah 7.10–17**.

This seed of hope – the miracle of Immanuel, 'God with us' – was far greater than Isaiah or Ahaz could imagine. There is a thread of hope woven through the whole book of **Isaiah**. For us it has a precious significance which far transcends the days of Ahaz. It is a beautiful and suggestive blueprint for the life, ministry and death of Jesus. The boy 'Immanuel' became the 'man of sorrows . . . pierced for our transgressions' (Isaiah 53.3–5).

As we read this Advent prophecy we are reminded that Bethlehem leads to Calvary.

✳ *Rejoice! Rejoice! Immanuel*
    Shall come to thee, O Israel.   *tr John M Neale*

Saturday December 8   Isaiah 8.19 to 9.7

'I have come to tell you,' St Oswald said, 'that day follows night and not night the day.' Isaiah's vivid description of a people overwhelmed by the crisis of no light and no authority is followed by a promise of hope. However dark the night, Isaiah never left his listeners without hope for the dawn.

Darkness was considered to be the environment of the underworld (see Job 10.20–22 and Psalm 143.3). God's people were in a desperate plight – 'distressed and hungry', they were caught in a whirlpool of anger and fear, and felt as if they had been 'thrust into outer darkness' (verses 21–22). However, Isaiah led them on to eternal truth – darkness would be banished by 'a great light' (verse 2). He told them that anger would turn to celebration of God's goodness, oppression vanish, and all because of the birth of a Davidic prince who would unite his people in godly and holy living.

For Christians, verses 6–7 have become one of the best known messianic prophecies in the Old Testament. The qualities of the prince and the promise of his peaceful and righteous reign, reflect Christ and his kingdom. His light stretches beyond the boundaries of darkness and death.

✳ *To hail thy rise, thou better Sun,*
    The gathering nations come.   *John Morison*

For group discussion and personal thought

Read **Isaiah 7.14–16** and **9.6–7**. What did these prophecies mean to people in Isaiah's time; and what do they mean to us today, especially during this season of Advent? In what ways can we meaningfully claim that they were fulfilled in Jesus Christ?

2nd Sunday in Advent, December 9   Isaiah 11.1–10
Bible Sunday

Our vicious assault on the environment, often inspired by nothing other than sinful greed, threatens our planet with calamity. Acid rain, holes in the ozone layer, the destruction of the rain forests, the pollution of rivers and seas, are grim reminders of our mismanagement of creation.

Isaiah knew nothing of ecological problems. In his society greed manifested itself in oppression and injustice (see 1.21–23). His vision unites his world and ours, for he saw a future of harmony under the reign of a Davidic king – Jesse (verse 1) was David's father. In this reign, justice, righteousness and integrity would flow out from social relationships into the whole created universe.

Healing for a crippled society and a threatened, limping planet is given by God, not fashioned by rulers or political philosophies. The 'rod of Jesse' for us is Jesus – born at Bethlehem, killed at Calvary, risen, ascended and reigning. Hope for us and our planet lies by way of his kingdom.

✳ *A prayer for Bible Sunday.*

> *O may these heavenly pages be*
>   *My ever dear delight;*
> *And still new beauties may I see,*
>   *And still increasing light.*   *Anne Steele*

Monday December 10

It is the Christian's vocation to live in two kingdoms, for our lives are miraculously 'hidden with Christ in God' (Colossians 3.3). Time and eternity continually merge together, then seem to move apart. Isaiah had a vision which seems to leave behind the hope that an actual king will bring peace and justice to

Judah. The picture of an earthly dynasty is translated into a messianic dream.

▶ Read **Isaiah 11.11–12**.

This is nothing other than a new exodus, a reuniting of the scattered people of God from the four corners of the earth. Israel and Judah, the northern and southern kingdoms, will again be one nation. At last there will be freedom from oppression and harm. God's enemies will be defeated and songs of praise and thanksgiving will echo and re–echo.

▶ Now read **Isaiah 12.1–6**, which is a hymn of praise.

George Herbert once called Christians, 'secretaries of God's praise' – those who complete the circle of creation by giving to God the thanks which is his due. Many years after Isaiah hymned the dawn of liberation, an old, devout man took a baby boy in his arms and sang with joy that he had seen God's salvation come to the earth (Luke 2.25–35).

✳ *Lord, may our carols ring out at the birth of Christ our King.*

Tuesday December 11　　　　　　　　　**Isaiah 14.1–8, 12–17**

Rulers, empires and philosophies often overreach themselves and usurp the sovereignty of God. In today's reading Isaiah pursues his theme of hope in God's liberating, active love. His celebration of God's power in a 'taunt song' (starting in verse 4) about a – perhaps imaginary – fallen king of Babylon may seem odd and distasteful to us. However, we must recall that Isaiah was a man of his times who did not know of Christ's teaching of 'turning the other cheek' (Matthew 5.38–39).

It is encouraging to hear from Isaiah that it is God who rules the nations; that one day oppression will end and the sinful arrogance of worldliness will be put to naught, for often it seems otherwise.

At the centre of this song (verses 12–14) is a picture of the king as the fallen morning star. In Canaanite mythology the morning star tried to climb above all the stars and set up his throne on the mountain of the assembly of gods, thus depriving the highest god of his rulership of the world. Inevitably his pride preceded a fall!

For Christians, Jesus is the bright morning star of the new creation (Revelation 22.16), and it is by the power of his suffering – his vulnerable, never-ending love – that the will of the Father will prevail over the dark forces of oppression.

❋ Come, bright morning star, be light to us.

Wednesday December 12   Isaiah 20.1–6

The prophets sometimes proclaimed the word of God by
actions rather than words. Their behaviour was occasionally
arrestingly strange (for example, see Ezekiel 5.1–4 and
Jeremiah 13.1–11), symbolising the fate of God's people.
These acted parables were intended to shock people and force
them to think.

One of Isaiah's persistent themes was the folly of placing
trust in foreign powers and not in God (see 7.3–9) and
31.1–3). His nakedness was meant to reinforce that theme
(verses 2–4). Ashdod, Egypt and Ethiopia (Cush) were strong-
holds of power. However, Ashdod, the most northerly of the
Philistine cities, was captured by the Assyrians in 711 BC, and
Egypt and Ethiopia were invaded in 701 BC. The record of
Isaiah's action invites us to see the hand of God in the movement of history and reflect that true security is to be found
only in him, not in the fortunes of the nations.

Some place their trust in wealth and property, others in
their abilities and skills, yet others in political movements.
Isaiah would encourage us to 'hold to Christ, and for the rest
be totally uncommitted'.

❋ Lord, teach me how to trust you.

Thursday December 13   Isaiah 22.1–14

The defeat of the great revolt against the Assyrians climaxed
in 701 BC when Jerusalem under King Hezekiah surrendered
after a siege (see 2 Kings 18.13–16). We know from Assyrian
sources that Hezekiah had to hand over troops, royal prin-
cesses and musicians as well as large sums of money. Senna-
cherib, the Assyrian king, described Hezekiah as 'shut in like
a caged bird in his capital Jerusalem . . . I made it hard for
him to go out of the gate of his city'. However, the people of
Jerusalem, far from sorrowing, rejoiced and feasted, relieved
that the siege had ended (verses 12–13).

While all around were losing their heads, Isaiah kept his.
Alone, weeping, comfortless (verse 4), it was left to Isaiah to
see below the surface of things, for God's people had missed
the meaning of their experience. Theirs was the rejoicing of
those without hope, those who live just for the present. They

243

did not hear the Lord of history calling them to repentance — to remember his love and holiness.

Standing against the current is never easy. Tears and crosses lie that way. But, at the end of the path, crying turns to laughter and crosses become symbols of victory.

✳ *Pray for those who are called to stand alone.*

Friday December 14   Isaiah 24.1–13

Today's reading is the opening part of a section — chapters 24–27 — which is called the 'apocalypse of Isaiah'. They give a panoramic poetic vision of the end of the world. Although verse 1 says that 'the Lord is going to lay waste the earth', verses 5–6 suggest that it is in fact people who will wreck the earth — plundering and destroying it and laying it to waste. Actions always have consequences. Rejection of God, following reckless self-interest, and failure to cherish creation as God intended, will curse and ruin the earth.

However, when we read Isaiah's words of devastation and destruction, we must realise that there is, as always in **Isaiah**, a counterbalance of hope (see 25.6–9 and 27.6). Even the anguish of universal desolation is encompassed by the love of God, for only so can he 'wipe away the tears from all faces' (25.8).

During Advent, we meditate not only on the first coming of Christ, but also on his return in glory at the end of time. We remember that he is both Alpha and Omega, the source of all that is, and the goal to which all shall return. The future of our world — and of all worlds — is in his nail-torn hands, and we know that nothing can separate us from his love.

✳ *Saviour, take the power and glory,*
   Claim the kingdom for thine own . . .
   Alleluia! come, Lord, come!   Charles Wesley

Saturday December 15   Isaiah 25.1–9

The 'city' whose destruction was celebrated by Isaiah symbolises all the principalities and powers which have resisted God's will (see also 'Babylon' in Revelation 18.1–8). The devastation of the capital of 'worldliness' is an inevitable result of God's nature — his holiness is inseparable from his righteousness. Therefore, he has a special concern for the weak and dispossessed and will silence the songs of the ruthless (verses 4–5). God's justice is his love worked out in action, and is therefore always tempered by tender mercy.

In verses 6–9, the witness of the Old Testament stretches longingly towards Bethlehem, for God's love reaches out to gather the whole of humanity to a magnificent banquet on Mount Zion. Isaiah pictured God destroying the veils of mourning and gently wiping away the tears from uncovered faces. Vintage wine was poured out; the choicest and richest of foods were there for all. As Lady Julian of Norwich said, 'All shall be well, and all manner of thing shall be well' when God is all in all. And what are the tokens that this shall be so? They are but simple things – a loaf broken and wine poured out.

✳ *Bread of heaven! on thee I feed.*   *Josiah Conder*

For group discussion and personal thought

Where do many people place their hopes today? Are these lasting hopes? Read **Isaiah 25.1–9**, and think of times when verse 9 has been true in your experience. Why do we sometimes find it difficult to trust and hope in God? How can we share the gospel message of hope with those whose lives seem hopeless?

3rd Sunday in Advent, December 16   Isaiah 26.7–19

It is never easy to live a godly life. In this prayer Isaiah explores some of the tensions which always seem to be a part of the pilgrimage of faith. In verse 10 he claims that God is ignored by the vast majority of people in spite of the grace lavished upon them and the ample evidence of God's majesty and power. Like Isaiah, we sometimes long that it should be otherwise and even harbour thoughts of revenge (verse 11). But, as we stand under the shadow of the cross, we know that God can weave even rejection into the fabric of his loving purposes.

In the same way that Assyria ruled Judah for a time, other lords have ruled us too (verse 13). Christians have to live with loyalties divided between secular authorities and the God who is Lord of all. Part of the discipline of discipleship is to learn how to 'honour' God's name in our political and social lives.

As with God's people of old, failure is ever present with us.

However sophisticated our programmes and activities, our success is minimal in comparison with our task. We, too, have failed to give 'birth' – life – to the people of the world (verse 18). But, like Isaiah we have to realise that is God's work, not ours.

✳ *Read Isaiah 26.17–19 slowly, as a prayer.*

Monday December 17   Isaiah 29. 13–24

In God's economy the last are the first, the poor inherit the earth, and a widow's mite is worth more than a treasury full of gold. God has a wonderful way of exploding our cherished assumptions and turning our expectations upside down. In today's series of prophecies, each dealing with the lack of understanding of Judah's leaders, Isaiah invites us to share the topsy-turvy world of God's love.

Worship needs order and form or else it may become unhelpful anarchy. However, form can easily become mere formality. The first prophecy (verses 13–14) tells of the consequences of Israel's worship which had literally become lip-service. Because of this hypocrisy, the wise who sought liberation in political manoeuvres would be confounded by God's 'wonders'. This time God would reveal himself to his people not in liberation, but in defeat.

The foolishness of such human wisdom is the theme of the second prophecy in verses 15–16. God the creator knows every secret of the human mind (see also Psalm 139.1–4). To think that God can be ignored is real foolishness.

Those who love God, know that he **is**. One day, Isaiah exulted, the world will understand that God is God. The blind will see; the deaf will hear; the humble will rejoice!

✳ *Lord, overturn our complexity with your simple love.*

Tuesday December 18   Isaiah 32.1–8

The perfect State has always eluded political planners. Somehow a gap always appears between a theory or a dream and its translation into reality. The poem in today's reading owes much to Israel's teachers of wisdom such as the writers of the book of **Proverbs**. It is a dream of an ideal kingdom. Imperfect understanding and frail human limitations will be no more (verse 4) and those who are just and noble will be recognised and honoured.

Such dreaming would be easily dismissed were it not for Isaiah's vision of a king ruling in 'righteousness' – that is to say, aware of his obligation to God and to his subjects. Perhaps written at a time of social chaos or when Israel's government was unjust, these words would have comforted their hearers and given them hope. Things would not always be so – the Messiah would establish a true kingdom of righteousness.

Christians – those who acknowledge that the Messiah came as a carpenter's son, and who live in his kingdom – know that here is 'no lasting city' (Hebrews 13.14, RSV). Only in Christ's kingdom – which is not of this world yet is in it – will true righteousness prevail.

✳ *Lord, help us to seek first your kingdom.*

Wednesday December 19   Isaiah 32.9–20

Joyful celebration was the hallmark of harvest and the Feast of Tabernacles (see Deuteronomy 16.13–15), for a successful harvest meant security and prosperity. However, Isaiah told the affluent women of Jerusalem that rejoicing would be transformed into mourning as order turned into chaos and the cultivated land into a wilderness. No clue is given about the cause of this desolation – it may have been military, political or spiritual.

The web of apprehension which Isaiah spun so deftly highlights his vision of salvation (verses 15–20). An outpouring of the Spirit of God will transform the nation's life, making deserts bloom. Justice and righteousness will flourish. God's kingdom is never our creation. We do not bring it about by our good works or religious attitudes. It is always the gift of God.

We are sometimes tempted to think that we can produce the kingdom of God by education or science or by using a specific political programme. Our ministry is rather to point the world beyond itself to God – the source of hope and peace – inviting all to journey with poor shepherds and wise foreigners to a stable in Bethlehem.

✳ *Lord, may your kingdom come!*

Thursday December 20   Isaiah 33.10–22

It is difficult for the human mind to understand the boundless nature of God. But Isaiah's frightening, majestic vision in today's reading – a vision of God's intervention in history to rout evil and establish Jerusalem as the permanent home of peace – reminds us of God's greatness and holiness.

God is God. His enemies will only destroy themselves by their opposition to him. Their self-destruction mirrors the 'consuming fire' of God's holiness (see verse 14 and also Psalm 50.3). At the heart of Isaiah's faith lay a passionate belief in the possibility of human goodness. Only a truthful, compassionate life can flourish in the fire of God's holy love. This vision gives us a sharp contrast between the fate of sinners (verse 14) and the righteous (verse 16) as they experience God's presence.

Although we know more of psychology and of people's potential for good and evil than Isaiah did, we nevertheless can learn from his vision. What we believe will shine forth in what we do; for it is by our attitude to others and to our world that we are known as Christ's and live lives that are pleasing to God.

✳ *Lord, may all that I do guide others to you.*

Friday December 21   Isaiah 34.1–2, 8–17

A God who loves and saves also judges, for salvation cannot be known apart from judgement – just as light has no meaning unless it can be compared with the darkness it dispels.

Speaking about the end of time, Isaiah used pictures and images to enlist his hearers' imaginations because such a theme stretches people's minds to the limit. In startling poetry Isaiah spoke about the devastation of Edom (verses 8–15), one of the traditional enemies of God's people. Although forged from the experience of oppression, this poem's tone of vengeance rightly disturbs us. We know God to be a God of love, emptying himself of glory and power so that as a helpless, vulnerable child he might be a light to the world.

Today's reading reminds us not to place our trust in human power but in God, for God's will of justice and peace cannot be defeated; he will be victorious. However, the price of that victory is beyond human comprehension. It is a price Jesus paid throughout his life from his cradle to Calvary.

✳   *Thou didst leave thy throne*
     And thy kingly crown
  When thou camest to earth for me . . .
    O come to my heart, Lord Jesus!
 There is room in my heart for thee.   *Emily E S Elliott*

The future is God's. Threat, fear, frailty – all that oppresses and destroys the human spirit will one day be no more and God's people will be liberated to sing his praise and enjoy him forever. Isaiah's vision reached beyond the human community to embrace the whole earth. The land and the people belong together. Just as blind eyes will be opened and mute tongues loosed (verses 5–6), so too the land will blossom like the desert after rain, and the glory of God be given to it.

People and places belong together. We, of all earth's generations, know how important the planet is – how delicately balanced is the ecology that gives us life and sustains us with air and food and resources. Isaiah knew that instinctively. At the centre of his perfect landscape is a pilgrimage path, 'the Way of Holiness' (verse 8), which leads to the nearer presence of God.

All that exists can lead us to that path; and we only truly find ourselves as we travel along it. However, the journey will be a surprising one. The path will wind through the small town of Bethlehem, past an undistinguished stable to the King of kings and Lord of lords.

✳ *As we draw near to the end of Advent, let us pray that we may experience a fresh wonder of all that God has done for us.*

For group discussion and personal thought

Christmas is a time for celebrating hope, peace and goodwill. Our readings from **Isaiah** have given us a picture of the nature of God's kingdom (for example, see **Isaiah 11.1–9; 32.1–8; 35.1–10**). Is the world any nearer to this ideal than it was in the time of Isaiah? During this Christmas season how can we show Christ to the world more effectively?

THE KING IS AMONG US

Notes by the Revd Ernie Whalley, MA

Ernie Whalley is a tutor at the Northern Baptist College in Manchester, having previously held a pastorate in the Central Bradford Baptist Fellowship.

The notes in this section are based on the Revised Standard Version.

A king was born into a peasant family. It seemed impossible, yet this was the setting for the birth of Jesus Christ. But what kind of king was he? How did he exercise his authority and power? What does his kingship have to say to us today? These are the questions we shall explore together in our Christmas readings as we celebrate the coming of Christ the King.

4th Sunday in Advent, December 23   Luke 1.26–38

A PROMISED KING

The baby promised to Mary was going to be a King. No wonder she found the whole situation impossible to take in.

The writer of **Luke**, a Gentile, writing a Gospel for Gentiles, stressed how God works in the lives of ordinary people, including poor peasants in a third-rate province of the Roman empire. The child would have a royal pedigree, going back through his father Joseph to the great King David himself. Since the golden era of David's kingship, many of the people of Israel looked forward to the birth of a king 'in David's line' (see Isaiah 9.6–7).

The idea of a Davidic Messiah was part of the popular hope of the Jews. He would inaugurate such a glorious reign that there would be no end to it. This long-awaited King was about to be born to a girl called Mary. Would he fulfil all these popular expectations of royal kingship? We shall have to wait and see.

We take promises seriously when we trust the person who makes them. With a spirit of expectancy we await the fulfilment of God's promises, but are we ready for the surprises?

✳ *Living God, keep us alive to your promises and ready to participate in their fulfilment.*

A KING WILL SAVE US
People are given their names for different reasons. Some
names are chosen because parents like the sound of them, and
some are named after relatives. Other names are selected
because of their meaning. The Hebrews attached great significance to choosing a name for a new-born child since the
name often indicated the role the child was to play in the
family or in the history of the people. This was the situation
for the child born to Mary.

- **Jesus** (verse 21). This name, popular among Jews, is the
  Greek form of the Hebrew word *Joshua*, meaning 'God is
  salvation'. The baby born to be King would deliver people
  from sin, bringing release from all kinds of oppression. As
  he grew up, the nature of this kingship became clear.
- **Emmanuel** (verse 23). **Matthew's Gospel**, written for
  Jews, shows how the coming of this royal child fulfilled
  prophecy. Isaiah wrote of Emmanuel – which means 'God
  with us' – in Isaiah 7.14. The living God is not against us,
  but alongside us. Our King is not confined to a palace but
  comes to our home.

✳ *On this Christmas Eve, ponder this: Jesus, Emmanuel, says
to you, 'I am with you always' (Matthew 28.20).*

WORSHIP THE KING
What a contrast between these two kings! Herod, a governor
of Palestine, was insanely jealous, getting rid of any potential
rival to his power, which included his wife, his mother-in-law
and his three sons. Here in this baby born in Bethlehem was
another threat to his love of power. Under the guise of
worship, he wanted to eliminate him.

Mary's child was so different. This King was born, not in a
palace or hotel suite, but in a shed reserved for animals. He
was surrounded, not by royal attendants, but by Mary and
Joseph, two ordinary peasant folk. Their child growing up
would demonstrate not the love of power but the power of
love. Visitors from the east came to worship and brought their
precious gifts, suitable for royalty.

- **Gold** – we offer in our worship, representing the stewardship of our material possessions.

- **Frankincense** – this fragrance can symbolise our whole-some influence in the world.
- **Myrrh** – used for embalming, signifying the offering of our sorrow and suffering because the King will bear this with us.

In our celebrations this Christmas Day, let us bring our offering of love:

✳ *Love shall be our token,*
   Love be yours and love be mine,
   Love to God and all the world,
   Love for plea and gift and sign.   *Christina Rossetti*

Wednesday December 26   John 1.1–14,18
ONE OF US

In 1873 Father Joseph Damien volunteered as a missionary to work with the six hundred people who had leprosy on the island of Molokai, Hawaii. They had been abandoned to this place and lived like animals in squalor and despair. Father Damien obtained building materials and made houses for them. He managed to secure a proper water supply to the camp. He worked tirelessly for the people's welfare, and per-suaded a doctor and nurses to come to help. Later, he built a small church where they could all gather together to worship God. Then, one day he put his foot into some warm water but did not feel anything. He realised he had caught leprosy, too. The following Sunday, he said in his sermon, 'Now I too am one of you.'

Father Damien's story is a parable of the incarnation. In the most profound of ways God in Christ has come amongst us. Today's reading from the prologue of **John's Gospel** seeks to express what this means in words. What a truth to cel-ebrate!

✳ *And he feeleth for our sadness,*
   And he shareth in our gladness.   *C Frances Alexander*

Thursday December 27   Romans 1.1–12
ALIVE IN HISTORY

Paul's letters usually deal with specific, pressing issues in the churches. The letter to the **Romans** is different. It is the nearest we have to a systematic outline of Paul's understanding of the gospel and has had a powerful impact on readers throughout the centuries, including Augustine and Luther.

It is interesting that, at the very beginning of **Romans**,Paul rooted the gospel firmly in history. This gospel centred on Jesus Christ and for the early Christians his royal pedigree was an important strand in the story.

We look to the past as Christians in order to understand the present and anticipate the future. Our Christian memory of the past prompts Christian hope in the future. We celebrate and confess the kingly rule of the God whom we see in Jesus.

Paul thanked God that, as he and his friends shared the story of faith in such a Christ, they encouraged one another. Our faith in Christ is sustained not only by words but by the support and encouragement of our Christian brothers and sisters.

✳ *Give thanks for those who have encouraged* **you** *on the journey of faith. How can you encourage someone today?*

Friday December 28   **Matthew 2.13–23**

MASSACRE OF INNOCENTS

In today's reading we pick up more evidence of Herod's jealousy and cruelty. Because of his threats, Mary and Joseph and the child Jesus became refugees in Egypt.

In this Christmas season, these verses about the killing of innocent children bring a cloud over the scene of joy. It reminds us of that suffering which is part of life even in a joyful time. All suffering is abhorrent, wherever it is seen and experienced. Yet innocent suffering, especially in children, touches a raw nerve. If this suffering is inflicted on a child in a deliberate way, even the most hard-hearted of people usually react with anger. Today we hear the cry of the holy innocents through the fury and rage of nations and communities at war, the sounds of the starving, and the children unwanted and unloved. On hearing the cry, are we willing to pledge ourselves to action?

When Jesus returned to the land of his birth, and grew up, he affirmed for all time the infinite value of every child: 'Let the children come to me, do not hinder them; for to such belongs the kingdom of God' (Mark 10.14).

✳ *Pray for those who have experienced this Christmas-time as an occasion of sadness; and remember children and adults who suffer, including refugees.*

Saturday December 29 **Galatians 3.23 to 4.7**

ALL ONE IN CHRIST

In his letter to the **Galatians**, Paul discusses the relationship between law and grace. Through the birth of Jesus, a new era has begun.

- We can call God, 'Abba' (verse 6). This is an Aramaic word, commonly used in the time of Jesus, which we can translate as 'Daddy'. The great God of all, far beyond our understanding, can be addressed in such an intimate way.
- An ancient Jewish prayer, familiar to Paul, thanks God that 'Thou hast not made me a Gentile, a slave or a woman.' According to Paul, the kingship of Christ turned this round completely. In Christ, human divisions were to disappear in a single new humanity. In Paul's day, he was most acutely aware of the barriers between Jew and Gentile. It took hundreds of years for the evil of slavery to be tackled, and there are still many forms of oppression around us today. The issue of the role of male and female is very much on our agenda at this time in our history.

✱ *Read again Galatians 3.28. What is God's Spirit saying through this verse to your culture today?*

For group discussion and personal thought

'Do not criticise your neighbour until you have walked half a mile in his shoes.' Discuss the implications of this statement in the light of **John 1.14**. What does this say to us (a) as individuals, and (b) as Christian communities, in our witness for Christ?

Sunday December 30 **Mark 3.31–35; John 19.17–27**

THE CRUCIFIED KING

The contrast between earthly kingship and Jesus Christ as King came to a climax in his crucifixion. Jesus was condemned to death as a common criminal, after mockery and insult. Nailed to a cross, the sign over his head, 'Jesus of Nazareth, the King of the Jews', was written in three languages for everyone in Jerusalem to understand: in Latin, the official language of administration; in Greek, the language for commerce and culture; and in Hebrew, the language of Palestinian Jews.

Yet to those with eyes to see, here was God at work in Jesus the King. This divine kingship came not through earthly power but through shame, not through earthly glory but through thorns. This humiliating death of the crucified King has, over the centuries, drawn people from every culture (John 12.31). In the anguish of innocent suffering, the King is among us. God identifies with human life in its weakness as well as its strength.

All who live for the values for which Jesus lived and died, are his brothers and sisters in the work of the kingdom. And note too that the words of the King on the cross include practical concern for his own family.

❋ *Did e'er such love and sorrow meet,*
   Or thorns compose so rich a crown.   Isaac Watts

Monday December 31   Philippians 2.1–13
THE SERVANT KING

How can the Christian Church live more faithfully the good news of the kingdom of God? Our reading today gives us some clues.

● **'Being of the same mind'** (verse 2). We are called to work together with a common purpose in living for Christ the King. Realistically this is not straightforward. In the search for truth, and appropriate ways of sharing this today, there will be different opinions. Humility is essential for we have so much to learn.

● **'The mind of Christ'** (verse 5). Faithful Christian obedience is focused on Jesus Christ, the servant King. In this early Christian hymn (verses 6–11) we have a dramatic picture of God in Christ as the servant – in humanity, humility, obedience until death, resurrection and exaltation. With this King, Easter is in Christmas; birth, death and resurrection are all bound together. In a world faced with uncertainty and fear, the life of Christ is the pattern for our discipleship. Forever he is King of kings and Lord of lords!

❋ *As we approach a new year let us pray: 'Lord, may we know you more clearly, love you more dearly, and follow you more nearly, day by day.' (from Richard of Chichester)*

SCHEME OF READINGS for 1991

Jan 1–12	BELONGING
Jan 13–Feb 23	JOHN'S GOSPEL 1–10
Feb 24–Mar 16	ISAIAH 40–55
Mar 17–Apr 6	JOHN'S GOSPEL 11–12, 18–21
Apr 7–27	EXODUS
Apr 28–May 18	ROMANS 1–8
May 19–25	SYMBOLS OF THE SPIRIT
May 26–June 8	2 CHRONICLES 1–9 The reign of Solomon
June 9–22	ROMANS 9–16
June 23–July 6	HOSEA
July 7–13	SONGS OF JOY AND SORROW Song of Songs and Lamentations
July 14–27	JOHN 13–17
July 28–Aug 10	DANIEL
Aug 11–24	1 PETER
Aug 25–Sept 7	GENESIS 1–11
Sept 8–14	RUTH
Sept 15–Oct 12	ACTS 13–21
Oct 13–Nov 2	2 CHRONICLES 10–36
Nov 3–23	2 CORINTHIANS
Nov 24–Dec 7	PSALMS
Dec 8–21	HEBREWS
Dec 22–31	CHRISTMAS THEME